Girls' Feminist Blogging in a Postfeminist Age

Girls' Feminist Blogging in a Postfeminist Age explores the practices of U.S.-based teenage girls who actively maintain feminist blogs and participate in the feminist blogosphere as readers, writers, and commenters on platforms including Blogspot, Facebook, Twitter, and Tumblr. Drawing on interviews with bloggers between the ages of fifteen and twenty-one, as well as discursive textual analyses of feminist blogs and social networking postings authored by teenage girls, Keller addresses how these girls use blogging as a practice to articulate contemporary feminisms and craft their own identities as feminists and activists. In this sense, feminist girl bloggers defy hegemonic postfeminist and neoliberal girlhood subjectivities, a finding that Keller uses to complicate both academic and popular assertions that suggest teenage girls are uninterested in feminism. Instead, Keller maintains that these young bloggers employ digital media production to educate their peers about feminism, connect with like-minded activists, write feminist history, and make feminism visible within popular culture, practices that build upon and continue a lengthy tradition of American feminism into the twenty-first century. *Girls' Feminist Blogging in a Postfeminist Age* challenges readers to not only reconsider teenage girls' online practices as politically and culturally significant, but to better understand their crucial role in a thriving contemporary feminism.

Jessalynn Keller is a Lecturer in Media Studies at the University of East Anglia, UK. Her research on girls' digital media cultures has been published in *Continuum: Journal of Media and Cultural Studies*; *Feminist Media Studies*; *Information, Communication & Society*; and *Celebrity Studies*, as well as in several edited anthologies.

Routledge Studies in New Media and Cyberculture

Girls' Feminist Blogging in a Postfeminist Age

Jessalynn Keller

Routledge
Taylor & Francis Group

NEW YORK AND LONDON

First published 2016
by Routledge
711 Third Avenue, New York, NY 10017

and by Routledge
2 Park Square, Milton Park, Abingdon, Oxon OX14 4RN

First issued in paperback 2017

Routledge is an imprint of the Taylor & Francis Group, an informa business

© 2016 Taylor & Francis

Library of Congress Cataloging in Publication Data

Keller, Jessalynn, 1982- author.
Girls' feminist blogging in a postfeminist age / by Jessalynn Keller.
    pages cm. — (Routledge studies in new media and cyberculture; 30)
Includes bibliographical references and index.
    1. Feminism—Blogs. 2. Girls—Blogs. 3. Online identities.
    4. Internet and women. I. Title.
HQ1178.K45 2015
004.67'8082—dc23   2015019537

ISBN 13: 978-0-8153-8640-7 (pbk)
ISBN 13: 978-1-138-80014-4 (hbk)

Typeset in Sabon
by codeMantra

To my mom, Mary, the most important feminist in my life …

Contents

List of Figures

Acknowledgments

This book would have been impossible to write without the passion and commitment of the feminist girl bloggers who shared their stories, insights, and writing with me for several years while I conducted this research. Their comments no doubt enriched the scope of this project and encouraged me to ask unexpected questions, think expansively, and perhaps most importantly, to have fun while doing it. It is the incredible voices of these girls that really make this book special, and for that I owe them my deepest thanks. These girls are already changing the world.

Warm thanks to everyone at Routledge who helped make this project happen, especially Felisa Salvago-Keyes and Katie Laurentiev who have graciously answered my questions and guided me through the process of publishing one's first book. I also appreciate the suggestions of the anonymous reviewers who read the proposal and the countless other scholars who have offered feedback at annual conferences where I've presented papers based on this research, including Console-ing Passions International Conference on Television, Video, Audio, New Media and Feminism, the Society for Cinema and Media Studies, and the Association of Internet Researchers. Finally, I am extremely grateful for the funding I received from the Social Sciences and Humanities Research Council of Canada to undertake this research.

This book began as my dissertation project at the University of Texas at Austin and I am thankful for the many fantastic colleagues and friends I met there. In particular, my Ph.D. supervisor, mentor, and friend Mary Celeste Kearney guided me through the shaping of this project and continues to inspire me with her belief in the power of feminist media scholarship. I'm also grateful for the guidance of my other internal and external committee members, including Mary Beltran, Nhi Lieu, Madhavi Mallapragada, and Leslie Regan Shade. During my time at UT-Austin I was lucky to have studied alongside many budding media scholars that have become fantastic friends who offered encouragement as I worked on this research, including Alex Cho, Charlotte Howell, Amanda Landa, Caroline Leader, Sarah Murray, and Jacqueline Vickery. I must extend an extra special thanks to my dear friend and girls' media studies colleague Morgan Blue, who has been reading and offering feedback on this research since its inception in 2010. I would be lost without her keen editing eye, her insightful critique and commentary, and most importantly, her unwavering belief in my work. Thank you!

I have been fortunate to be surrounded by fantastic feminist media studies colleagues since moving to the UK, many who have read chapter drafts and/or provided support as I've completed this book. These include my former Middlesex University colleagues Feona Attwood, Mariam Kauser, Giovanna Puppin, and Alison Winch; as well as Alison Harvey, Jo Littler, Kaitlynn Mendes, Jessica Ringrose, and Tamara Shepherd. Cheers to you all! I also want to recognize the MDX FemGenSex network for creating space for exciting feminist scholarship at Middlesex University, including a symposium in November 2013 where I presented work from this book.

The decision to write about teenage feminists was influenced by my own experience as a teenage feminist growing up in Saskatoon, Saskatchewan, Canada. I'd like to acknowledge my close friends during this formative time in my life as being influential in the development of my feminist politics: Amanda Hughes, Niki Sutherland, and Jennifer Logan. Jennifer passed away unexpectedly in January 2015, yet her passion for feminist social justice work will always be inspirational to me.

Finally, I'd like to thank my family for their steadfast support throughout not only the writing of this book, but my life. My parents, Mary and Wilf, have always encouraged me to pursue my passions, both ones that were 'sensible' and those perhaps more … 'far-fetched'. They have not only made sacrifices to help with the logistics of academic success (two international moves and countless plane tickets come to mind …) but most importantly, they (still!) always pick up the phone when I call. I would never have written this book without their unwavering love, genuine enthusiasm, sound advice, and continual confidence in me. I'm also so lucky to have my sister Lorilee as a best friend who has taught me much about living life mindfully and with conviction. And finally, my cat Bella has not only been a loyal companion throughout long days of writing and revising, but never fails to remind me of the importance of an afternoon nap.

Introduction

Transforming Feminist Conversations? Girls, Blogging, and Feminist Politics in the Twenty-first Century

> "Lacking editors (whose intolerance for insanity tends to sand off pointy edges), lacking balance (as any self-publishing platform tends to do), laced with humor and fury (emotions intensified by the web's spontaneity), the blogosphere has transformed feminist conversation, reviving in the process of an older style of activism among young women ..."
> —Emily Nussbaum, "The Rebirth of the Feminist Manifesto"

> "Feminists still have a lot of work to do in terms of countering the negative stereotype of feminism in the media and the overarching idea that feminism is dead, but I think that teen girls today are completely ready and willing to take on that fight."
> —Julie Zeilinger, 19, feminist blogger, email interview

The quote from journalist Emily Nussbaum is from an October 2011 article she penned for *New York Magazine* and is telling in its insistence that the Internet has fundamentally altered contemporary feminism. Whether or not Nussbaum is correct, her argument raises significant questions about the relationship between the Internet, specifically the blogosphere, and feminism – both past and future. Nussbaum goes on to describe a feminist blogosphere that is passionate and messy, yet unequivocally political. She writes,

> These sites inspired an even sharper cadre of commenters, who bonded and argued, sometimes didactically, sometimes cruelly, but just as often pushing one another to hone their ideas – all this from a generation of women written off in the media as uninterested in any form of gender analysis, let alone the label 'feminist' (n.p.).

Nussbaum's analysis is exciting to many of us invested in feminist politics and is indicative of a recent popular interest in feminist activism employing new media technologies and web 2.0 platforms. To wit: The global spread of Slutwalk in 2011, the digital circulation of the 2012 "I Need Feminism Because" university campus initiative, and the success of the #FBRape campaign in 2013 have all received attention from mainstream press in the United States, Canada, and the United Kingdom, generating a resurgence of public debate about feminist politics that has been largely absent from mainstream public discourse since the start of the twenty-first century.

But despite this increasing recent public attention to feminist politics, postfeminism remains a hegemonic cultural discourse that continues to be influential in public perception of contemporary gender politics. The idea that feminism is no longer necessary, the grounding logic of postfeminism as I will later outline in detail, is most often discussed in relation to teenage girls' perceived lack of investment in feminism. Indeed, it is young women in their mid-late twenties and thirties that are most often characterized as participants in the feminist blogosphere and recent activist campaigns. The exclusion of *girls'* voices from many feminist organizations and from mainstream journalism's reporting on feminist activism inadvertently reinforces the dominant perception that younger girls are not feminist. Frequent stories, such as a November 2012 article on *CNN.com* asking, "Where are all the millennial feminists?" further advance the notion that few millennial feminists exist, and often forecast an uncertain future for feminism (Weinberger 2012).

However, Julie's comment that I cite hints at a very different reality – one where teenage girls are eager participants in contemporary feminism, committed to proud feminist identities, and striving to make progressive social change in their communities through activist initiatives. It is the often-unheard voices of Julie and her feminist peers who are active new media producers that I explore in this book, which asks several questions: How are teenage girls articulating a feminist politics and crafting their own identities as feminists and activists within this emergent feminist blogosphere celebrated by women like Emily Nussbaum? *Why* have online spaces become significant spaces with which to do so? And finally, *how* are teenage girls in fact negotiating and resisting these postfeminist and neoliberal discourses by acting as feminist digital media producers?

Girls' Feminist Blogging in a Postfeminist Age is the first book-length study to investigate these questions by exploring how girls are engaging in feminist activism using new media platforms, including blogs, Twitter, Facebook, and Tumblr. It aims to contextualize girls' blogging as part of a lengthy tradition of girls' media production and American feminism, mapping the continuities between blogging and feminist practices such as zine-making, consciousness-raising, and media production such as *Ms. Magazine*. The book then addresses contemporary concerns about girls' supposed lack of commitment to feminist politics (McRobbie 2009) and panics surrounding girls' risky uses of online technologies (Shade 2007, 2011; Ringrose and Eriksson-Barajas 2011; Cassell and Cramer 2008), complicating them by demonstrating how some girls are in fact savvy new media producers who are using digital media as political agents and specifically, feminist activists.

This book carves a unique space in the intersection of digital media studies, cultural studies and girls'/women's studies. It draws together current scholarly debates about the prevalence of postfeminist discourses and the new feminine technologies they produce within contemporary culture (McRobbie 2009), the potential power of new media technologies to be employed for purposes of social change and activism, and the agency of today's youth who have grown up amid cultural fragmentation marked by individualization, commercialization, and consumer citizenship (Harris 2008). This analytical space allows for the interrogation of multiple modes of power and resistance that are characteristic of our cultural moment, a necessary task for feminist media scholars interested in understanding the cultural implications of new media technologies. Thus, this book is an inherently political project that aims to acknowledge, document, and theorize girl bloggers' significant contributions to contemporary feminism, while focusing on their use of new media technologies and platforms to do so.

Positioning a 'Girl' Subjectivity

Given the topic of this book, it is necessary to outline what I mean by the subjectivity of girl. Who 'fits' into this subject position of girl? Who can claim girlhood? And finally, how can we understand the subjectivity of girl as offering a fresh perspective on feminisms and contemporary feminist activism? I understand the subjectivity of girl through a feminist poststructuralist position, which theorizes girlhood as discursively produced through historical, cultural, and social contexts, rather than a static and biological or age based category that is universally valid (Pomerantz 2009; Eisenhauer 2004; Driscoll 2002). Furthermore, the subjectivity of girl is complicated by intersecting identities, such as race, class, age, sexuality, and nationality, further problematizing the notion that a singular understanding of girlhood is possible or even desirable (Pomerantz 2009). Yet, for research purposes, I requested participants be aged twenty-one or younger at the start of the study and identify with the discursive construct of girl, the definition of which no doubt varies across participants. Consequently, this project aims to understand how girls situate themselves within girlhood and deploy a girl subjectivity within blog spaces and in relation to feminism.

Although the previous discussion points to the difficulties in employing the category of girl for research purposes, I focus on girls, rather than young women or women, for several reasons. Girls have been historically marginalized within feminist research, leading to a dearth of knowledge on girls' participation in feminist activism and the continued assumption that girls distance themselves from feminism. Jessica Taft (2011, 5) argues, "Girl activists' ideas, stories, and theoretical contributions thus remain largely hidden from view. They continue to appear in both the public and academic domain only as occasional images – as visual objects rather than as intelligent and intelligible political subjects." While recent work in the growing field of girlhood studies is beginning to complicate and challenge these assumptions, girls as historical and contemporary political subjects remain understudied.

In her seminal book *Girls: Feminine Adolescence in Popular Culture and Cultural Theory*, Catherine Driscoll (2002) argues that girlhood must be a focus of analysis for feminist researchers not only because of its previous marginalization within the field, but because of the way girlhood can enable a reflection on feminist relations to dominant discourses. She writes,

> As soon as feminist theory – analytic or activist – begins to look only for its own repetition, as soon as it is certain of where it comes from and what its effects are, then it begins to expect merely its own repetition. It also thus ceases to be a vital force in political life, let alone in the daily lives of women and girls. A feminist focus on girls is thus desirable for pragmatic reasons, but it also draws attention to the model of subjection presumed by feminist theory and the ways the Woman-feminist subject is formed, deployed, or avoided within the experience of individuals (304).

Driscoll's insistence that the process of researching girls and girlhoods must move beyond merely talking about girls to "considering their interaction with discourses that name and constitute them" encourages an analytic mode that can be used to explore how girlhood is mobilized within larger cultural discourses of agency, citizenship, and authority (304). Thus, studying girls and girlhood helps us to understand the production and evaluation of gendered subjectivities and the ways in which major public discourses get folded into the highly visible construction of late modern girlhood (Driscoll 2002).

This point is particularly salient with regard to this project, as girls are highly visible and celebrated within both neoliberal and postfeminist discourses, as I'll describe later in this introduction. Girls themselves recognize this, and several of my study participants spoke specifically about how the word girl is often employed in media and commercial discourses to signify hegemonic femininity and/or a 'girl power' rhetoric that Emilie Zaslow (2009) describes as being informed by tenets of postfeminism. Several of the bloggers I discuss in this book echoed my concern about this problematic equation of girls and girlhood with such a narrow image of hegemonic femininity. Consequently, I employ girl in part as a political strategy to counter the limited images of girlhood that we often see in commercial popular culture, with the hopes of depicting alternative girlhood subjectivities being performed by adolescent girls today.

In this sense I take up Monica Swindle's (2011, para. 47) call to understand girl as an affect with political potential, whereby "the pleasurable power that girl now modulates has great ability to affect in the global affective economies of the twenty-first century, especially considering the possibilities for distribution through technologies and new media." According to Swindle, girl has a political traction that we as feminist scholars must pay more attention, something I aim to do in this book. Yet, I employ girl acknowledging that my participants have complex relationships with this identity; some enthusiastically embrace the label, while others expressed ambivalence toward a girl subjectivity. Consequently I employ girl not as an accurate descriptor of my participants, insomuch as an imperfect theoretical concept that allows me to explore the connections between identities such as gender and age and their intersection with feminism and digital media.

Why Feminism Now?

Within the past decade there has been an increasing scholarly interest in young women's identification with the label 'feminist' (Harris 2010). Much of this work, such as that by Shelley Budgeon (2001), Madeleine Jowett (2004), and Emilie Zaslow (2009), has focused on young women's attitudes toward feminism, concluding that while most girls do not identify as feminists, many support feminist ideals. It is this seeming contradiction that has perplexed many feminist scholars, who often discuss these findings in reference to the context of a postfeminist culture that celebrates choice and individual empowerment, while distancing itself from feminism as a political movement. While this work has no doubt been important in understanding girls' attitudes toward feminism and the more commercially inclined 'girl power,' it has not specifically addressed the actual activist practices of girls.

Anita Harris (2010, 475) argues that this focus on young women's attitudes toward feminism has overshadowed "a more productive investigation into contemporary young feminist practice, including its continuities with the past," suggesting that feminist researchers must ask different questions in order to get at the complexity of girls' feminist practices. Harris contends that the varied nature of contemporary feminist practices requires researchers to be open to the ways that "narratives of choice and individualization, conditions of decollectivization and globalization, a pervasive media culture and the emergence of new information and communication technologies" shape what young women do, rather than what they merely say about feminism. She concludes, "What is required, I think, is an openness in our ideas about what constitutes feminist politics today, especially a greater understanding of the function of micro-political acts and unconventional activism in this historical moment as well as recognition of links with past practice. Such an approach might enable us to yet move beyond generationalism to forge a new feminism we do not yet know" (481).

Harris' critique provides the starting point for my own research on girls' feminist activism, and the ways that girls' blogging and participation in the feminist blogosphere have the potential to be activism. Consequently, this book makes an important intervention into the research on girls, feminism, and postfeminism by positioning girls' media production as feminist activism. This idea builds off of the foundational work of Mary Celeste Kearney (2006), whose book *Girls Make Media* was the first feminist scholarship to comprehensively explore the varied practices of girl media producers and to take this cultural production seriously. In doing so, Kearney challenged hegemonic discourses that recognized girls as only cultural consumers and encouraged feminist media studies scholars to recognize the potential for resistance and agency within girls' media production practices.

My approach also asks new questions specifically about the relationship between girlhood and feminist activism, an area that has been unexplored in existing research, which often includes girls under the broader category of 'young women.' Whereas Taft (2011) provides a useful analysis of girlhood in relation to activist identities, she does not address how girlhood relates to the identity of a feminist activist. Thus, this book builds on Taft's important work by focusing on girls' performances of feminist and activist identities through blogging. These topics are the focus of the first and second chapters. I position these ideas alongside a discussion of the history of feminist media production and activism in order to draw out continuities and discontinuities, rather than maintaining a strict divide between second wave and third wave activist practices.[1]

Blogging as a Practice of Girlhood Media-Making

A 'blog' is an abbreviated term for 'weblog,' which refers to a website that is organized by reverse-chronological written entries (also called 'posts') usually focused on a particular topic or issue. Although writing is certainly an important part of a blog, Jill Walker Rettberg (2008) argues that a blog must be understood holistically as constituting writing as well as layout (including visuals), connections/links, and tempo. I do not believe it's useful to employ a narrow definition of what constitutes a blog and throughout this book I use the term flexibly, discussing girls' use of social media platforms such as Facebook as part of their blogging practice. There are, however, some defining features of blogs that are important to highlight: Blogs are frequently updated (and thus constantly changing), personal in nature (often written in the first person), and contain a social aspect via their embedded links to other websites and comment sections. Consequently, Rettberg describes blogs as a social genre that can facilitate conversations within a single blog or between multiple blogs. The connections between blogs addressing a particular topic are popularly referred to as a 'blogosphere,' a term that I will occasionally employ in this book. Indeed, I emphasize the social aspect of blogging here as it is of particular importance to my analysis of girls' feminist blogs, and I'll be returning to an in-depth discussion of it in chapters one and three.

The feminist blogosphere is certainly not the sole site with which girls are engaging in feminist activism. However, for several reasons I have chosen to use girls' feminist blogs as a productive site from which to ask questions about girls and feminism. First, blogging has been a practice that has been tremendously popular with middle-class North American teenage girls since the early incarnations of the Internet. According to a Pew Internet Research study from 2008, American teenage girls outnumber their male counterparts as bloggers, with 41 percent of girls ages 15–17 claiming to have a blog (Lenhardt, Arafeh, Smith, and Macgill 2008). The popularity of blogging among girls may be due to the connection between diary/journal writing, a longstanding part of girl culture. For example, one of the first free blogging platforms popular in the early 2000s was called LiveJournal, drawing an explicit connection between journaling and blogging.

Young women also tend to use social networking sites more than both their male peers and adult generations (Duggan and Brenner 2013).[2] The increasing popularity of social networking sites, such as Facebook, Twitter, and Tumblr, over the past five years has meant that girls will also often use these platforms to blog or circulate their blog posts via these platforms, as I discuss in chapter three with regards to girls' use of Tumblr. Despite these statistics, it is necessary to recognize that blogging is not an opportunity afforded to all girls equally, and that social inequalities continue to limit who has the leisure time, resources, and literacy skills to blog, an issue that I will return to throughout this book.

Second, writing has been a longstanding part of girls' culture, and writing practices, such as keeping a diary, having a pen pal, and writing fan letters, are dominant girlhood tropes with both historical and contemporary significance (Hunter 2002; Kearney 2006). Many of girls' writing practices, from the diaries kept by Victorian girls to the zines created by 1990s riot grrrls, have a liberatory effect on girls, allowing them a sense of freedom, a source of pleasure, and site of fantasy and identity exploration (Kearney 2006). Thus, I aim to position blogging within this lengthy history of girls' writing practices, and specifically analyze the importance of writing as a way for girls to foster feminist and activist identities.

Third, there has recently been considerable scholarly and mainstream interest in the use of blogs and social networking sites to facilitate social movements, such as the Arab Spring, the Occupy Movements, and SlutWalks. In fact, Nussbaum's (2011) article that I cite earlier in this chapter, begins by describing her experience at New York's Slutwalk, relating the physical march itself to its online representations. She writes,

> And Slutwalk is more public still: Even as we march, it is being tweeted and filmed and Tumblr'd, a way of alerting the press and a way of bypassing the press. I am surrounded by the same bloggers I've been reading for weeks. And though bystanders cheer us on (two gray-haired women dance topless in a window), this is very much a march for young women, that demographic that has been chastised throughout history for seeking attention – and ever more so in recent years, as if publicity itself were a venereal disease, one made more resistant by technology (n.p.).

Thus, the relationship between digital technology and social protest warrants serious scholarly attention and raises interesting questions about online networks and connections, publicness, and activism, topics I investigate in chapters two and five.

While blogs are my object of analysis in this book, this project is not merely about how girls use the Internet to engage with feminisms. Instead, I strive to draw connections between contemporary culture and feminism, parsing out the ways in which girls' online engagements with feminism are integrally related to their 'offline' daily experiences within a neoliberal cultural context. In this sense, I challenge two dominant, yet problematic, discourses that circulate in both academic and mainstream discussions regarding youth and their Internet practices: narratives of risk resulting from supposed effects of new media, and escapist discourses that position young people's online practices as unrelated to their offline lives. I will discuss these two discourses in turn.

While media scholars have long refuted technological determinism, it nonetheless continues to shape dominant discourses on new technologies, including the Internet. These effects-centered arguments privilege the presumed properties of the technology itself as producing direct effects on society, excluding the recognition of the social context that gives technologies meaning and the complexity with which individuals interact with technology (Williams 1974; Marvin 1990; Gray 2009). Consequently, we often hear reports in the mainstream media that the Internet has caused deviant youth behavior, such as cyberbullying or sexting. This discourse is often gendered, with girls often portrayed in media accounts as 'at risk' when online or using other new communication devices such as mobile phones, and are portrayed in media accounts as potential victims of online sexual predators, sexting scandals, or life-threatening cyberbullying from classmates (Shade 2007, 2011). For example, in a 2009 article in the Canadian national newspaper *The Globe and Mail*, Judith Timson writes, "The Internet has made girl-on-girl viciousness so much more virulent, with mass shunnings, false rumour-mongering and online slagging of each other."

Leslie Regan Shade (2011) notes that these discourses have led to a gendered 'protectionist' rhetoric that posits girls' online practices in need of adult surveillance and supervision, denying girls' autonomy and agency within online spaces. Additionally, I would also suggest that this protectionist discourse fails to address societal power structures by positioning technology as the problem girls face in online spaces rather than patriarchy, sexual harassment, and violence against women and girls. Most recently, we can see this discourse reproduced through public discussions of the Amanda Todd case, which resulted in Canadian government action to implement policy on cyberbullying rather than addressing the sexual harassment and misogyny experienced by Todd.[3] I will return to further discuss this protectionist discourse related to girls' Internet practices in chapter five.

It is worthwhile returning to Raymond Williams' (1974, 129) concern with the ahistorical nature of technological determinism: "Any cancellation of history, in the sense of real times and real places, is essentially a cancellation of the contemporary world, in which, within limits and under pressures, men (sic) act and react, struggle and concede, cooperate, conflict and compete." Williams advocates for analyzing technologies as cultural, recognizing the complex intersection of media as a practice, intentionally developed in relation to social needs and historical specificities. This approach complicates simplistic media effects arguments by privileging the complex relationship between culture and media. By situating my discussion within the competing cultural contours of neoliberalism, post-feminism and contemporary feminism, I draw on Williams' framework to make apparent the ways that cultural context frames and informs girls' blogging practices.

In this sense, a cultural studies theoretical framework informs this book, focusing on the interaction between text, production, reception, and socio-historical context, and analyzing the ways that power is discursively produced and circulated throughout these sites (Kellner 1995; D'Acci 2005). While cultural studies has been the dominant approach in television studies, it has been used less widely within Internet studies, resulting in a lack of research that adequately positions Internet practices as part of a complex terrain of social, cultural, political, and economic processes. Critical Internet scholar Mary Gray (2009, xiv) highlights this absence, arguing that researchers must "decenter media as the object of analysis in new media research" by employing ethnographic research that will allow us to better understand the use and meaning of media within the "everyday lives of people." I take up Gray's call by adopting an ethnographic approach to my project in order to understand how digital media production functions in the everyday lives of feminist girls. I will return to a discussion of my methods later in this introduction.

The second, albeit related, assumption about the Internet practices of youth is based on an escapist discourse which posits that youth use the Internet to 'escape' their 'real lives,' creating online identities that are disconnected from their offline practices and experiences. In her ethnographic study of the media practices of rural queer youth, Gray (2009, 86) problematizes this escapist discourse by drawing on the work of Nancy Baym (2006), to argue that "[f]ocusing on new media as spaces that produce online worlds fails to respond to the call of critical cyberculture researchers to examine how 'offline contexts permeate and influence online situations, and online situations and experiences always feed back into offline experiences.'" Thus, I have chosen an ethnographic approach to my research in order to "contextualize media engagements as part of a broader social terrain of experience," disrupting the false boundary between online and offline worlds (Gray 2009, 14).

This discussion alludes to the importance of studying blogs as media that encompass significant ideas about contemporary girlhood, feminism, and new media technologies. Thus, I envision this book as a cultural interrogation rooted in the logic of cultural studies as opposed to merely an in-depth examination of a particular medium, understanding girls' feminist blogs as a 'hub' that centers and makes visible larger cultural narratives about girls' engagements with feminism today.

Neoliberalism, Postfeminism, and New Gendered Technologies

A significant goal of this book is to situate girls' blogging practices within the larger cultural context of neoliberalism. In *The Twilight of Equality: Neoliberalism, Cultural Politics, and the Attack on Democracy*, Lisa Duggan (2003, 70) argues that neoliberalism is not a "unitary system" but a "complex, contradictory cultural, and political project created within specific institutions, with an agenda for reshaping the everyday life of contemporary global capitalism." Neoliberalism is characterized by privatization, deregulation, a celebration of individualism, and a rejection of the social welfare model of state governance popularized in the early twentieth century. David Harvey (2005) argues that since the 1980s neoliberalism has "become hegemonic as a mode of discourse. It has pervasive effects on ways of thought to the point where it has become incorporated into the common-sense way many of us interpret, live in, and understand the world" (3). Harvey's insistence on understanding neoliberalism as a hegemonic discourse is particularly useful for this project, as I'll be discursively analyzing neoliberalism in relation to contemporary feminist discourses.

Duggan and Harvey contend that, contrary to popular logic, neoliberalism is not politically neutral, blind to identities, or solely about economics. Both scholars map how neoliberalism as a project continues to create power inequalities both between nations and among national citizens. Harvey argues that neoliberalism has not generated worldwide economic growth, but has merely redistributed wealth to favor already economically privileged individuals and nations, perpetuating a greater class disparity. He maintains, "It has been part of the genius of neoliberal theory to provide a benevolent mask full of wonderful-sounding words like freedom, liberty, choice, and rights, to hide the grim realities of the restoration of reconstitution of naked class power, locally as well as transnationally, but most particularly in the main financial centers of global capitalism" (119). Harvey's guiding argument that class power is restored via neoliberalism as an economic and cultural project is convincing, yet must be considered alongside the ways in which it relates to gender.

Lauren Berlant (1997), Angela McRobbie (2009), and most recently Rosalind Gill and Christina Scharff (2011) demonstrate that it is essential to understand neoliberalism as a gendered construct, producing specifically gendered subjects that reaffirm normative gender, race, class, and sexual identities. For example, McRobbie (2009) argues that femininity – particularly *youthful* femininity – is being reshaped to align with emerging neoliberal social and economic arrangements. She explains, "From being assumed to be headed toward marriage, motherhood and limited economic participation, the girl is now endowed with economic capacity ... [expected to] perform as [an] economically active female citizen" both by working in paid employment and consuming commercial goods (58). Girls and young women then, are "weighted toward capacity, success, attainment, enjoyment, entitlement, social mobility, and participation" that dovetails with neoliberal discourses privileging individualism, freedom, choice, and consumer citizenship (McRobbie 2009, 57).

Media scholars such as Laurie Ouellette and Julie Wilson (2011) have examined the relationship between neoliberalism and gender specifically in relation to contemporary media, exploring how new media facilitates the production of gendered neoliberal subjects. Ouellette and Wilson analyze how media convergence – bolstered by new media platforms – often continues to rely on the unpaid domestic and affective labor of women, rather than provide the freedoms, creativity, and flexible interactivity that new media scholars such as Henry Jenkins (2006) have celebrated. They argue,

> Converging media technologies and platforms facilitate an expectation that women make enterprising use of books, television and the web as interconnected resources for self-work and successful family management. Women's 'active' participation in the evolving media landscape – including the mastery of new technologies such as the Web – does not liberate us from top-down cultural control or parallel the labor into women's media reception practices. The implications of this extension are not only limited to the sexual division of labor and the gendering of citizenship but also include the forms of leisure, fantasy, pleasure, and escape available to women in a 'can-do' enterprise culture (559).

This work highlights the importance of examining new media in relation to gendered neoliberal subjectivities, a connection I use as a guiding contextual framework throughout this book.

Alongside neoliberalism, I also characterize our contemporary moment as being marked by what Rosalind Gill (2007) calls a "postfeminist sensibility." Although postfeminism has been the subject of debate and multiple definitions within feminist scholarship, I find Gill's characterization of it as a cultural sensibility, rather than a theoretical position, a type of feminism after the women's liberation movement, or a regressive political stance, to be most useful for my own analysis. I understand postfeminism as a cultural sensibility promoted throughout contemporary popular media culture that takes feminism into account while simultaneously repudiating it as "harsh, punitive, and inauthentic, not articulating women's true desires" (Gill 2007, 162; McRobbie 2009). Postfeminism can be further characterized by several themes, including: femininity as a bodily property; a shift from objectification to subjectification; an emphasis on surveillance, monitoring, and self-discipline; a rhetoric of individualism, choice, and empowerment; a dominance of makeover paradigms; and a resurgence of ideas about natural sexual difference (Gill 2007). Although it is beyond the scope of this introduction to explore each of these themes, I will return to several of them throughout this book.

Gill and Scharff (2011) argue that postfeminism is ultimately related to neoliberalism in three ways. First, both discourses privilege individualism, regarding individuals as free agents that are unfettered by social, political, or economic restraints. Second, the autonomous, calculating, and self-regulating neoliberal subject is similar to the active, freely choosing, and self-reinventing postfeminist subject. And third, it is specifically women that are taken up by both neoliberalism and postfeminism and encouraged to "work on and transform the self, to regulate every aspect of their conduct, and to present all their actions as freely chosen" (7). Thus, it is necessary to understand postfeminism as not only a response to feminism, but also integrated within a larger neoliberal cultural climate that shapes the kinds of ideal subjectivities that are promoted to girls and women.

This is especially important to consider when studying girls' media practices. For example, Sarah Banet-Weiser (2011, 2012) analyzes how girls perform neoliberal and postfeminist subjectivities within new media platforms such as YouTube, demonstrating that girls are encouraged to brand themselves through visible displays of normative femininity, which can be circulated on the web. Building on the earlier work of Anita Harris (2004), Banet-Weiser argues that the ability for a girl to "put herself out there" signifies not only a successful performance of postfeminist femininity, but also an adoption of an idealized neoliberal subjectivity via the opportunity to generate income and to become an entrepreneur of the self. Although this is an important argument, it tells us little about girls' agency and those girls who, in fact, complicate neoliberal postfeminist girlhoods through their feminist identities and politics. This book aims to better understand these feminist girls and how they utilize digital platforms to perform alternative girlhood identities.

Doing Feminist Ethnography in Digital Spaces

In addition to the theoretical interventions this book makes, I also hope to begin to map a method for conducting feminist ethnography within online spaces – a practice that remains poorly articulated within existing digital and feminist media studies literature. This is despite the importance of ethnography as a feminist method, especially within girls' media and cultural studies. For example, several girls' studies scholars have recently published rich ethnographic studies that provide useful models from a cultural studies perspective for conducting ethnographic research with girls. Jessica Taft's (2011) *Rebel Girls: Youth Activism & Social Change Across the Americas*, Emilie Zaslow's (2009) *Feminism, Inc: Coming of Age in Girl Power Media Culture*, and *'Girl Power' Girls Reinventing Girlhood* by Dawn Currie, Deirdre Kelly, and Shauna Pomerantz (2009) all utilize ethnographic methods including focus groups, interviews, and participant observation to examine issues such as girls' activism, interaction with girl power media culture, and enactment of girlhood, femininity, and feminism, respectively. These studies inform my own ethnographic approach that takes girls' voices as a starting point for my research inquiry, and I have modeled my own project, specifically the use of open-ended interviews and focus groups, after them.

Whereas the previously mentioned studies are useful because of their focus on girls, none offer a sustained and focused discussion on the relationship between girls and new media. Here, Mary Gray's (2009) book *Out in the Country: Youth, Media, and Queer Visibility in Rural America* offers an excellent methodological model for thinking about the relationship between girls and new media. Gray's ethnography examines the ways in which rural queer youth navigate their identities through new media engagements, relationships, and their local cultural context, demonstrating her commitment to "ethnographic approaches that contextualize media engagements as part of a broader social terrain of experience" (14). This specific ethnographic approach – what Gray terms "in situ" – differs from the more common ethnographic approach to media reception by broadening the focus of study beyond the relationship between media text and audience. Gray explains,

> Instead of examining audiences' reactions to specific programs or websites, I attempt to map the relationship between rural young people's experiences of a cluster of media engagements and a milieu that is constitutive of its meaning. An in situ approach to media takes as the object of study the processes and understandings of new media among people within the context of their use ... [and] focuses on how media engagements fit into a larger mosaic of collective identity work (127).

Whereas other scholars (McRobbie 1991; Drotner 1994) have advocated for similar approaches to media research, Gray's work has been particularly pertinent to shaping my approach to this book because of its focus on new media, specifically youth Internet practices. Thus, this "in situ" ethnographic approach allows me to better investigate questions of girls' media production practices and the cultural context that informs them, rather than solely their media reception. The questions that guide my ethnographic work will then be informed by this specific methodological standpoint.

I do not position this book as an ethnography per se, but instead a project that combines ethnographic methods with discursive and ideological textual analyses of girl-produced media and popular media commentary that focuses on girls, feminism, and/or new media technologies between 2009 and 2013. I conducted monthly in-depth, semi-structured Skype and email interviews with five self-identified girl feminist bloggers over a six-month period in 2012, as well as follow-up interviews with the bloggers in July 2014. Most interviews lasted between 30 and 60 minutes and were recorded and transcribed prior to data analysis. I also employed what I'm calling an 'online focus group blog' with a group of eight bloggers, which included the five bloggers who participated in the interview component. The focus group blog functioned as a secured online space where my study participants and I held regular conversations about blogging, feminism, and girlhood over the research period and generated over sixty printed pages of discussion, which I organized thematically using discursive and ideological textual analysis. This method allowed bloggers the opportunity to engage with one another, ask their own questions, and direct the project in ways that traditional interviews do not allow. In this sense, this book also contributes methodologically to new/digital media studies by outlining a model for ethnographic research in digital spaces that privileges collaboration, media production, and community-building as part of the research process.

I supplemented my ethnographic methods with a discursive and ideological textual analysis that focused on the eight blogs authored by my study participants, as well as *Rookie Magazine*, edited by teenage feminist blogger Tavi Gevinson who I discuss in chapter five. I primarily focused my analysis on the written text, including both the blog posts and comments. However, I also analyze images that are incorporated into blog posts, blog logos, color schemes, links, and other visual content when relevant to my discussion. I read the entirety of each blog up until the end of my data collection period (blogs ranged from being a few months old to over four years) and purposefully selected entries to analyze based upon their relevance to the themes I am addressing in this project. Whereas my sample size is no doubt small, I want to emphasize that I am not attempting to make generalizations about *all girls* or even *all feminist girls* in this project – a task that would be impossible. Instead, I employ a small group of participants and their blogs in order to do justice to their detailed stories and experiences as feminist bloggers in a way that wouldn't be possible with a large pool of participants.

Organization of Chapters

The chapters of this book are organized thematically around primary themes that emerged from conversations with my study participants throughout the course of the research. However, I also hope that the chapters speak to one another and together produce a coherent story that highlights the exciting contributions of girl bloggers to feminist activism today. Chapter one explores how blogs function as a discursive space for girls to perform feminist identities that may be unwelcome in school, home, or peer group environments. I analyze how these performances of feminist identities work affectively and politically as a strategy for girls to resist normative postfeminist femininities. The second chapter continues my discussion of identity but focuses on girl bloggers' activist identities, mapping how blogging functions as an accessible form of activism for girls. Chapter three addresses how feminist girl bloggers form communities through their use of new media technologies, connections that I analyze as 'networked counterpublics.' The chapter also considers issues of friendship and diversity within bloggers' networked counterpublics. The fourth chapter traces how feminist girls creatively engage with the history of feminism through their blogs, and in doing so, produce feminist history through their blogging. Finally, chapter five explores how feminist girl bloggers create a space within popular culture to perform feminism publically, a practice I analyze as a form of citizenship. In the Conclusion I position my analysis as an initial, necessary step in mapping a cultural history of girls' participation in feminism in the early twenty-first century. I draw on follow-up interviews with several of my participants and examples of recent feminist digital activism campaigns to reflect on what the current visibility of popular feminism might mean for both girls and feminist media studies scholars as we move through the second decade of the twenty-first century.

Notes

1. See chapter four for a detailed discussion of feminist waves.
2. This recent study surveyed only those over the age of eighteen, and, therefore, this statistic refers to young women between the ages of eighteen and twenty-nine, a slightly older demographic than my study participants.
3. Amanda Todd, a fifteen-year-old British Columbia high school student committed suicide on October 10, 2012 after being sexually harassed online. For three years an unknown man continuously circulated a topless photo of Todd to her family, classmates, and teachers. The photo led to Todd being harassed, threatened, and physically assaulted at school. A month before her suicide, Todd created and posted a video to YouTube explaining her situation through the use of flash cards, which quickly went viral upon news of her death. In response to Todd's suicide a motion was introduced in the Canadian House of Commons that proposed more funding for anti-bullying organizations and a study of bullying in Canada.

References

Banet-Weiser, Sarah. 2011. "Branding the Post-Feminist Self: Girls' Video Production and YouTube." In *Mediated Girlhoods: New Explorations of Girls' Media Culture*, edited by Mary Celeste Kearney, 277–294. New York: Peter Lang.

Banet-Weiser, Sarah. 2012. *Authentic TM: The Politics of Ambivalence in a Brand Culture*. New York: New York University Press.

Baym, Nancy. 2006. "Finding the Quality in Qualitative Research." In *Critical Cyberculture Studies*, edited by David Silver and Adrienne Massanari, 79–87. New York: New York University Press.

Berlant, Lauren. 1997. *The Queen of America Goes to Washington City: Essays on Sex and Citizenship*. Durham: Duke University Press.

Budgeon, Shelley. 2001. "Emergent Feminist(?) Identities: Young Women and the Practice of Micropolitics." *European Journal of Women's Studies* 8 (7): 7–28.

Cassell, Justine, and Meg Cramer. 2008. "High Tech or High Risk: Moral Panics About Girls Online." In *Digital Youth, Innovation, and the Unexpected*, edited by Tara McPherson, 53–75. Cambridge: MIT Press.

Currie, Dawn, Deirdre Kelly, and Shauna Pomerantz. 2009. *'Girl Power:' Girls Reinventing Girlhood*. New York: Peter Lang.

D'Acci, Julie. 2005. "Cultural Studies, Television Studies, and the Crisis in the Humanities." In *Television After TV: Essays on a Medium in Transition*, edited by Lynn Spigel and Jan Olsson. Durham: Duke University Press.

Driscoll, Catherine. 2002. *Girls: Feminine Adolescence in Popular Culture and Cultural History*. New York: Columbia University Press.

Drotner, Kristen. 1994. "Ethnographic Enigmas: 'The Everyday' in Recent Media Studies." *Cultural Studies* 8(2): 341–357.

Duggan, Lisa. 2003. *The Twilight of Equality? Neoliberalism, Cultural Politics, and the Attack on Democracy*. Boston: Beacon Press.

Duggan, Maeve, and Joanna Brenner. 2013. "The Demographics of Social Media Users – 2012." Pew Internet & American Life Project. Washington, DC. Accessed November 13. http://www.pewinternet.org/Reports/2013/Social-media-users.aspx.

Eisenhauer, Jennifer. 2004. "Mythic Figures and Lived Identities: Locating the 'Girl' in Feminist Discourse." In *All About the Girl: Culture, Power, and Identity*, edited by Anita Harris, 79–90. New York: Routledge.

Gill, Rosalind. 2007. "Postfeminist Media Culture: Elements of a Sensibility." *European Journal of Cultural Studies* 10 (2): 147–166.

Gill, Rosalind, and Christina Scharff. 2011. "Introduction." In *New Femininities: Postfeminism, Neoliberalism and Subjectivity*, edited by Rosalind Gill and Christina Scharff, 1–17. New York: Palgrave MacMillan.

Gray, Mary. 2009. *Out in the Country: Youth, Media, and Visibility in Rural America*. New York: New York University Press.

Harris, Anita. 2004. *Future Girl: Young Women in the Twenty-first Century*. New York: Routledge.

Harris, Anita. 2008. *Next Wave Cultures: Feminism, Subcultures, Activism*. New York: Routledge.

Harris, Anita. 2010. "Mind the Gap: Attitudes and Emergent Feminist Politics since the Third Wave." *Australian Feminist Studies* 25 (66): 275–284.

Harvey, David. 2005. *A Brief History of Neoliberalism*. Oxford: Oxford University Press.

Hunter, Jane. 2002. *How Young Ladies Became Girls: The Victorian Origins of Girlhood*. New Haven: Yale University Press.

Jenkins, Henry. 2006. *Convergence Culture: Where Old and New Media Collide*. New York: New York University Press.

Jowett, Madeleine. 2004. "'I Don't See Feminists As You See Feminists:' Young Women Negotiating Feminism in Contemporary Britain." In *All About the Girl: Culture, Power, and Identity*, edited by Anita Harris, 91–100. New York: Routledge.

Kearney, Mary Celeste. 2006. *Girls Make Media*. New York: Routledge.

Kellner, Douglas. 1995. "Cultural Studies, Multiculturalism, and Media Culture." In *Gender, Race, and Class in Media: A Text-Reader*, edited by Gail Dines and Jean M. Humez, 5–17. Thousand Oaks: Sage Publications.

Lenhardt, Amanda, Sousan Arafeh, Aaron Smith, and Alexandra Macgill. 2008. "Writing, Technology, and Teens." Pew Internet and American Life Project, Washington, DC. Accessed December 12, 2012. http://www.pewinternet.org/Reports/2008/Writing-Technology-and-Teens/06-Electronic-Communication/04-Blogging-and-social-networking-are-dominated-by-girls.aspx.

Marvin, Carolyn. 1990. *When Old Technologies Were New: Thinking About Electric Communication in the Late Nineteenth Century*. Oxford: Oxford University Press.

McRobbie, Angela. 1991. *Feminism and Youth Culture*. New York: Routledge.

McRobbie, Angela. 2009. *The Aftermath of Feminism: Gender, Culture and Social Change*. Thousand Oaks: Sage.

Nussbaum, Emily. 2011. "The Rebirth of the Feminist Manifesto." *New York Magazine*, October 30. Accessed November 14, 2011. http://nymag.com/ news/ features/feminist-blogs-2011-11/.

Ouellette, Laurie, and Julie Wilson. 2011. "Women's Work: Affective Labor and Convergence Culture." *Cultural Studies* 25 (4–5): 548–565.

Pomerantz, Shauna. 2009. "Between a Rock and a Hard Place: Un/Defining the 'Girl.'" *Jeunesse: Young People, Texts, Cultures* 1(2): 147–158.

Rettberg, Jill. 2008. *Blogging*. Malden: Polity.

Ringrose, Jessica, and Katarina Barajas. 2011. "Gendered Risks and Opportunities? Exploring Teen Girls' Digital Sexual Identity in Postfeminist Media Contexts." *International Journal of Media and Cultural Politics* 7(2): 121–138.

Shade, Leslie. 2007. "Contested Spaces: Protecting of Inhibiting Girls Online?" In *Growing Up Online: Young People and Digital Technologies*, edited by Sandra Weber and Shanly Dixon, 227–244. New York: Palgrave MacMillan.

Shade, Leslie. 2011. "Surveilling the Girl via the Third and Networked Screen." In *Mediated Girlhoods: New Explorations of Girls' Media Culture*, edited by Mary Celeste Kearney, 261–275. New York: Peter Lang.

Swindle, Monica. 2011. "Feeling Girl, Girling Feeling: An Examination of 'Girl' as Affect." *Rhizomes*, 22. Accessed March 3, 2013. http://www.rhizomes.net/ issue22/swindle.html.

Taft, Jessica. 2011. *Rebel Girls: Youth Activism & Social Change Across the Americas*. New York: New York University Press.

Timson, J. 2009. "Feminism in the Web Era: It ain't pretty." *The Globe and Mail*, March 24. Accessed October 4, 2012. http://www.theglobeandmail.com/life/ feminism-in-the-webera-it-aint-pretty/article977261/.

Weinberger, Hannah. 2012. "Where are all the Millennial Feminists?" *CNN.com*, November 10. Accessed November 12. http://www.cnn.com/2012/11/09/living/ millennialsfeminism.

Williams, Raymond. 1974. *Television: Technology and Cultural Form*. London: Fontana/Collins.

Zaslow, Emilie. 2009. *Feminism INC: Coming of Age in a Girl Power Media Culture*. New York: Palgrave MacMillan.

1 Click Moments and Coming Out

Girl Bloggers and the Performance of Feminist Identities Online

I'm a feminist. Man, that feels good.

I've been a feminist all my life but didn't realize it until a few weeks ago when I checked out a twenty-pound stack of books from the library ... Somewhere along the line something clicked; maybe it wasn't as glamorous as the whole light-bulb-over-the-head charade, but it was pretty dang life-changing ...

When I realized I was a feminist I thought "what do I do now"? I was honestly scared to tell anybody about my new "discovery" because I wasn't sure how they'd react. ... But why did I have to feel this way? Like I was unearthing a dirty secret, my own straight girl's version of coming out of the closet? Why am I scared for the future, of what people will think of me? The fact is, today's world is dangerous for teenagers like me (and you, if you're reading this) because the "f-word" is marred by too many stereotypes to count ...

So I wanted to write a blog about something I actually understand. I'm not an award-winning physicist or world-renowned psychologist (yet!), but what I do understand is the stuff swishing around in my noggin. I want to write about life from my perspective – a feminist teen just trying to make sense of the world – and hopefully appeal to others who feel the same way ...

—Renee, Sunday June 27, 2010, blog post

I've quoted the inaugural post of Renee's blog at length because it provides a useful introduction to many of the issues I will discuss in this chapter: the private process of identifying oneself as feminist, the public assertion and performance of a feminist identity, the unique needs of teenage girl feminists, and the 'good' feelings that a feminist identity can generate. It also reveals how girls like Renee adopt blogging to explore – and, as I will argue, perform – emerging feminist identities. It is this relationship between feminist identities and blogging that informs the guiding questions of this chapter: How do girl bloggers understand their own feminist identities? In what ways do girls use blogging to better articulate and explore these identities? How do girls' feminist identities challenge normative constructions of both girls and feminists? And what benefits do girls receive from performing a feminist identity?

Renee's blog post also exposes the tension that the feminist label continues to carry in contemporary culture. Indeed, stereotypes of man-hating, bra-burning, and hairy-legged feminists still exist within popular consciousness, including within high school environments where feminism is often not part of the daily lexicon (Ringrose and Renold forthcoming 2016). Feminism itself is too often misunderstood as a movement about taking away men's rights, promoting women as better than men, or a politics of times past, no longer relevant to North American women who supposedly have achieved equality. While these dominant discourses certainly inform the cultural climate of contemporary teenage girls and the way they understand feminism, I am suggesting that the feminist bloggers I discuss are actively changing this context, in part through their public embracing of feminist identities. Thus, this chapter maps how the performance of feminist identities reveals not only ruptures within postfeminist logic, but also the ways in which online spaces such as blogs have been significant spaces to problematize the charicature of the feminist found within postfeminist popular culture.

Within the past fifteen years there has been significant scholarly and popular interest in girls' understandings of feminism, particularly in what has been dubbed the "I'm-not-a-feminist-but" phenomenon, characterized as a popular stance among girls and young women (Budgeon 2001; McRobbie 2009; Zaslow 2009; Harris 2010; Zeilinger 2012). The seemingly contradictory identity positions taken up by young women – supposedly desiring feminist gains for equality yet ambivalent about feminism as a political movement – have been confusing for scholars and have led to a focus on the cultural contexts that inform such subjectivities. For example, Shelley Budgeon (2001) maintains that contemporary young women may not choose to identify as a feminist, but their actions or "life politics" and identities remain informed by feminist ideals. She argues that it is the cultural tensions, contradictions, and fragmentation of our neoliberal, cultural context that prevents young women and girls from adopting the feminist label. She writes,

> Non-identification may display a refusal to be fixed into place as a feminist, but may also be a sign of the inability to position oneself as feminist because of confusing and contradictory messages about what feminism really is. This is a point of major significance. What is feminism? When an answer to such a question is so difficult to produce is it surprising that young women do not identify themselves as feminist? (23)

Likewise, recent ethnographic work examining girls and feminism, such as a large-scale study with eighty girls conducted by Emilie Zaslow (2009), also highlights the complexity of the feminist label for many contemporary girls. Zaslow found that while the majority of her teenage study participants agree with feminist ideals and are not hostile to feminism, many are ambivalent about embracing the feminist label, and instead describe their beliefs using a discourse of individual rights and choice, rather than a collectivist or redistributive approach to gender equality (See Fraser 2013). Zaslow understands this finding in relation to the postfeminist commercial girl power rhetoric popular during her participants' youth, which focuses on individualism and choice as markers of an empowered feminine identity.

Similarly, Christina Scharff (2012) argues that young women are encouraged to repudiate feminism through prominent cultural discourses of postfeminism and neoliberalism, both of which privilege an individualist rhetoric that is in tension with the collectivist approach to structural inequalities that feminism takes up. Her study, based upon interviews with forty young women in the UK and Germany, reveals the "contested space that feminism occupies within the cultural space of postfeminism," making visible two interpretive frames through which young women understand feminism; as valuable, but no long necessary, or as extreme and ideological (Scharff 2012, 40). Scharff's most significant intervention is the way in which she theorizes repudiations of feminism within the heterosexual matrix, arguing that the "trope of the feminist" as unfeminine, man-hating, and lesbian is imagined as a constitutive outside of the heteronormative order, "haunting" her participants, despite the lack of tangible evidence that such a feminist exists. According to Scharff then, the trope of the feminist is not merely a negative stereotype, but reveals the complex ways that performances of gender and sexuality shape dis-identification with feminism.

Defining the "F-word"

The previously mentioned studies highlight how problematic both defining feminism and defining who is a feminist can be, issues that are certainly not new but are constantly shifting in relation to both broader cultural contexts and particular social situations (Scharff 2012). While it is clear that limited definitions are not desirable for my research, it nonetheless remains important to have a focused understanding of the word 'feminism' that can inform this book. I add my own voice to this debate with caution and focus my discussion on how my participant bloggers define feminism and their own feminist identity, rather than my own understanding of these terms. I take up Scharff's (2012) insistence that feminism must be approached "flexibly" and that we should understand feminism as a discursive category, which recognizes the multiple iterations of the word, better understood as feminisms in the plural (Scharff 2012; Butler 1990).

This approach is necessary in part due to the varying responses I received from bloggers when I asked them to define feminism. Several of my research participants articulated definitions of feminism that align with a liberal feminist ideology, while alluding to the complexity that arises when putting feminism into practice. For example, Courtney, a twenty-one-year-old college student says that "[m]y definition of feminism is simply gender equality. Not only under law, but also socially. Just because we have laws that say everyone is equal, not everyone is treated as such." Here, Courtney recognizes that feminism must be more than just formal laws, but a cultural shift in attitude that involves "treating a woman who works and a woman who stays home with the children with the same respect. It's accepting women who don't shave or wear makeup as well as those that prefer those things [sic]. It's seeing an equal distribution of women of different colors, shapes, and sizes in the media."

In a similar vein, nineteen-year-old Madison claims, "My definition of feminism is the belief in women's economic, social, and political equality." However, she stresses an attention to intersectionality as a central part of her feminism. "I think it's important to remember that there are lots of different types of women. Feminism should help ALL women. We cannot be free if one of our sisters is still bound by her race, sexual orientation, or gender identity. Intersectionality plays a large role in the feminism I practice and believe in." It is not surprising that liberal feminist ideology is prevalent amongst my participants. As Bonnie Dow (1996) notes in her study of television programming from the 1970s and 1980s, it is liberal feminism that is most often incorporated into popular media, making the tradition's individualist discourse of equality, opportunities, and rights the most familiar feminist discourse to many Americans.

Liberal feminist values also align with perceived American values, and are consequently more palpable to the public than the rhetoric of radical or socialist feminists, for example. Because liberal feminism emphasizes legislative changes in order to open up opportunities to women rather than a more substantial alteration of unequal social relations, it is non-threatening to the status quo, particularly men. Indeed, scholars such as Lisa Duggan (2003) have analyzed the ways in which 'equality' has recently become a central part of conservative neoliberal rhetoric that privilege a "'color-blind' anti-affirmative action racial politics, conservative-libertarian 'equality feminism,' and gay 'normality'" (44). And while Duggan's discussion of the neoliberalization of equality is markedly different from the liberal feminism that supported suffrage, the Equal Rights Amendment and sexual harassment lawsuits, it is important to recognize how discourses of equality remain prevalent in both ideologies.

Nonetheless, comments like Courtney and Madison's also point to the influence of third wave and U.S. third world feminisms to my participants' definitions of feminism. As Leslie Heywood and Jennifer Drake (1997) note, third wave feminists acknowledge the necessity of complicating the category of 'woman' by recognizing the multiple experiences and oppressions women face based upon race, class, sexuality, ethnicity, age, religion, national identity, ability and other identities. This third wave perspective owes much to the U.S. third world feminists who have rightfully problematized the notion of 'sisterhood' and made visible the experiences of women of color within feminism since the early 1980s (Sandoval 2000; Moraga and Anzaldua 1981). As a result, I've discovered that the language of intersectionality is common among many young feminists today.

Given that the rhetoric of choice is a central part of postfeminist culture (Scharff 2012; McRobbie 2009; Gill 2007), I was surprised that only one of the bloggers I interviewed emphasized choice as a central part of her definition of feminism, although others, such as Courtney, certainly allude to it. Amandine, a seventeen-year-old high school senior suggests that "[f]eminism is all about giving people choices. Women can keep or terminate a pregnancy without being judged either way. Men can become fashion designers without people automatically assuming they're gay. Women can become CEOs and balance a healthy family life too." While Amandine's definition problematically glosses over the structural inequalities that present certain men and women with more 'choices' than others, her definition makes sense considering not only the potential influence of postfeminist discourses on girls today, but also the ways in which third wave feminism has conceptualized feminism as more fluid, flexible, and individually shaped (Dicker and Piepmeier 2003; Karlyn Rowe 2003; Heywood and Drake 1997).

In their introduction to *Catching a Wave: Reclaiming Feminism for the 21st Century,* Alison Piepmeier and Rory Dicker (2003) caution against what they call a "feminist-free-for-all," where any choice a woman seemingly makes is positioned as feminist, without an analysis of broader social power structures. Indeed, scholars such as Zaslow (2009) have demonstrated that this free-for-all stance toward feminism is prevalent among their young research participants. It also shares some similarities with Tavi Gevinson's articulation of feminism. While I will discuss the eighteen-year-old blogger and her feminist publication, *Rookie,* in chapter five, her definition of feminism is important to consider here. In a March 2012 TedxTeen talk, Tavi argues that, "feminism is not a rulebook, but a discussion, a conversation, a process."[1] I asked my participants for their comments on Gevinson's take on feminism, and their thoughts reveal important elements of their own understandings of feminism.

For example, eighteen-year-old Kat, says that she "semi-agree[s]" with Gevinson, explaining that "[w]hile [feminism] isn't a book of rules, I think there are certain things you have to believe in order to be a part of the feminist community, including equal pay, reproductive rights, LGBTQ rights, etc. There are certain things you have to agree with." Kat's comments reveal that to her, feminism must address larger structural inequalities (e.g. equal pay), and attention to intersectional oppressions (e.g. LGBTQ rights). Kat's feminism, then, is not only about individual choices and actions, but is tied to a social analysis that recognizes the complex ways that power works, revealing the influence of both third wave and radical feminisms.

While Renee agrees with Kat, maintaining "there are certain beliefs that basically come with the feminist job description," she stresses a definition of feminism that still leaves room for growth and, as she states, "ever-changing identities." She explains,

> When I first started writing, for example, I saw feminism more as a set of rules or beliefs that I should follow and explore. But as I blogged more and started having conversations with other feminists, I started seeing feminism as something much more broad and abstract that could be applied to many areas of my life – whether as a confidence

boost, a sense of internal drive and accomplishment, or a lens through which I could view the things life was throwing at me. In this way, feminism has become much more personal. It's no longer a club I feel I have to prove myself to be a part of, it's something I can mold and shape to work for me.

Renee's comments suggest how important accessibility is to her understanding of feminism, something that seems appropriate considering her age. To Renee, discourses of feminism must be something that she can access and apply to her own life in order for it to make sense to her.

The responses I have described earlier point to what Scharff (2012) calls the "multiplicity of engagements with feminism," and reveals the diverse ways that feminist identities and feminism is imagined by the bloggers I interviewed. There are numerous reasons for these varying understandings of feminism – race, class, sexuality, and other identities, home environment and social location, specific interests and activist engagements, and education – to name a few. I will address these issues throughout this book, parsing out the multiple ways that girl bloggers negotiate, produce, and articulate feminisms in order to demonstrate that girl feminist bloggers are not a homogenous group or subculture, but representative and productive of the differences folded into contemporary feminisms. However, I now turn to discussing some of the similar sentiments about feminism shared by the bloggers I interviewed, including an enthusiastic investment in their own feminist identity.

A "First Dose of Feminism": Considering Feminist Identities

Because my study consists of a purposefully chosen sample of girls who identify as feminist, it is not surprising that a feminist identity is a significant part of their lives. Nonetheless, I believe that it is important to stress the enthusiastic response I received when I asked girls about their feminist identities, because these expressions reflect an affective dimension of a feminist identity that I will take up later in this chapter. Renee tells me, "I'm not exaggerating when I say that feminism is a HUGE part of my overall identity" and that she views her feminist identity as "a very, very positive thing." Likewise, Amandine describes her feminist identity as "extremely important" to her overall identity. While my participants' experiences cannot be generalized across girls as a group, their interest in identifying as feminists remain significant in light of dominant discourses suggesting girls today are not interested in feminism (Budgeon 2001; Zaslow 2009; Scharff 2012).

In fact, I suggest that the teenage feminists I discuss in this book may potentially signal the shifting position of feminism in North American society – from one of feminism in retreat as theorized through postfeminism by scholars such as McRobbie (2009) to one where the ruptures of neoliberalism have created opportunities for feminism to re-emerge as viable and even desirable. Within this context public feminist identities become signifiers of these neoliberal ruptures, and thus it is necessary to pay attention to girls' performances of *feminist* identities, rather than just the *non-feminist* girls that have been the focus of academic research.

This interest in and enthusiasm for thinking about their own feminist identities, including the 'click moments' when girls discovered that they're feminist, and tales of 'going public,' when they publicly share their new identity, is clearly reflected in many of the girl-authored blogs I analyzed. Similar to Renee's posting with which I opened this chapter, many girls choose to blog about how they became feminist and what their newfound feminist identity means to them. Several of these stories are detailed on the *FBomb*, an online community for teenage girl bloggers to which several of my participants regularly contribute. For example, in a June 2, 2010 post called "My Click Moment," Julie Z. recounts, "I can't pinpoint a moment, let alone a day, week or month, but I eventually 'clicked' sometime near the end of my freshman year of high school. I wasn't afraid of being a feminist, and I wasn't afraid to tell people that I was. And I've been happy with myself and my life ever since."[2]

Similarly, an *FBomb* post titled "Why I Became a Feminist" by Rachel F. on October 26, 2009 details how the author became a feminist after receiving a sexist comment from a male classmate. And a November 2, 2010 posting by Anna R., a sixth grade girl, begins with, "In fourth grade I had my first dose of feminism. I had read an article in a local feminist magazine that spoke of the expected roles and stereotypes of a modern female. The issues they were talking about bothered me. I could feel it." These types of stories are a regular part of the *FBomb* and other feminist blogs, and suggest the importance of these first experiences with feminist identities in the lives of feminist girls. Indeed, many of these experiences are described as transformative to the blogger's identity and become the first necessary step in connecting with a larger feminist community, an issue I will discuss in more detail in chapter three.

But despite the enthusiasm with which my participants talked about their feminist identities, they were very much aware of the potential tensions that their feminist identity could raise in their daily lives. For example, Renee explains that once she realized that she wanted to identify as feminist, she felt like she was hiding a secret. She tells me, "I wondered how my family would react, or my friends, or what this new label meant for my life as a whole." And while she was pleasantly surprised by her own family and friends' reactions to her going public as a feminist, she maintains that, "Once you put yourself out there as a feminist you WILL deal with mixed reactions, but [you can't] let that get you down." In fact, Renee claims that the positive experiences she's had – like receiving a hand-written letter from a girl thanking her for introducing her to feminism through her blog – far outweigh the negative comments that she's received on her blog's comments section.

Other bloggers reveal more contentious experiences with family and friends upon disclosing their feminist identity. Courtney tells me that her religious family tried to curb her feminist leanings by telling her "the Church isn't an advocate of feminism." Likewise, Kat claims that her classmates and even her teachers in her rural conservative Midwestern high school would give her "crap" about being a feminist, mocking her feminist beliefs in AP History class. And while Amandine found her mom to be "totally cool" with her feminist identity, her friends think feminism is "a load of garbage," although Amandine admits that some are actually what she calls "practical feminists," interested in women's rights, like equal pay, rather than the feminist theory which fascinates her.

Eve Sedgwick's (1990) *Epistemology of the Closet* provides useful insight into how girls' disclosures of their feminist identities constitute a key part of transformative identity work. Indeed, we must ask what the difference is between Amandine and her friend who may support equal pay but refuses the feminist identity. Sedgwick reminds us that the act of "coming out" does not require the revelation of new information or actions, but the discursive articulation of a subjectivity that may or may not be known. In doing so one's identity is produced as "discursive fact" that carries both transformative potential on an individual and social level, as well as risk (Sedgwick 1990; Foucault 1978). In other words, while girls like Amandine and Renee may have always espoused feminist values and actions, the public performance of a feminist identity within the discursive framework of a revelation, constitutes a shift that carries both power, and as Renee mentions in her inaugural post, danger. And while several of the bloggers did mention negative experiences upon disclosing their feminist identity, the power that many felt upon identifying as feminist suggests an empowering transformation that several bloggers experienced, which I will discuss in more detail later in this chapter.

We don't know much about Amandine's friend, who she describes as a "practical feminist," although Amandine claims her friend doesn't personally identify as such. Of course, it is not my objective to state that her friend is or is not a 'real' feminist. Nonetheless, Sedgwick claims that "'[c]losetedness' itself is a performance initiated as such by the speech act of a silence – not a particular silence, but a silence that accrues particularity by fits and starts, in relation to the discourse that surrounds and differentially constitutes it" (3). Thus, the speech act of not identifying as feminist – remaining closeted, so to speak – reflects the ambivalent positioning of many feminists within contemporary culture. The silence around identifying as feminist – whether one believes one is or not – must then be considered as "a weighty and occupied and consequential epistemological space" worthy of careful analysis (77).

Scharff's research on young women's disavowal of feminism accomplishes this and even suggests a productive link with Sedgwick's scholarship. Scharff argues that young women's refusal of a feminist identity is rooted in maintaining the heteronormative order, whereby "the 'feminist' acts as a constitutive outside of the heterosexual matrix" (87). In this sense, "coming out" as a feminist – language that Renee herself uses in the blog post that opens this chapter – is very much situated within discourses of sexuality that can be acknowledged or unacknowledged. Although none of my participants specifically mentioned a fear that they'd be assumed to be lesbian once they publicly identified as feminist, the pervasive nature of the 'lesbian feminist' stereotype may indeed have caused some of the bloggers anxiety about coming out, suggesting some productive scholarly commonalities between being out of the closet as gay or feminist.[3]

These stories point to the diversity of experiences that girl bloggers have had with regard to going public with their feminist identities and suggest that it is impossible to generalize across even this small group of girl feminist bloggers. Indeed, social contexts informed by geographical location and familial beliefs appear to shape the responses that my participants received to their identity claims, and research also suggests that identity categories such as race, class, and sexuality inform engagements with a feminist identity (Scharff 2012; Kearney 2006). What connects my participants however, is how they have used blogging as a strategy to "try out" feminist and activist identities (Crowther 1999). I will turn to this idea now in order to discern how blogs function as a discursive space for the performance of feminist identities.

Feminist Identities in Flux: Exploring Feminism Through Blogging

While several scholars have explored the connection between girls' identity exploration and media production (Mazzarella 2005, 2010; Thiel Stern 2007; Stern 2002), most of this research does not focus on the political identities that girls cultivate through media production, inadvertently reinforcing the notion of girls as apolitical. Of course, there are some notable exceptions, including some excellent analyses of riot grrrl culture by Jessica Rosenberg and Gitana Garofalo (1998), Mary Celeste Kearney (2006), Kristen Schilt and Elke Zobl (2008), and Alison Piepmeier (2009); as well as Dawn Currie, Deirdre Kelly, and Shauna Pomerantz's (2009) study of girl skaters and "Online Girls." I build on this work by focusing on the relationship between feminist identities and blogging in order to map the productive possibilities of this relationship.

While all of my participants acknowledge an important link between their feminist identities and their blogging, the process of becoming a feminist blogger varies. In some cases, it was the process of identifying as a feminist that directly led some girls to start blogs in order to perform and experiment with a feminist identity. "The whole reason I started my blog was to document the life of a new feminist, and all the mistakes and misgivings I might have along the way. Writing, blogging, and receiving feedback from older feminists has allowed me to understand and appreciate the movement more," Renee tells me.

Other girls, like Madison, claimed that her own transformation to feminist blogger "just sort of happened." Madison, who began blogging four years ago at the age of fifteen, originally wrote about a variety of topics while following other feminist blogs because of her general interest in feminism. She recalls, "I slowly started to blog about feminism [myself] and then it totally blew up in my face! I went from having, like, twenty followers that were mainly friends from school to having a thousand followers in two months ... I realized that I was the only – or at least one of only a few – teenagers blogging about feminism on Tumblr." She changed her blog's name to reflect the new focus on feminism and has considered herself a feminist blogger since. Four years later, her blog continues to be a hub for feminist activity on Tumblr, and she has been actively using her position as a blogger to advocate for the reproductive rights of women in her home state of Michigan.

Like many of her blogging peers, Madison's commitment to feminist blogging was only the beginning of a process of engagement with feminism that would result in multiple, shifting, and complicated feminist identities, what I've referred to as "feminist identities in flux" (Keller 2012). Indeed, several of my participants revealed that the blogging process itself, including writing one's own posts but also reading others' posts and commenting on others' blogs, has changed the ways in which bloggers perform their feminist identities. Madison claims that connecting with likeminded peers has made her more confident in her feminist beliefs. She says, "I thought I was the only one when I first started. I really thought it was me and Jessica Valenti and that was it. I love blogging because now I know all these people – tons and tons of people who agree with me, which is great. I've become more sure [of myself] and less apologetic I think ... it has made me more confident."

While I will elaborate on the connection between feminist identities and one's sense of self later in this chapter, I want to highlight how Madison's comments can allow us to think productively about the ways that blogging can facilitate a shift from understanding one's feminist identity as an individual feminist identity to part of a collective feminist identity. Likewise, Courtney tells me, "Since beginning my blog, my feminist identity became a lot more than just being [a] personal [thing] ... Up until then it was just something that I identified as because I believed in gender equality, but I think after that as a feminist I can be part of a larger community and actually share what I think and talk to people about these things and get other people interested in these issues. So it became more about community issues than just about myself." Thus, while scholars have described digital media as inherently narcissistic, implying that young women who use these technologies are more interested in individualized identities and actions (Banet-Weiser 2012b), the comments I have been analyzing complicate these assumptions, suggesting that blogging may facilitate communal feminist identities that build productive solidarities, something I will discuss further in chapter three.

Courtney's comments also relate to the other main point that several of my participants made when I asked about how blogging has changed their performance of a feminist identity; namely, that blogging has served to complicate their performances by introducing them to a range of new feminist issues. For example, Kat admits that she learned a lot about LGBTQ issues after she began blogging and can now understand her feminist identity as supportive of LGBTQ rights. Madison also claims that her participation in the feminist blogosphere has complicated her own feminist identity by exposing her to the experiences of women of color and queer women. In this sense, many of these bloggers began to learn about issues like intersectionality and privilege through their blogging and have had to reconsider their own feminist identities and values in relation to this new knowledge. In Madison's case, this knowledge has altered her definition of feminism to recognize the importance of difference and intersectionality, which I described above. Finally, Renee summarizes her own changing identity as follows:

> Blogging continually shapes my feminist identity. Blogging requires one to research topics they may not be familiar with and also consider the views of those responding to their writing via comments, emails, etc. Blogging, then, allows us to continually learn and form new opinions. These revised opinions help mold our ever-changing identities.

While Renee uses the word "experiment" to describe her blog, Barbara Crowther (1999) has used the language of "trying out" identities in relation to her work on girls' diaries, and Mary Celeste Kearney (2006) has applied this idea to grrrl zines, films, and websites. Both scholars discuss how these mediums serve as performative spaces for girls' identity work, facilitating the expression of fluid, shifting, and experimental identities.[4] Although I'm suggesting that girls' blogs work in similar ways, I'd like to build on Crowther and Kearney's ideas by thinking about the performance of feminist identities as specifically being a resistant, political, or even an activist act, an idea I will elaborate on in the next chapter. I employ this move in order to recognize how identities function as political markers that girl bloggers are mobilizing in order to produce social change. In this sense, a feminist identity also serves as a tool that girl feminist bloggers use to chip away at postfeminist constructions of feminism and femininity that populate their daily lives.

The Faces of Feminism: Challenging Feminist Stereotypes

The bloggers that I interviewed were very much aware of the dominant discourses about feminism, particularly those about feminists. Several of my participants referred to 'the feminist stereotype,' which suggests feminists are masculine, lesbian, and "man hating" as being the prevalent characterization of feminists within popular culture and high school life. Theoretically, I return to Scharff's (2012) work, which conceptualizes the "trope of the feminist" as mobilizing a range of affective responses and performances that suggest 'the feminist' must be understood as more than a negative stereotype that must be eradicated, but instead as an identity intimately bound within larger normative discourses about sexuality and gender. However, I have chosen to utilize the language of my participants here, most of which use the term 'stereotype' to talk about the ways that feminists are commonly constructed in public discourse within the U.S. I suspect that this term is employed due to their familiarity with it, because it is a concept often taught in primary and secondary education.

Whereas it may be easy for adult feminists and scholars to dismiss problematic feminist stereotypes as indicative of ignorance, these stereotypes serve as the awkward backdrop against which girl feminists often articulate their own feminist identities and therefore warrant scholarly attention. Indeed, several of the bloggers I spoke to were very concerned with challenging feminist stereotypes and asserting their own feminist identities in ways that demonstrate the diversity the feminist label carries, or 'new' feminist identities. Of course, as Scharff (2012) details, feminist stereotypes and challenges to these stereotypes have a lengthy history in Western feminisms dating back to the early suffragette movements. Consequently, I employ the term 'new' with a knowing wink, fully realizing that contemporary girl bloggers are perhaps only the most recent cohort of feminists to rally against feminist stereotypes. Yet we must recognize the need to take their concerns about and challenges to the stereotype of the feminist seriously, as these objections may reveal further insight into the cultural positioning of young feminists.

For example, Renee tells me, "I would say that feminism for me is advocacy for young people, telling them what [feminism] is [because] it's a scary word to a lot of people. Just trying to dispel those stereotypes is what I'm focusing on through my blog." She describes her blogging as an attempt to present a more realistic picture of what a feminist is with the goal of helping younger girls to identify with the movement. This strategy can be clearly seen throughout the two years her blog was active. For example, several posts point to Renee's interest in encouraging others to think about feminists beyond the narrow stereotypes as hairy-legged man-haters. In "This is What a Feminist Looks Like," Renee blogs, "My point is, you can't make assumptions about an entire group of people just because they call themselves something. So instead of assuming that I hate men (yes, I have actually been accused of hating men), take a minute to really hear me out. Look at what I am fighting for. Me. Renee. Not those so-called 'feminists' on TV."

Her references to "feminists on TV" suggest that Renee is very much attuned to media representations of feminists and is particularly invested in asserting her own performances of feminism in contrast to these so-called media stereotypes. Interestingly though, Renee makes a plea to her reader as an individual – as Renee – drawing on her individual attributes to challenge feminist stereotypes. Here, she mobilizes a discourse of individual agency that suggests we can understand feminism through her own image and actions, without having to deal with the messiness of feminism as a larger social movement.

In a November 24, 2011 posting called "The Faces of Feminism," Renee published pictures she solicited from over 100 people that identify as feminist (Figure 1.1). However, in contrast to the individualistic framing I describe earlier, Renee discusses her feminist identity within this context of a broader community of feminists. She introduces the post as follows:

> I've said this in the past, but I'll say it again: sometimes identifying as a feminist can be tough when there are so many people in this world dead-set on tearing you down. This post is for any feminist who's ever felt alone in their struggle. The 100+ people pictured below are here to tell you that you're not alone.
>
> Feminists: We're out there. Everywhere.
>
> One of my main hopes for this post is to show how diverse the feminist community really is. Scroll down and you'll see we've got quite the eclectic mix of nationalities, styles, genders, pets (heh), etc. It sounds lame, but as I scroll through these pictures I'm overwhelmed by a sense of awe and admiration. These are real people, dangit. They're not air-brushed. They're not paid spokesmodels.
>
> They're just like you and me.

It is important to recognize the way in which Renee employs the visual element of her blog in this posting, relying on images rather than words to suggest the diversity of the feminist movement. We see pictures representing different races, ages, genders, abilities, and body sizes that not only reveal feminism as diverse, but also function as a public declaration of readers' feminisms. By sending Renee one's image, readers are explicitly 'coming out' as feminists in much the same way that I previously discussed in relation to the bloggers. However, by grouping these images together as one posting (rather than individual revelations), Renee draws attention to the "constitution of collective feminist identities" and the affective power they hold "to tell [readers] that [they're] not alone" (Gunnarsson Payne 2012, 69).

Renee is certainly not the only girl blogger concerned with feminist stereotypes. In addition to discussions of 'click moments,' feminist stereotypes are also a popular and frequent topic of conversation on the *FBomb*. In a February 1, 2011 *FBomb* post called "This is What a Feminist Looks Like," Liz P. writes, "I know that my Miley Cyrus CD-buying, perezhilton. com-reading, shaved-legs self breaks a lot of feminist stereotypes. I am also aware that my yelling-at-people-across-tables, giver-of scary-looks-after

THURSDAY, NOVEMBER 24, 2011

THE FACES OF FEMINISM

What does a *feminist* look like?

(Scroll down to find out.)

I can't believe this day has finally come - I'm proud to present **The Faces of Feminism!** This project is the product of many months of planning, advertising, and worst of all *waiting*, but it turned out better than I'd hoped. I set out to collect at least 100 photographs of "self-proclaimed feminists" and by joe, I've done it!

I've said this in the past, but I'll say it again: sometimes identifying as a feminist can be tough when there are so many people in this world dead-set on tearing you down. **This post is for any feminist who's ever felt alone in their struggle. The 100+ people pictured below are here to tell you that you're not alone.**

Feminists: We're out there. Everywhere.

One of my main hopes for this post is to show how diverse the feminist community really is. Scroll down and you'll see we've got quite the eclectic mix of nationalities, styles, genders, pets (heh), etc. It sounds lame, but as I scroll through these pictures I'm overwhelmed by a sense of awe and admiration. These are real people,

Figure 1.1 "Faces of Feminism" blog post, author screen shot. Used with permission of blog owner.

offensive- comments, opinionated self keeps some of these stereotypes up ... but, what can I do?" She concludes:

> With more awareness, more people will come around to calling them-selves feminists. And having friends and role models (like YOU all) who are fun, funny, interesting and nice who identify as feminists will certainly speed up that process.
> So don't get frustrated. Perceptions change, and the pride you feel in being a teenage feminist will only grow.

Likewise, in a September 17, 2012, posting titled, "Dealing with a New Type of Feminist Stereotype," Jane G. argues that feminist stereotypes are "evolv-ing" to include feminists being depicted as "angry women just looking for something to be angry about," "women who can't take a joke," and "women who are bitter towards one ex-boyfriend and are taking it out on all of mankind." Although I would suggest that these stereotypical characteristics are actually not new, the author's main point remains consistent with much of the other commentary on feminist stereotypes written by girl bloggers, namely, that feminist bloggers must consistently work to dismantle these stereotypes by educating others about feminism and making visible feminist identities that do not align with the supposedly negative feminist stereotypes. Blogging, according to several of these pieces, is an excellent way to do this because of the public nature of the practice.

I am particularly interested in what it means for girl bloggers to be so invested in combating negative feminist stereotypes, and why they may choose blogging as a practice by which to do so. Indeed, as Scharff (2012) demonstrates, "the spectre of the man-hating feminist" may lead even well-intentioned feminists to redefine feminism in ways that may inadvertently position 'older' styles of feminism as emblematic of manhating, lesbianism, and unfeminine behavior in contrast to 'newer' feminist image that seemingly includes consumption of popular culture and smooth legs. Drawing on these theoretical interventions by Scharff (2012) as well as Angela McRobbie's (2009) theorizations about postfeminism, I am arguing that girl bloggers' investment in challenging what they call "feminist stereotypes" reflects the lingering postfeminist cultural context in which they grew up, where girls and women are rewarded for performing a visible heterosexual femininity (Gill 2007; McRobbie 2009).

When bloggers claim that they shave their legs or post a photo of themselves with makeup, they publicly perform hegemonic femininity. However, in contrast to Scharff's participants, most of whom did not identify as feminist and therefore claimed femininity and heterosexuality as reasons for their disidentification with feminism, my own participants' public claiming of both feminism yet rejection of many feminist stereotypes, reveals a key negotiation that is resistant to traditional femininity without rejecting all hegemonic gender and sexuality norms. In this sense, many girl feminist bloggers use blogging as a tool to negotiate the conflicting cultural expectations placed on themselves as girl feminists in order to live publicly as a feminist.

Performing "Femidox": Exploring Intersectional Feminist Identities

While feminist identities are clearly important to girl feminist bloggers, it is imperative to note that girls' feminist identities do not exist in isolation from girls' other identities, and must be understood "intersectionally" (Crenshaw 1989). This was constantly emphasized by one of my participants in particular, Amandine, whose religious and cultural identity as Orthodox Jewish greatly influences the way in which she understands her feminist identity. During our first interview Amandine tells me, "I usually use the terminology Jewish feminist [to describe myself] rather than just feminist since Judaism is as integral to my identity as feminism is. Another word I jokingly use is 'femidox' – feminist Orthodox!"

While Amandine seems confident with her "femidox" identity, she claims that it was her experience with feminist blogging that made her more thoroughly consider the ways in which her feminist and Jewishness intersect. In a September 2011 posting on her blog about the recent makeover of the feminist blog *Jewesses with Attitude* Amandine describes why the site was so influential to her own identity as a Jewish feminist. She writes,

> I first became involved in feminism the year before I went into high school, when I was working on a paper about the Second Wave. Dorky as it sounds, reading books like *The Feminine Mystique* lit a fire in me that I couldn't extinguish. As a result, I began to identify as a feminist. I didn't think it was compatible with Judaism, though, especially not Orthodoxy. It made me feel uncomfortable to think of one when I thought of the other. I completely compartmentalized myself: one box was for my devotion to women's rights, and the second box was where I kept Judaism. The two were equal parts of my identity, but separate, never overlapping. ...
>
> While I loved the [Jewish Women's] Archive at first sight, it was the *Jewesses with Attitude* blog that fascinated me. I had never seen any sort of blog or website dedicated to celebrating Jewish women from a feminist perspective, and the idea drew me in. I began borderline-obsessively reading past posts, drinking in the Jewish feminism that I had been isolated from for so long. Since it was the first Jewish feminism I was exposed to, and the first feminist blog I officially followed, it greatly shaped my attitudes and opinions. Because feminism is something I want to dedicate my entire life to, I don't think it's melodramatic when I say that JWA truly changed my life. (Okay, maybe it's a little melodramatic. But it's still true.)

I quote from Amandine's post at length because her narration highlights the importance of blogs as creating a space where intersectional identities can be performed in new ways. Amandine clearly recognizes that in many mainstream spaces her Jewish and feminist identities seem incompatible, however, she discovered that they are in fact compatible within the space created by *Jewesses with Attitude*. This has important implications for thinking about feminist blogs as spaces for intersectional, political identity performance and suggests that blogs may facilitate this process in unique ways.

The issue of intersectional identities complicating feminist identities is certainly not new and has a lengthy history within feminist movements. However, the previously mentioned case study suggests that intersectional identities may be performed more flexibly online because of the ease in which girls can produce their own media and network with other media producers. Alison Piepmeier (2009) argues that while most contemporary feminist scholarship acknowledges the importance of intersectionality, fewer "grapple" with intersectionality in a way that tracks "symbolic and institutional power structures and their influence on individual lives" (127). For the purpose of my discussion, I am most interested in Piepmeier's assertion that zines provide the opportunity to "describe and mobilize identities that are so unspoken in popular discourses they they're often invisible" (130). In this sense, it is zines' (and, I'd suggest, blogs') ability to make invisible identities visible to both mainstream culture and the feminist community that becomes a central way that they facilitate the performance of intersectional identities.

For Amandine, it was the visibility of a Jewish feminist identity – a subjectivity that had previously seemed impossible to her – that encouraged her to rethink her identity in new ways. In a phone interview Amandine explains how blogging became the next logical step in trying to understand and articulate her identity as a Jewish feminist: "I hadn't yet become a Jewish feminist, I was more like a feminist that happened to be a Jew, and then I found Jewish feminist blogs like *Jewesses with Attitude*, and they really impacted a lot of my philosophies … [Then] writing my blog has really made me explore my connection to both Judaism and feminism and develop my own philosophy."

This idea of developing her "own philosophy" is important to consider in relation to the idea of a feminist identity. Indeed, several of the bloggers that I interviewed revealed a fear of not enacting a proper feminist identity, or in other words, not performing feminism 'correctly.' In Amandine's case, she was convinced that a feminist could not be religiously Jewish, and that being a Jewish feminist would somehow mark her as a lesser feminist. Amandine navigated this dilemma by creatively using the space of her blog to work out her own philosophy of feminism that takes into account both of the political identities that she privileges in her daily life. The identity work described by Amandine is an on-going process, something that several of the bloggers I spoke to discuss. For example, in a February 2012 post Amandine discusses the upcoming U.S. election, weighing the pros and cons of each party's stance on women's rights and Israel. Realizing that neither party sufficiently meets her feminist and pro-Israel leanings she writes, "So this leaves me, as a pro-Israel Jewish feminist, in a bit of a pickle." Nonetheless, it is this "pickle" that makes Amandine's blog such an interesting case study for thinking about the complex nature of feminist identities.

While Amandine's blog provides a rich example of intersectionality because of the way she performs four marginalized identities (a young, female, feminist, Orthodox Jew), it is important to consider how intersectionality functions for bloggers who may possess normative identities. Amandine's own recognition of her marginal ethnic and religious status meant that she considered the intersection with her feminist identity early in her feminist journey. But what about bloggers who may possess privileged identities, such as whiteness, heterosexuality, or normative body type? Has participating in the feminist blogosphere altered the ways in which they think about and perform these identities?

It was significantly more difficult for me to discern how feminist bloggers with privileged identities navigated intersectionality through blogging. This is not surprising considering that normative identities are often invisible to those who possess them, and therefore my participants did not verbally articulate their normative identities in the same explicit ways in which they addressed their marginalized identities. For example, few bloggers commented on their whiteness or heterosexuality, without being specifically asked. However, several conversations revealed that blogging did encourage some girls to begin to recognize their privileged identities, specifically in terms of race, sexuality, and gender identity. For example, Courtney describes how her own privileged position as a white, cis-gendered college student allowed her to easily perform a feminist identity without confronting issues of exclusion or tensions within feminism. She explains,

> Eventually I started to discover a lot of feminist blogs on the Internet, and I learned more about the history of feminism, which was a shocker. I learned about the whiteness of feminism, the cis-genderedness of feminism. At that point, it made me feel selfish because up until then, feminism had always just been a personal identifier. After I read accounts of women of color in feminist movements who had largely been ignored or trans* men and women and other who don't fit binary genders being excluded, I started to feel ashamed that I wasn't doing anything about these issues and I had been largely ignorant of them because I am white and cis-gendered.

Courtney tells me that recognizing her privilege has changed the ways in which she performs her own feminist identity by becoming more "proactive" in confronting injustice in the movement and recognizing the complexity that a feminist identity may carry for others. She reflects, "[My participation as a blogger] has helped me get over the whole 'if you believe in equality you HAVE to be a feminist and identify as such' phase" (caps in original).

This discussion highlights the worrisome fact that while blogging provides a useful opportunity to explore intersecting identities, girl feminist bloggers tend to focus on their marginalized identities of gender and age rather than reflecting on privileged identities. Of course, this doesn't mean that bloggers are ignorant of issues of race, sexuality, class, ability and other identities. As I will discuss in the third chapter, all the bloggers recognize the predominantly white young feminist blogosphere as being problematic and an issue that must be addressed. Nonetheless, it is apparent that while bloggers are well versed in critiquing a lack of diversity, they also lack a language to reflect back upon their own privilege and how this may shape their feminist and activist identities – an issue worthy of further exploration by feminist media studies scholars.

"A License To Be Me": Revisiting the Feminist Killjoy

The bloggers I spoke to were clearly keen on mobilizing their feminist identities to critique their relationships with others, a finding that is not necessarily surprising, considering the emphasis that feminism places on relational equality, such as the importance of equality between girls and boys in educational settings and the necessity for romantic relationships based on equality and mutual respect. For example, Courtney tells me that her feminist identity "solidified" after being in an abusive romantic relationship in high school. "It was awful and it makes me so sad knowing that I let all of these things happen because I didn't know what abuse was. I wish I had been stronger, and I know now that feminism really gives me a much stronger attitude than I had before … It's almost as if feminism made me realize my worth as an actual person." This comment indicates that gaining a feminist consciousness provided Courtney with both an understanding of structural power and the language (what she calls a "stronger attitude") to critique her previous abusive relationship. Today she is in a fulfilling relationship with a supportive partner in part because of the confidence, self-respect, and understanding of power she gained from feminism.

In addition to providing girls with the conceptual and discursive tools to critique relationships, several of the bloggers emphasized that feminism's influence on their own sense of self was one of the most positive aspects of their feminist identity. Madison's discussion of this is worth citing at length:

> Oh my god. I can't even begin to describe how calling myself a feminist has changed me … I used to do extreme things in order to lose weight. Binging and purging and the like … Becoming a feminist introduced me to a whole new sector of society that told me there was nothing wrong with the way I looked. It brought out a totally new side of me.
>
> Discovering feminism answered so many questions for me. I have a very tough, abrasive personality, and a lot of people have called me a "bitch." It always frustrated me that my male best friend could get away with things I could never try without being chastised, especially in leadership positions. Being a feminist made me realize that it's not me who is the problem, it's society.

Madison also often blogs about feminism's positive influence on her life. For example, in a 2011 post she describes her struggle with developing large breasts at age ten and how awful she felt when adult men would stare at them. She writes, "The feeling of being leered at and cat-called is not a pleasant one … This is what happened to my boobs. I hated the attention they brought to me. I have since recognized that the men leering are wrong, not my body. I now understand that my body is mine … I love my boobs, and I love feminism."

Madison is not unique among these bloggers in her insistence that feminism has been an overwhelming positive force in her life that has helped her challenge sexism that she experiences in her everyday life. Renee also elaborates on how identifying as a feminist gave her the tools to understand social power structures. She explains,

> On a personal level, I think that feminism is one of the most positive forces in my life, if not the most positive ... Simply put, feminism has given me license to be who I am and treat myself better ... Once you start reading more feminist books, checking out feminist blogs and websites online, and learning about various causes pertaining to women's rights, your priorities begin to change. My feeling was almost like, 'Well, if feminists accept me the way I am – intelligent, sarcastic, compassionate, bigger than a size 0 – why can't others accept me this way, too?' Maybe I'm not the problem. Maybe society is the problem. Maybe, just maybe, I'm already good enough.

Abby, a fifteen-year-old newly self-identified feminist concurs, reflecting, "My feminist identity has impacted my sense of self mainly by helping me name an aspect of myself, the part of me that yearns for equality and justice. This is such a crucial part of me, and it makes me proud that most of my friends see 'feminist' as an integral part of who I am."

These conversations were particularly interesting and inspiring to me, because they draw attention to the emotional strength that a feminist identity gives to several of the bloggers. I return to Piepmeier's (2009) research on girl zines here, as she convincingly argues that girl zines contain an affective dimension, which she describes as a "pedagogy of hope" (also see hooks 2003). Piepmeier's key intervention here is recognition of the political work being done by the pedagogies of hope articulated in girls' zines, functioning as "small-scale acts of resistance" to a cynical culture that disregards the political significance of girls' cultural practices. According to Piepmeier, the affective responses generated via zinemaking – hope for a better world, the pleasure of struggle to make social change, an empathy toward others – function as a "new mode of doing politics" that privileges the connection between affect and political change. Jessica Taft (2011, 154) articulates a similar idea in her research on girl activists, arguing that a "politics of hope" and "positivity" informs her participants' activist strategies. She writes, "Hopefulness as a political strategy and set of practices fuses strongly with girls' identity claims, particularly their narratives about their youthful and girlish idealism." While Taft (2011) discusses these affects as outward looking – imagining a better world and believing that it is possible, for example – I'm interested in the ways in which these feelings operate as affective resources that girls use to perform and maintain feminist identities.

This is particularly provocative to consider in relation to the negative affects that often "stick" to feminism, which Sara Ahmed (2010) discusses through the theoretical figure of the "feminist killjoy." She describes how feminists are understood as killing joy, "spoiling" the happiness of others by bringing "bad feeling" into the room "not only by talking about unhappy topics such as sexism but by exposing how happiness is sustained by erasing the very signs of not getting along" (66). Ahmed's assertion that "to inherit feminism can mean to inherent sadness" (75) is significant, yet requires some rethinking. I am not refuting Ahmed's insightful intervention here; indeed, the feminist killjoy lingers throughout many of the blog posts and interview comments I've analyzed in this chapter, and is arguably a key part of the feminist stereotype that the bloggers discussed at length. I'm also not suggesting that feminism is 'easy' to do – or doesn't come with emotional costs. Yet, the empirical data I present here also suggests another operative of the feminist killjoy, one where feminism offers 'good' and even 'joyful' feelings of relief, positivity, and confidence to feminist girls. While some feminist scholars have highlighted these joyful and even "feisty" feelings that stick to girl feminists (see Ringrose and Renold forthcoming 2015), there remains a need to theorize the teenage girl feminist as an agent of social change.

Thus, I aim to draw Ahmed in conversation with Piepmeier and Taft here to argue that positive affects may "stick" (Ahmed 2010) to the figure of the girl feminist due to her social, discursive, and affective positioning as *girl* in ways that the (presumed adult) feminist killjoy may prevent us from seeing. As Monica Swindle (2011) reminds us, girl carries affect, a "pleasurable power … [that] is a distinct way of feeling, an orientation toward oneself, objects, and other that creates a (shifting contingent) collective, an affective community." The positive affects that "stick" to girlhood, including "happiness" (Swindle 2011), "hope" (Taft 2011), and "optimism" (my participant Renee) then complicate the feminist killjoy as we might understand her in relation to girls. Thus, we need to re-read the figure of the 'girl feminist' and the affects associated with girls who self-identify as feminist through an analytical lens that privileges the feeling of feminism through the experience of youth, and specifically, girlhood – a strategy I employ in the following section.

The Politics of Affect for Girl Feminists

I am suggesting that the affective dimension of a girlhood feminist identity produced through blogging has important political implications that have been overlooked by feminist scholars. Indeed, Swindle (2011) argues "the political now seems to be not only or even mostly a project of consciousness raising, awareness of oppression, but more a question of affect." In other words, we must ask how might the positive feelings about oneself generated from a feminist identity be politically useful. Based upon my interviews with girl feminist bloggers, I am proposing that an introduction to feminism and the subsequent performance and maintenance of a feminist identity may encourage girls to view themselves more positively by providing them the language and tools to better understand themselves through social structures rather than the individualized frameworks commonly used in popular consumerist and psychological discourses as I discuss later in this chapter.

To reiterate Madison's significant realization: "Being a feminist made me realize that it's not me who is the problem, it's society."

This finding is especially important as it points to the unique discursive positioning of girls within contemporary American society, and suggests the need to understand girls' feminist identities and their affects in relation to these discourses – discourses which often circulated within popular media culture. To wit: For over twenty years there has been considerable public debate about a perceived loss of girls' self-esteem as they enter adolescence, a discourse that led to a popular understanding that adolescent girls were "in crisis" and in need of protection and empowerment by adult women (Pipher 1995).[5] This 'girl in crisis' discourse has been followed more recently by moral panics about girls' sexualization in the media (Levin and Kilbourne 2009), princess culture (Orenstein 2012; Hartstein 2011), and gender stereotyping (Wardy 2013), all which adopt similar protectionist rhetoric that emphasize individualized solutions implemented within the family unit rather than the structural critiques offered through the performance of a feminist identity.[6]

Girls' studies scholars have critiqued these individualized discourses (Kearney 2006; Currie, Kelly, and Pomerantz 2009; Schilt 2003), suggesting that we must instead recognize the power and cultural agency that girls already possess and express in creative and innovative ways, such as through media production (Kearney 2006; Schilt 2003) and alternative subcultures (Kearney 2006; Currie, Kelly and Pomerantz 2009). Nonetheless, while girls will often take up feminist issues through these practices and within these subcultural contexts, feminist identities often remain unarticulated, a key difference from the feminist bloggers I am discussing.[7]

Research on the feminist youth subculture riot grrrl also illuminates how performing a feminist identity may generate positive feelings of power, confidence, and inner strength amongst girls.[8] Jessica Rosenberg and Gitana Garofalo (1998) note that the term 'riot grrrl' was chosen to "reclaim the vitality and power of youth with an added growl to replace the perceived passivity of 'girl'" (809). This performance of strength is important to riot grrrl's feminist politics, which aimed in part to 'reinvent' girlhood as a powerful subjectivity from which girls could speak, rather than one marked by the hegemonic notions of girlhood as a position of victimhood and dependence (Kearney 2006). This sense of power, confidence and agency can be seen in the responses of riot grrrl participants when asked how being part of the movement has affected them personally. For example, one riot grrrl tells Rosenberg and Garofalo (1998),

> [Riot grrrl] has changed who I am and my opinions. It gave me the ability to say, 'I'm not going to kill myself. I'm not a victim.' Made me more obnoxious. Speakout and say whatever. Opened me up to a lot of stuff that I've been reading –books, authors, political issues. I'm Indian; Riot Grrrl has given me a sense of self and identity. Before I was uncomfortable being nonwhite in a 95 percent white suburb. It has changed my life. (840)

Kearney argues that the responses to riot grrrl, such as the one just mentioned, demonstrate how a riot grrrl identity has functioned as a "preliminary step for female adolescents attempting to regain the confidence, assertiveness, and self-respect they lost due to abuse or the onset of puberty" (83). However, she notes that this is different from the 'girls in crisis' approach that I previously discussed. Instead of individualizing girls' problems and offering adult-initiated solutions, riot grrrls develop their own voice within a community of peers via feminist social critique and do-it-yourself punk ethos, "creating a common knowledge of the larger systemic problems associated with being young and female in a predominantly adultist, patriarchal, capitalist, and heterocentric society" (Kearney 2006, 83).

This research on riot grrrl points to positive and 'good' feelings, including confidence, assertiveness, and a sense of agency that the performance of a riot grrrl identity – which I am understanding as a specific type of feminist identity – generates for girls. My own findings build on this scholarship by suggesting that identifying as a feminist helps girls to perform political agency that allows them to navigate the challenges of adolescence in ways similar to riot grrrls. While I'm not suggesting that contemporary girl feminist bloggers are directly comparable to riot grrrls, I am pointing to a historical trajectory of girls' performance of feminist identities through media production and arguing that the positive affects produced through these practices are politically significant in and of themselves, as they demand a new framework for understanding feminist girls as positive and agential figures of social change. I will return to a discussion of affect in chapter three in relation to the ways in which affects circulate between girls through their networked counterpublics.

Resistant Feminist Identities: Making Sense of Postfeminist Contradictions

The bloggers I interviewed often frame the 'feminist feelings' of agency and confidence they derive from performing a feminist identity as helping them makes sense of the ways in which postfeminist discourses privilege a model of aspirational femininity that is almost impossible to achieve, including norms related to the ideal feminine body (Gill 2007; McRobbie 2009). For example, Renee tells me, "As a plus-size gal, [feminism has] also given me license to see beauty beyond pant size and accept it in many forms. Though I'd be lying if I said I felt like a goddess every second of every day (you know how it goes), for the most part feminism has made me feel better about my body than any cheesy commercial telling me to 'love my curves' ever has."

Renee often expresses this sentiment on her blog as well. For example, in a June 2010 entry Renee describes how her experiences as the 'fat girl' in elementary and middle school left her self-conscious and feeling as though she failed at proper bodily femininity. She explains how a feminist consciousness, evident throughout her post as she critiques impossible hegemonic feminine body norms, has increased her confidence and respect for herself and her accomplishments. She writes,

> I'm a lot different than I was in elementary school, even middle school. I'm not a wallflower. I speak my mind. I don't put myself down. I try not to care what people think about me. I respect myself. I surround myself with people who really care about me, and work hard to be a good student, citizen, sister, daughter … you catch my drift. In other words, I'm proud to be me! It just sucks it's taken me a decade to realize it.

Both Renee's comments to me and those in her blog post are significant because they suggest that her feminist identity serves as a resource that she can draw on to be more confident and resist normative femininity. Conversely, her confidence continually produces her feminist identity, making her more comfortable in publicly performing feminism. Thus, Renee is able to see the contradictions embedded within postfeminist advertising campaigns like Dove's Campaign for Real Beauty telling her to love her body while attempting to sell her 'body-improving' products. Feminism provides her with the discourse, knowledge, and agency to critique the postfeminist idea that 'empowerment' can be attained through the consumption of beauty and fashion products.[9]

Similarly, Courtney reports that her feminist identity has made her much more confident in herself and her ability to resist the bodily maintenance prescribed by postfeminism. "I don't freak out if I haven't shaved in a few weeks and I'm less afraid to speak up about what I believe in," she tells me. Madison's comments about her struggle with body image and weight previously discussed are also worthy to return to as another example of how performing a feminist identity has generated feelings that have inspired her resistance to social pressures to be "perfect." She explains, "Before feminism I was always frustrated or angry or upset because I couldn't fit into what society wanted me to be. I wasn't submissive or skinny or popular, but I was constantly trying to fit into those things. Feminism is what told me that I didn't have to be those things, so it finally brought me happiness. I feel like feminism allows me to be myself."

Madison's comments are particularly provocative because they highlight the ways in which the aspirations for girls most visible within postfeminist media culture – a "skinny" body, for example – are almost always unattainable, just out-of-reach. Yet, it is the *promise* of a skinny body if you engage in the constant labor of dieting and exercise (or self-harm practices like purging or starving oneself as Madison previously discussed), that circulate throughout postfeminist media culture, generating the feelings of frustration and anxiety that Madison acknowledges. We may understand these aspirations as part of a larger affective dimension of neoliberalism that Lauren Berlant (2011) refers to as "cruel optimism"; those optimistic attachments that become cruel when the object that draws one's attachment actively impedes the aim that brought one to it initially. Yet it is feminism and her identification with the movement that allows Madison to pull apart, question and ultimately sever her attachment to the ideal of the skinny body. In this sense, it is Madison's feminist identity that provides her another option ("feminism is what told me that I didn't have to be those things") and allows her to understand the impossibility of postfeminist ideals not as personal failure, but as part of a problematic social system that disadvantages girls and women.

Bloggers also discussed how their feminist identities have provided them a language to critique media representations of girls and women, an issue that is of particular importance to young feminists, according to my study participants. Abby says, "I now have feminist critique so ingrained in myself that I cannot watch a movie or television show or read a book without analyzing the portrayal of women and their relationships, and this has only been for the better for me." Additionally, participants described how their feminist identity has encouraged them to engage in intersectional media analyses that take account how race, sexuality, and class intersect with gender representations. Renee says, "The teens in [popular television] shows … are usually attractive, well-dressed, middle-to upper class, heterosexual, white and focused on fashion and dating. I want to see more diversity, more authenticity, and more body sizes (and not that size 10 is plus size crap!)." My textual analysis of girls' blogs reveals a similar sentiment, with posts such as one on the *FBomb* by Elizabeth M. entitled "Female Bodies and Positive Rhetoric," exemplifying the ways in which young feminist bloggers are gaining the power and confidence to critique media representations of women and girls in sophisticated and thought-provoking ways.

Renee also points out how her feminist identity has helped her to resist the notion that girls shouldn't be smarter than boys in the classroom and simultaneously "nurture her internal strength." The discussion that the girls and I had about this in the focus group reminds us of the continual pressures girls can have to perform hyper-femininity in school to fit into peer gender and sexual cultures, and gain popularity status, which can contradict with openly achieving and performing intellectual and academic identities (Ringrose 2013). As adult feminists outside of the high school classroom it is easy for us to overlook this reality. Renee explains,

> From my experience, there seems to be a subtle yet pervasive phenomenon in high school girls: many of them don't want to be seen as over-achievers. I can't count the number of times I've seen girls 'play dumb' in class rather than admit they do have ideas to share. Are these girls scared that boys won't like them if they have a better handle on the material or get higher test scores? … I never want to deny all that I've accomplished in school or pretend I don't know an answer when I actually do. I wish more girls could experience this internal strength and pride brought on by feminism. I wish more girls knew that it's okay to dream big.

Based upon these examples, I suggest that the performance of a feminist identity can be viewed as a resistant practice in itself, as it provides bloggers a platform from which to problematize and challenge hegemonic, postfeminist femininity, specifically body image, media representations of women/girls and "playing dumb." In this sense, a feminist identity offers girls a political subjectivity to make sense of the world, including postfeminist media culture, which few other normative girlhood identities offer. As Julie aptly summarizes, "Basically the movement gave me confirmation that I wasn't crazy!"

Conclusion: Resistant Feminist Identities

In this chapter I outline the ways in which girls perform feminist identities through the practice of blogging, mapping how this form of digital media production grants girls the opportunity to learn about feminism, experiment with fluctuating feminist identities, challenge feminist stereotypes, and grapple with intersectionality. I pay particular attention to how the bloggers' feminist identities inform their ability to not only critique their relationships with others but also to reevaluate their feelings about themselves, a process often resulting in newfound confidence and 'good' feelings. I suggest these strong affects must be understood as political resources, and have become significant to the ways in which girls challenge postfeminist discourses and practices. Finally, I advocate for understanding the performance of a feminist identity as a resistant practice that girls are engaging in via their role as bloggers.

Framing the performance of a feminist identity as a practice of resistance builds upon a feminist cultural studies model that understands resistance at the level of everyday practices and emphasizes the power of collective strategies of resistance rather than merely resistant reading models (McRobbie 1994; Durham 1999). By positioning feminist identity performances as resistant in themselves, I open the possibility for girls to perform a political agency in the *present*, rather than understanding their practices as potentially inspiring *future* political action, the dominant framework used to discuss the relationship between girls and politics (Schilt 2003; Harris 2008). Consequently, this chapter demonstrates the need to recognize the value for girls in performing feminist identities in a cultural context that where postfeminist narratives of empowerment make increasingly little sense to girls who are confronting sexism in their everyday lives – and to take seriously the practice of blogging as producing a space in which to do so.

Notes

1. Because I use only first name pseudonyms to refer to the bloggers in my study, I have also chosen to refer to Tavi by her first name as well throughout this book.
2. All posts from the *FBomb* are cited as they appear on the blog, with the author's first name and last initial. These names may or may not be used by individual writers as pseudonyms, and therefore their identity remains protected.

3. I am not suggesting that a gay and a feminist identity are directly comparable, as I do not believe they are. The systemic discrimination LGBTQ people continually face differs from the shunning of feminists within contemporary culture that I describe here. Nonetheless, some of the affective responses discussed by my participants can be better understood using Sedgwick's framing, paying attention to how the heterosexual matrix structures both "coming out" experiences. Additionally, we must also recognize how girls are often under particular pressure in adolescence to participate in heterosexual romance culture and perform heterosexual identities at a time when their own emerging and changing desires may be not fully understood or known. These pressures and uncertainties likely complicate a teenager's 'coming out' as feminist in ways that adults may not experience.

4. Crowther and Kearney's approach is rooted in a poststructuralist cultural studies perspective that understands identities as always "in process" (Hall 1989, 68) and "becoming" through discourse, rather than already "being" or able to be discovered (Hall 1996). In addition to Hall (1989, 1996), see McRobbie (1994).

5. First articulated by psychologists Lyn Mikel Brown and Carol Gilligan (1992) and later popularized by Mary Pipher (1995) in her bestselling book *Reviving Ophelia: Saving the Selves of Adolescent Girls*, these works described girls' transition to adolescence as a difficult process resulting in a loss of self confidence, voice, and ambition. Pipher's (1995) book stressed that girls require adult intervention to "save" them from this process, which she argued could result in poor body image, and unhealthy habits, like dieting, drinking, drugs, and self harm. See Zaslow (2009) for an extensive discussion of this discourse.

6. Over the past year, this concern has focused on the online practices of teenage girls and potential risk from 'cyberbullying' and cyberharrassment. These discourses often stress the need for adult surveillance and monitoring in order to protect girls from potentially troublesome situations. I will be returning to this issue in chapter five.

7. Kearney (2006) demonstrates how girls' media production provides an opportunity for girls to challenge female beauty standards, negotiate racial and ethnic identities, and gain technical skills, amongst other resistant practices. However, she notes that feminist identities often remained marginal within these media production practices, despite such texts often addressing what we might deem 'feminist issues.' See also Schilt (2003) and Currie, Kelly, and Pomerantz (2009).

8. It is important to note the significant role that media production played in this subculture, because riot grrrls were encouraged to create their own music, zines (including early incarnations of blogs called e-zines), films, and other forms of media.

9. See Banet-Weiser (2012a) and Dye (2009) for critiques of Dove's Campaign for Real Beauty.

References

Ahmed, Sara. 2010. *The Promise of Happiness*. Durham: Duke University Press.

Banet-Weiser, Sarah. 2012a. "'Free Self-Esteem Tools?' Brand Culture, Gender, and the Dove Real Beauty Campaign." In *Commodity Activism: Cultural Resistance in Neoliberal Times*, edited by Roopali Mukherjee and Sarah Banet-Weiser, 39–56. New York: New York University Press.

Banet-Weiser, Sarah. 2012b. *Authentic TM: The Politics of Ambivalence in a Brand Culture*. New York: New York University Press.

Brown, Lyn Mikel, and Carol Gilligan. 1992. *Meeting at the Crossroads: Women's Psychology and Girls' Development*. Cambridge: Harvard University Press.

Budgeon, Shelley. 2001. "Emergent Feminist(?) Identities: Young Women and the Practice of Micropolitics." *European Journal of Women's Studies* 8 (7): 7–28.

Butler, Judith. 1990. *Gender Trouble*. New York: Routledge.

Crenshaw, Kimberle. 1989. "Demarginalizing the Intersection of Race and Sex: A Black Feminist Critique of Antidiscrimination Doctrine, Feminist Theory, and Antiracist Politics." *University of Chicago Legal Forum* 140: 139–167.

Crowther, Barbara. 1999. "Writing as Performance: Young Girls' Diaries." In *Making Meaning of Narratives*, edited by Ruthellen H. Josselson and Amia Lieblich, 197–220. Thousand Oaks: Sage.

Currie, Dawn, Deirdre Kelly, and Shauna Pomerantz. 2009. *'Girl Power:' Girls Reinventing Girlhood*. New York: Peter Lang.

Dicker, Rory, and Alison Piepmeier. 2003. *Catching a Wave: Reclaiming Feminism for the 21st Century*. Boston: Northeastern University Press.

Dow, Bonnie. 1996. *Prime-time Feminism: Television, Media Culture, and the Women's Movement Since 1970*. Philadelphia: University of Pennsylvania Press.

Duggan, Lisa. 2003. *The Twilight of Equality? Neoliberalism, Cultural Politics, and the Attack on Democracy*. Boston: Beacon Press.

Durham, Meenakshi Gigi. 1999. "Articulating Adolescent Girls' Resistance to Patriarchal Discourse in Popular Media." *Women's Studies in Communication* 22 (2): 210–229.

Dye, Lauren. 2009. "Consuming Constructions: A Critique of Dove's Campaign for Real Beauty." *Canadian Journal of Media Studies* 5(1): 114–128.

F., Rachel. 2009. "Why I Became a Feminist." *FBomb*, October 26. http://thefbomb.org/2009/10/why-i-became-a-feminist/.

Foucault, Michel. 1978. *The History of Sexuality, Volume 1*. New York: Random House.

Fraser, Nancy. 2013. *Fortunes of Feminism: From State-Managed Capitalism to Neoliberal Crisis*. London: Verso.

G., Jane. 2012. "Dealing with a New Type of Feminist Stereotype." *FBomb*, September 17. http://thefbomb.org/2012/09/dealing-with-a-new-type-of-feminist-stereotype/.

Gill, Rosalind. 2007. "Postfeminist Media Culture: Elements of a Sensibility." *European Journal of Cultural Studies* 10 (2): 147–166.

Gunnarsson Payne, Jenny. 2012. "Feminist Media as Alternative Media?" In *Feminist Media: Participatory Spaces, Networks and Cultural Citizenship*, edited by Elke Zobl and Ricarda Drueke, 55–72. Germany: Transcript.

Hall, Stuart. 1989. "Cultural Identity and Cinematic Representation." *Framework* 36: 68–81.

Hall, Stuart. 1996. "New Ethnicities." In *Stuart Hall: Critical Dialogues in Cultural Studies*, edited by David Morley and Kuan-Hsing Chen, 441–449. New York: Routledge.

Harris, Anita. 2008. "Young Women, Late Modern Politics, and the Participatory Possibilities of Online Cultures." *Journal of Youth Studies* 11(5): 481–495.

Harris, Anita. 2010. "Mind the Gap: Attitudes and Emergent Feminist Politics since the Third Wave." *Australian Feminist Studies* 25 (66): 275–284.

Hartstein, Jennifer. 2011. *Princess Recovery: A How-to Guide to Raising Strong, Empowered Girls Who Can Create Their Own Happily Ever Afters*. Ohio: Adams Media.

Heywood, Leslie, and Jennifer Drake. 1997. *Third Wave Agenda: Being Feminist, Doing Feminism*. Minneapolis: University of Minnesota Press.

hooks, bell. 2003. *Teaching Community: A Pedagogy of Hope*. New York: Routledge.

Karlyn Rowe, Kathleen. 2003. "*Scream*, Popular Culture, and Feminism's Third Wave: 'I'm Not My Mother'." *Genders Online Journal* 38. http://www.genders.org/ g38/g38_rowe_karlyn.html.

Kearney, Mary Celeste. 2006. *Girls Make Media*. New York: Routledge.

Keller, Jessalynn. 2012. "Virtual Feminisms: Girls' Blogging Communities, Feminist Activism and Participatory Politics." *Information, Communication & Society* 15 (3): 429–447.

M., Elizabeth. 2012. "Female Bodies and Positive Rhetoric." *Fbomb*, October 26.http:// thefbomb.org/2012/10/female-bodies-and-positive-rhetoric/.

Mazzarella, Sharon. 2005. *Girl Wide Web: Girls, the Internet, and the Negotiation of Identity*. New York: Peter Lang.

Mazzarella, Sharon. 2010. *Girl Wide Web 2.0: Revisiting Girls, the Internet, and the Negotiation of Identity*. New York: Peter Lang.

McRobbie, Angela. 1994. *Postmodernism and Popular Culture*. New York: Routledge.

McRobbie, Angela. 2009. *The Aftermath of Feminism: Gender, Culture and Social Change*. Thousand Oaks: Sage.

Moraga, Cherrie, and Gloria Anzaldua. 1981. *This Bridge Called My Back: Writings by Radical Women of Color*. London: Persephone.

Orenstein, Peggy. 2012. *Cinderella Ate My Daughter: Dispatches from the Front Lines of the New Girlie-Girl Culture*. New York: Harper Paperbacks.

P., Liz. 2011. "This Is What a Feminist Looks Like." *FBomb*, February 1. http://thefbomb.org/2011/02/this-is-what-a-feminist-looks-like/.

Piepmeier, Alison. 2009. *Girl Zines: Making Media, Doing Feminism*. New York: New York University Press.

Pipher, Mary. 1995. *Reviving Ophelia: Saving the Selves of Adolescent Girls*. New York: Penguin.

R., Anna. 2010. "Young Feminism: The Fire Inside Me." *FBomb,* November 2. http:// thefbomb.org/2010/11/young-feminism-the-fire-inside-me/.

Ringrose, Jessica. *Postfeminist Education? Girls and the Sexual Politics of Schooling*. London: Routledge.

Ringrose, Jessica, and Emma Renold. Forthcoming 2016. "Teen Feminist Killjoys? Mapping Girls' Affective Encounters with Femininity, Sexuality, and Feminism at School." In *The Politics of Place: Contemporary Paradigms for Research in Girlhood Studies*, edited by Claudia Mitchell and Carrie Rentschler. New York: Berghahn Books.

Rosenberg, Jessica, and Gitana Garafalo. 1998. "Riot Grrrl: Revolutions from Within." *Signs: Journal of Women in Culture and Society* 23 (3): 809–841.

Sandoval, Chela. 2000. *Methodology of the Oppressed*. Minneapolis: University of Minnesota Press.

Scharff, Christina. 2012. *Repudiating Feminism: Young Women in a Neoliberal World*. Surry: Ashgate.

Schilt, Kristen. 2003. "'I'll Resist with Every Inch and Every Breath:' Girls and Zine Making as a Form of Resistance." *Youth & Society* 35(1): 71–97.

Schilt, Kristen, and Elke Zobl. 2008. "Connecting the Dots: Riot Grrrls, Ladyfests, and the International Grrrl Zine Network." In *Next Wave Cultures: Feminisms, Subcultures, Activism,* edited by Anita Harris, 171–192. New York: Routledge.

Sedgwick, Eve. 1990. *Epistemology of the Closet.* Berkeley: University of California Press.

Stern, Shayla Thiel. 2007. *Instant Identity: Adolescent Girls and the World of Instant Messaging.* New York: Peter Lang.

Stern, Susannah. 2002. "Virtually Speaking: Girls' Self-Disclosure on the WWW." *Women's Studies in Communication* 25 (2): 223–253.

Swindle, Monica. 2011. "Feeling Girl, Girling Feeling: An Examination of 'Girl' as Affect." *Rhizomes* 22. http://www.rhizomes.net/issue22/swindle.html.

Taft, Jessica. 2011. *Rebel Girls: Youth Activism & Social Change Across the Americas.* New York: New York University Press.

Wardy, Melissa. 2013. *Redefining Girly: How Parents Can Fight the Stereotyping and Sexualizing of Girlhood, from Birth to Tween.* Chicago: Chicago Review Press.

Z, Julie. 2010. "My Click Moment." *FBomb*, June 2. http://thefbomb.org/2010/06/my-click-moment/.

Zaslow, Emilie. 2009. *Feminism INC: Coming of Age in a Girl Power Media Culture.* New York: Palgrave MacMillan.

Zeilinger, Julie. 2012. *A Little F' d Up: Why Feminism Is Not a Dirty Word.* Berkeley: Seal Press.

2 "Still Alive and Kicking"
Defining a Girl-Centered Feminist Activism

"I think an activist is anyone who works towards any kind of societal change. This definition allows for more people to claim the word 'activist,' which I think is a good thing ... The activist label is important to me because I like to feel that I am making a change. I've written before about how feminism helped fill a void in my life, well activism helps ensure that the void stays full."
—Madison, focus group blog

"I guess I'm an activist. I've never been to a protest yet, but I'm dying to. I've been to a number of speeches and webinars and conferences and panels on feminism. I suppose that I would classify myself as an activist because I'm so involved in making sure that women have all the rights we deserve, whether it's by talking about feminist candidates on my blog or going to a webinar about pregnant students' rights. I don't know if I ever consciously took on the label of activism but I guess it's important to me. I don't think the title of it is important, what's important is that you get stuff done."
—Amandine, focus group blog

I begin this chapter with Madison and Amandine's comments, as they hint at the precarious positioning of activism within our contemporary society. Indeed, the proliferation of new media technologies in most countries around the world have added to this uncertainty about what types of actions are needed to produce social change. Amandine's comment points to the continued privileging of the protest in many people's imaginings of activism, even as she concedes that her own activist practices vary from this dominant image. In contrast, Madison suggests the need to think of activism in broad terms, understanding the practice of working toward social change as the defining feature of an activist. Yet, what constitutes "working toward" social change? How do girl feminist bloggers come to perform an activist identity, and why is this identity important to them? How does the performance of an activist identity by girl feminist bloggers challenge normative modes of activism? What activist practices are undertaken by girl feminist bloggers? And finally, how does this activism both continue and diverge from feminist activism historically?

I address these questions in this chapter by analyzing how girl feminist bloggers understand their activist identities and how they mobilize these identities to engage in activist practices. Drawing on cultural studies scholarship on youth politics and feminist literature discussing women's participation in political activism, I suggest that the discrepancy between girls' perceived notions of an activist and their own experiences of activism reveals particular gendered and aged cultural narratives about activism that shape the ways that girls understand their own practices. I explore my participants' experiences with coming to perform activist identities in relation to this discussion, demonstrating how their feminist and activist identities are intricately related yet often yield tension within the larger feminist community due to girls' preference for using new media technologies for feminist activism.

Based upon this analysis I argue that feminist blogging constitutes a form of *accessible activism* for some girls. This framing acknowledges how girls have limited resources – often due to age, but also perhaps gender, class, race, location, and ability – to participate in activism. Through various examples, I outline three key activist practices that girls engage in via blogging: education, community-building, and the production of feminist visibility. I maintain that rather than view these strategies as new practices determined by digital media, we must historicize them as continuing longstanding feminist activist practices. Finally, I contend that recognizing girls' feminist blogging as activism decenters masculine and adult-focused conceptions of activism, opening space for girls to perform political subjectivities that are accessible to their social positioning as girls. I now turn to reviewing some of the literature on activism that contextualizes my arguments in this chapter.

Theorizing the Changing Practices of Activism

Activism has been – and continues to be – a contentious concept within both scholarly literature and mainstream culture. A basic definition suggests that activism is the action of advocating for political, social, economic, or environmental change via any of an array of possible strategies (Klar and Kasser 2009; Corning and Myers 2002). In this sense, activism involves the goal of improving some aspect of society through active political intervention (Klar and Kasser 2009). Joss Hands (2011, 5) also argues for recognizing *power* as a contested part of activism, which is "directed against prevailing authority as domination and exploitation, whether in personal relations of micro-power, or in the form of institutional domination." But what constitutes *political* intervention? Or *improving* society? Or even *action*?

Although it is beyond the scope of this chapter to provide an extensive historical analysis of changing modes of activism, it is worthwhile to consider briefly how scholars, primarily in the disciplines of political science, psychology, and sociology, have conceptualized activism. Pippa Norris (2009) notes that early North American and European research during the 1960s and 1970s on "traditional political activism" understood activism primarily through the lens of participation in electoral politics, such as voting, campaigning, and party membership. Participation in trade unions was also often considered political activism during this time. According to this traditional conceptualization, which continues to linger even today, *girls cannot even be activists* because they are prevented from engaging in political activism due to their minor status. Whereas girls may be able to campaign and lobby despite not being eligible to vote, their contributions remain marginalized because their opinions are not formally recognized through the voting process.

Civic activism is defined by participation in voluntary organizations, community associations, and social movements, such as the women's liberation, environmental, and anti-globalization movements (Inglehart and Norris 2003). Ronald Inglehart and Norris (2003) distinguish such forms of civic activism from traditional activist organizations (primarily parties and trade unions) via their looser networks and decentralized structures, modes of belonging based upon shared issue concerns and identity politics, and mixed action repertoires to achieve goals. Nonetheless, civic activism can often be identified through clearly articulated goals and arguably remains representative of activism within public imagination, as we will see later in this chapter. Finally, Inglehart and Norris recognize what they call "protest activism" as another type of activism based around participation in activities like demonstrations, boycotts, and petitions, although civic and traditional activists may also use these types of tactics. While protest activism has gained prominence as a scholarly focus since the early 1970s, Norris notes that it often remains distinguished from literature on "traditional" activism, even as protest activism is now "mainstream" and "widespread" in many countries (639).

The categorizations mentioned earlier reveal a limited focus on what has been considered activism, based primarily around the experiences of white, middle-class, heterosexual, Western, adult men. Consequently, academic studies of activism often revealed that women participated *less* than men in political activism, reinforcing hegemonic binaries that positioned women as personal and private and men as civic and public (Norris and Inglehart 2003). Norris and Inglehart provide a rather unsatisfactory explanation for this discrepancy. They correctly suggest that women's unequal status in public and private life has alienated women from conventional politics, yet they fail to adequately address methodological issues related to definitions of activism, data gathering techniques and historical analyses that privilege men over women and adult over youth.

Jessica Taft (2011) maintains that feminist sociologists of social movements have argued for expanded conceptions of activism in order to better understand the various ways in which women, including women of color, girls, working class and poor women, as well as non-Western women, have participated in activism. I'd also suggest that the primarily quantitative methodology employed by political scientists, sociologists, and psychologists neglects to capture the diverse experiences of women activists. For example, it excludes women who may be participating in activism that falls outside of narrow survey definitions or questions based on traditional activism. Finally, the quantitative approaches often privileged in these disciplines do not historicize their findings, erasing the historical activism of women, such as the suffrage movement in the early twentieth century or mobilizing for public childcare after World War II.

I outline traditional definitions of activism in order to contextualize my analyses of girl bloggers' activism, as well as to better distinguish my own approach from dominant studies of activism. I conceptualize girls' activist identities by employing a cultural studies approach, which moves beyond definitions of traditional and civic activism to account for the vast array of activist practices including *cultural* practices used by (often marginalized) people. As evident by my previous discussion, youth have been excluded from traditional and civic definitions of activism, resulting in cultural studies scholars' interest in studying how youth practice politics – a focus that became foundational to the field of cultural studies.

Since the 1970s, cultural studies scholars have researched youth subcultures, which soon became a dominant framework for studying youth politics and resistance (see Hebdige 1979; Willis 1977; Hall and Jefferson 1976). Although it is not possible to discuss these texts comprehensively here, it is the attention that this work paid to various forms of youth politics that is important for my discussion. This literature was the first to address issues of the social meaning of style, the oppositional politics embedded in cultural practices such as rock shows and cultural objects such as motorbikes, and the ways in which marginalized groups (primarily due to class and race) exercise creativity from their subordinated positions to enact cultural agency within subcultures. Significantly, this research created new ways to think about youth, culture, and politics, as well as methodological approaches such as action research and ethnography (McRobbie 1991).

However, whereas these early studies often addressed issues of class and race, they ignored gender as an identity category, resulting in the exclusion of girls as agential subjects from many of these youth studies. Angela McRobbie (1991) argues subcultural theorists' lack of attention to the ways that gender hierarchies structure subcultures has allowed for youth cultures to be understood as *male*, and issues such as sexism, violence, the sexual division of labor, and heterosexism to be made invisible in subcultural analysis. Despite her criticism, McRobbie nonetheless recognizes the potential that subcultures hold for girls' feminist politics, arguing, "To the extent that all-girl subcultures, where the commitment to the gang comes first, might forestall these processes [early marriage, child birth, housework] and provide their members with a collective confidence which could transcend the need for 'boys', they could well signal an important progression in the politics of youth culture" (42). Thus, McRobbie's insistence that feminist scholars must not dismiss work on subcultures, but instead "read across" these works, highlights the relevance that these subcultural theories may have for studying girls' cultural politics – including the practice of feminist blogging that I focus on here.

Despite critiques such as the one described above by McRobbie, there remains a dearth of work on girls within male dominated subcultures, both historically and contemporarily. The work that does exist, however, provides important insight into the feminist practices of girls in these alternative spaces. For example, punk is one subculture where girls have engaged in feminist activism and political agency through cultural production practices as musicians, artists, and writers (Kearney 2006), participating in events such as Rock Against Sexism and pro-choice marches (O'Brien 1999), and challenging feminine beauty norms through dress and style (O'Brien 1999; LeBlanc 1999). Kearney (2006) notes that girls' participation in punk is particularly significant, as girls were able to create their own feminist and activist identities *outside of the mainstream women's movement*, which many girls found alienating due to their age, race, class, and sexuality. Thus, punk became a space for girls to resist both normative feminine and feminist identities, while often exercising political critiques that were indeed feminist.[1]

Punk was not the only youth subculture that served as a space for political mobilization of young people. In his book *Hip Hop Matters: Politics, Pop Culture, and the Struggle for the Soul of a Movement* S. Craig Watkins (2005) notes that hip hop's "oppositional ethos" allowed hip hop culture to be a "political resource" for youth, fostering a political consciousness rooted in urban racial politics (149). While Watkins rightly critiques contemporary commercial hip hop as often promoting misogyny and degrading images of women, feminist scholars (Guevara 1987; Rose 1994; Kearney 2006) emphasize that girls and women have *always* been participants in hip hop culture, often acting as cultural producers through practices such as rapping, graffiti art, and breakdancing. Many black and Latina girls in hip hop were uncomfortable with identifying as feminist due to its connotations as a white movement, but they were able to use the subcultural space of hip hop to practice a reconfigured feminist and activist agenda related to their identities as women of color (Rose 1994; Kearney 2006). Thus, Kearney (2006) argues that "Like punk, hip hop provided an alternative place for girls' resistance to both patriarchal and feminist constructions of femininity during the 1970s, as well as a space for their more active engagement in cultural production" (45).[2]

While these examples of girls' activism within subcultures are useful in demonstrating a lengthy history of girls' involvement with feminist activism, recent cultural studies research has complicated the concept of the subculture in order to better analyze contemporary youth politics. David Chaney (2004) argues that the once accepted division between subcultures and dominant culture has dissolved, giving way to a "plurality of lifestyle sensibilities and preferences" that facilitates a widespread engagement with media and consumer industries once limited to niche subcultures (47). Sometimes called "post-subculture studies," this recent body of scholarship aims to understand contemporary youth cultures that are situated within a globalized world marked by fluidity, mobility, shifting identities, emerging technologies, and new consumption patterns characteristic of neoliberalism (see Muggleton and Weinzierl 2003).

Thus, new concepts such as neotribes, lifestyles, scapes, scenes, networks, citizenships, and communities have become more favored frameworks of analysis because of their ability to account for the lack of structure found in many contemporary youth cultures, such as ravers, Goths, or online fan cultures (Harris 2008a). Consequently, even the less formal practices of civic activism that I discussed at the beginning of this section appear markedly different today than they did thirty or forty years ago. Anita Harris (2008a) reflects on this shift in relation to young women, arguing:

> Whereas once young people's resistance politics, and young women's feminist activism in particular, could be easily identified, today these seem obscure, transitory and disorganized ... young women have new ways of taking on politics and culture that may not be recognizable under more traditional paradigms, but deserve to be identified as socially engaged and potentially transformative nonetheless (1).

Harris' emphasis on looser, more disparate activist networks as characterizing contemporary feminism aligns with much of the literature on third wave feminism (Garrison 2000, 2010; Piano 2002) and provides a useful starting point for thinking about how girls take up activist identities and practices through their blogging, the focus of the remainder of this chapter.

Activist Identities and the Politics of "Doing Something"

In addition to the feminist identities I discuss in the previous chapter, the bloggers I interviewed articulated an investment in an activist identity, often understanding this identity as being intimately connected with their feminism. Madison mentions that for her, feminist and activist identities are "so ingrained with one another" that she "finds it hard for someone to claim one without the other because I personally can't separate those identities." Activism, for many of the bloggers, was the part of feminism that involved "doing something." This sentiment was repeated in both the focus group and in personal interviews when many of the bloggers adamantly argued that being an activist involved not just being passionate about an issue, but *acting* on it.

For example, Amandine tells me that her definition of an activist is "someone who has a cause and does something about it." Likewise, sixteen-year-old high school student Carrie claims, "My definition of an activist is someone who responds to an issue they care about with action. Though thinking and talking about issues privately is important and a legitimate form of responding to issues, I don't think that doing that makes someone an activist." Whereas these explanations are rather simple, my further conversations with the girls and analysis of their blogs reveal more complex articulation of their activist identities, consisting of certain activist practices made possible through the girls' roles as media and cultural producers.

Being an activist is now a significant part of how many of my participants think about themselves, but it is important to note that most of them did not take on the activist identity until they began to blog. Similar to becoming feminist, taking on the activist label was a process that involved navigating dominant perceptions of activism with the bloggers' own experiences and feminist goals. Julie explains,

> I think of myself as a somewhat reluctant activist. Before I started blogging, I never really thought of myself as a leader or really as somebody terribly involved in 'causes.' I identified as a feminist of course but that came more from a place of trying to describe my ideologies and finding a community than actively trying to change policies. It was through blogging that I realized changing policies isn't the only way to define activism – I think activism is also about changing hearts and minds, which is what I do (or try to do) when I blog.

In this sense, the activist label was made intelligible for Julie through the practice of blogging, a relationship that is the focus of the remainder of this chapter.

The previous quote from Julie highlights a key tension that was continually raised throughout our conversations about activism and centered on what practices are legitimately 'activist.' This tension was made clear when I asked the bloggers to describe what they think of when they hear the word 'activist.' Amandine tells me that she visualizes a "person standing outside an official-looking building with a protest sign" and most likely protesting environmental issues, animal rights, or gay rights. She elaborates, "it's funny, but the first thing that comes to mind isn't in terms of women's rights or civil rights. I think that might be because environmentalism and gay rights are things that are very publicized when people are protesting about them now, but civil and women's rights are depicted by the media as more of a thing of the 1960s and 70s." Amandine wasn't unique in this regard, as several of my participants characterized activists as people who protest, leaders of social movements, like Martin Luther King, Jr. (a figure that several bloggers mentioned), or those who attract media attention because of outrageous acts, such as members of the Westboro Baptist Church.[3] The bloggers' associations reflect the prevalence of protest activism as a dominant signifier of activism in public consciousness. Interestingly, when these bloggers imagine an activist, they don't immediately picture themselves – or even other girls or women.

Activist as a Gendered and Aged Construct

I suggest that this discrepancy between girls' perceived notions of an activist and their own experiences of activism reveals particular gendered and aged cultural narratives about activism that shape the ways girls understand their own practices. As I previously noted, girls are often characterized as apolitical (also see Taft 2011), reflecting larger traditional gendered binaries that position the public sphere of politics and activism as a masculine domain. Even within the realm of feminist politics, girls, as "'the other' of feminism's womanhood" have been regarded as not sufficiently feminist (Currie, Kelly, and Pomerantz 2009, 4). In order to understand girls' political engagements, we must look beyond normative expressions of political participation, as defined by adults. Indeed, girls' feminist activism has often looked different than activist practices taken up by adult women and men. Harris (2008b) argues that girls' political participation has often taken place through less formal activities and private spheres, becoming invisible if we understand activism as a solely public activity within a public/private binary (a binary that is also, as Harris notes, highly gendered). In addition to their gendered identities, girls are also subject to age-based exclusions, marginalized as political subjects within both formal politics, and also often, social movements (Taft 2011; Harris 2008b).

Finally, several scholars (Aapola, Gonick, and Harris 2005; Harris 2008b; Taft 2011) have argued that adult-centric notions of what activism should be and where it should occur will often dismiss girls' activisms as "generational rebellion" rather than serious, meaningful political action, or will problematize girls' actions as dangerous or inappropriate. Harris (2008b) writes,

> Often, 'good participation' is defined as young people's membership, taking part, or sharing decision-making in pre-existent programs, forums, bodies and activities that have been crafted by adults, such as youth roundtables, liaison with government representatives, and involvement in local council initiatives. Young people's participation in activities with one another, outside adult control, is often trivialized and/or problematized … Similarly, the decision of many young people not to participate in conventional civic and political activities is frequently constructed as apathy and cynicism that can be corrected through education and access, rather than as a rational choice to dissociate themselves from alienating and impotent institutions (484).

Although Renee describes her own perceptions of an activist as very "positive," she explains that in contrast, "society's view of an activist is someone who is very annoying, nagging, not grounded in reality." Renee's description corresponds with the figure of the "bad activist," as elaborated by Jacqueline Kennelly (2011), who studied youth activists in Canada in the mid-2000s. According to Kennelly, dominant discourses about young activists often position youth activists as "troublemakers" and "rabble rousers," contrasting them with popular notions of the "good citizen," whose activist practices do not challenge social structures and instead rely on apolitical, middle-class practices like community service, philanthropy, and commodity activism.

However, Kennelly does not adequately analyze the gendered implications of the "bad activist," missing an important opportunity to theorize who may become an activist and who may not. If, according to both Renee and Kennelly, activists are viewed so negatively, who is willing to take on the label? Renee suggests to me that it is the dominant perceptions of an activist, as abrasive, confrontational, and annoying that may prevent many girls from identifying as activists. She elaborates,

> High school is really tough, especially for girls. Girls always want to be liked by everybody … I don't want to generalize too much, but I think girls get a lot of stress thinking that people don't like them, they spend a lot of time maintaining relationships. And so, being an activist that is stereotyped as nagging and annoying would really turn girls off because they would think it would be a turn off for other people. That's really sad.

Renee's discussion is interesting because it implies that it is specifically the *unfeminine* qualities associated with being an activist – loud, abrasive, confrontational, annoying – that are unappealing to girls, who are dealing with tremendous pressures to fit into normative feminine identities within high school environments. While "nagging" may be commonly understood as a feminine quality, it is one associated with an undesirable feminine stereotype – that of the shrill, nagging, and often unattractive wife. Of course, I do not want to portray girls as passively accepting these stereotypes and modifying their own behavior accordingly, and we cannot generalize that all girls are doing this. Indeed, we may understand many girls' hesitancy to avoid the activist label as a conscious and active strategy to make their high school life as easy as possible – understandable to most of us who felt pressure to conform during our formative years. Nonetheless, the tension between dominant understandings of an activist and normative feminine qualities remain important to consider.

Thus, it is not surprising that most of my participants agreed that girls are discouraged from being activists by parents, teachers, or friends. Yet, several of my participants discussed how girls *are* expected to participate in *particular kinds of activist practices*. Madison explains: "I think we're [girls] encouraged to do activism with what I call 'soft topics' like animal rights or children's rights, not harder topics like poverty, racism, or things of that nature." When I ask her about her own experience with activism while growing up, she claims that despite having a father who was active in conservative politics, she was not expected to be an activist herself. "I think I was always encouraged to help people. To help people, to volunteer, things like that," she says. My discussion with Madison reveals how activism is commonly understood in gendered ways, with girls expected to take on traditionally feminine practices often involving caring and emotional labor (volunteering at a seniors home, for example), and topics that are apolitical, and relatively non-controversial.[4]

It is perhaps not surprising then that none of my participants were specifically encouraged to participate in *feminist* activism as young girls or teenagers, most likely due to the controversial and political nature of feminism, as well as its connection to adult women. Nonetheless, as children of the 1990s, most of my participants were taught that girls were equal to boys, and told by their parents that they could be anything they wanted to be. Several of the bloggers I interviewed credit this upbringing with making them open to feminist politics as they got older and experienced sexism, despite the word 'feminism' itself being absent from their childhood environments. For example, Abby explains how angry she felt as a second grader when her teacher gave out coloring illustrations showing Jewish holiday scenes that featured only boys praying, celebrating, and performing ritual acts – actions that Abby claims are done by both genders in the religion. She tells me, "My nine-year-old self quickly realized that 'that's not fair!' and on many of those pages, the boys were colored in to look like girls instead!"

While Abby's action may not reflect dominant – masculine – understandings of activism, her example nonetheless demonstrates an activist trajectory on which Madison elaborates. She says, "I think a lot of girls get into [feminism] through soft issues again ... girl power, more women in the government, things like that. I got into feminism through the less controversial end of it, and once I got ingrained in the philosophy of it I became more invested in other issues, like being pro-choice and things that are more controversial." This comment echoes Rebecca Hains' (2012) findings in her ethnographic study of girl power media. Hains argues that the Spice Girls, probably the most notable girl power media franchise, served as a "pathway to feminism" for several of her research participants.

Emilie Zaslow (2009) offers a more nuanced argument, arguing that her study participants' engagement with girl power media culture encouraged them to adopt what she calls a "performance of feminist identity" informed by individual strength, confidence, and ambition, rather than a practice of feminist politics or activism. While I am not making an argument here about commercial girl power specifically, I am suggesting that while girls may not be encouraged to be activists in many circumstances, they are nonetheless often taught that they are equal to their male peers and expect to live out this ideal in their daily lives. Consequently, when girls encounter inequality in their lives, feminist consciousness can begin to emerge, as it did for Abby.

Given the many sectors of society where gender inequality persists, we might expect more girls to eventually become feminist activists. Indeed, feminism is one political sphere dominated by female activists, making it a space that would be seemingly appealing to girls based upon their gender alone. However, my conversations with the bloggers revealed that their age is a factor that has prevented several of them from participating in what may be seen as more traditional feminist activism. A conversation I had with Madison reveals that girl feminists often feel not *sufficiently activist* in comparison to their older feminist counterparts whom Madison describes as not taking younger feminists' activism seriously. She claims,

> Older feminists do not understand online activism; therefore, they don't think that online activism is true activism. If you go to a feminist conference and they're talking about ways to get young people involved, young feminists will say you need to create an online presence … but they'll say that that's not real, that's not real activism. Or they'll say that bloggers aren't doing anything for our cause, so they don't value them.
>
> And that just pushes young feminists away because that's where we spend the majority of our time, our organizing and our consciousness raising. Especially with consciousness raising – that's a big one. Older feminists are still in favor of getting in a room together and talking about sexism and patriarchy, but that's not how young feminists do it anymore – they do it online, through blogs, and Facebook. And they [second wave feminists] don't take that seriously … it's very contentious. As a young feminist I blame the older generation and think they need to start taking us seriously.

While Madison laughs as she says this, it is clearly an issue of contention for her – and rightly so. While Madison's activist identity is important to her, she feels as though her practices are marginalized within the larger feminist community. To Madison, ideas about activism, and specifically feminist activism, are shaped by age in a way that often position younger feminists as not *real activists* or not *sufficiently activist* in practice.

Madison's experience within the feminist community aligns with discourses about other types of youth activism that I previously discussed; these include the framing of activism in adult-centric terms that dismiss young activist's politics as merely "generational rebellion" (Taft 2011), and discourses that contrast the image of the "youth activist" with that of the "youth citizen" – the former image attached to notions of "rabblerousing" and "troublemaking" and the latter representing characteristics desirable to the neoliberal state (Kennelly 2011). Consequently, while adult activists are often afforded a certain respect for their supposed rational political beliefs, youth activists are positioned as lacking in knowledge, utilizing inappropriate activist tactics, and/or out to just cause trouble. These discourses exist in contrast to another dominant discourse about youth and activism – that which suggests youth are not interested in being politically active (Kennelly 2011).

This issue is further compounded by the increasing prevalence of 'online activism' over the past decade, including both public and academic debates about the merits of activism that are primarily enacted through digital media and/or new media technologies. Often framed in the press as "slacktivism" or "clicktivism," online activism is frequently described as lacking in authentic participation and clear, sustainable social change (Christensen 2011; Chattopadhyay 2011). For example, in his oft-cited *New Yorker* piece "Small Change: Why the Revolution will not be Tweeted," journalist Malcolm Gladwell (2010) argues that social media cannot facilitate the "high risk" or direct-action activism of the civil rights movement. He explains this as due to a lack of strong personal connections forged through online media and the decentralized nature of online activist networks. Gladwell concludes, "Facebook activism succeeds not by motivating people to make a real sacrifice but by motivating them to do the things that people do when they are not motivated enough to make a real sacrifice. We are a long way from the lunch counters of Greensboro." The older feminist activists mentioned by Madison seem to align with Gladwell's position, questioning younger feminist's motivation and dedication to the cause because of their use of digital media technologies.

New media scholars have also been interested in the possibilities for social change through online activism. While it is beyond the scope of this chapter to substantially engage in these debates, it is worthwhile highlighting some of these arguments. Richard Kahn and Douglas Kellner (2004) document how activists have successfully used the Internet to organize, facilitating what they call an "international protest movement" against neoliberal institutions, such as the World Trade Organization, in the late 1990s and early 2000s. They conclude their celebratory article by arguing that online activism has created a "vital new space of politics and culture" which have produced "new social relations and forms of political possibility" (94). Similarly, some feminists were also eager to use new media technologies for activism, including the cyberfeminists active in the 1990s who were enthusiastic about the networking and organizational abilities afforded by new media and used these technologies for activist purposes (Shade 2002).

More recently, new media scholars have been more nuanced in their analyses of online activism, demonstrating how it facilitates connections between online and offline activism and raises awareness of political issues, while remaining cautious about the potential for sustained social movements. For example, Paolo Gerbaudo (2012, 160) argues that activists use social media as a means of mobilization, "reweav[ing] a new sense of public space, refashioning the way in which people come together on the streets." Gerbaudo's ethnographic research contradicts Gladwell's assertions that social media lacks personal connects and structure. Instead Gerbaudo writes,

> Social media have become emotional conduits for reconstructing a sense of togetherness among a spatially dispersed constituency, so as to facilitate its physical coming together in public space. This finding clearly goes against much scholarship on new media, which has tended to locate them in a 'virtual reality' of in a 'cyberspace,' or in a 'network of brains' detached from geographic reality (159–160).

By analyzing social media within its cultural context of depleting public space, Gerbaudo recognizes that social media offers important opportunities for activists that go beyond merely organization purposes; yet he cautions that the continuity of social movements such as the Arab Spring cannot be sustained through social media alone. Unfortunately, Gerbaudo's book does not address gender, race, class, age, and other identities as categories of analyses, and therefore, we get little understanding of girls' roles in these movements.

It is also necessary to ask *whom* online activism may benefit most. My suggestion throughout this book, that blogging is an activist practice especially useful to marginalized people (in the case of this study, girls), is supported by other feminist research. For example, Saayan Chattopadhyay (2011) uses the online 2009 Pink Chaddi Campaign in India as a case study to demonstrate how Indian women who may face constraints to organizing in public spaces have successfully mobilized using digital media instead. Whereas Chattopadhyay recognizes the limitations of online activism, such as unequal access to technologies, he nonetheless argues that it "opens up innovative modes of belonging and perhaps equally atypical ways of approaching politics, individual communities, and cultural difference" (66). Similarly, Carrie Rentschler (2014) outlines how feminists have used social media to challenge rape culture, holding perpetrators accountable when the media, police officials, and school authorities do not. Such studies remind us that online activism cannot be approached through binary logic, which suggests that online activism is 'real' or 'not real,' but must be analyzed as part of changing cultural conditions that require multiple modes of resistance, avenues of communication, and strategies of knowledge production.

Exploring Girl Feminist Bloggers' Activist Practices

My discussion of activism has so far analyzed the activist identities cultivated by girl feminist bloggers. But how are these activist identities mobilized into actual activist practices facilitated through blogging? Taft (2011) argues that girl activists' political identities and strategic activist practices are interrelated, and that we therefore must understand girls' identity claims in order to truly understand how and why they do activism in particular ways. Nonetheless, Taft is careful to avoid the charge of essentialism. She writes,

> Identity does not shape strategy due to anything inherent in a group's identity. Rather, it shapes strategy through a group's negotiated and active assertion of the political meaning of that identity. I do not argue that identity determines strategy, but I do suggest that there is a relationship between the two, and that this relationship is best understood through looking at the mechanism of identity narratives and identity claims (182–183).

Thus, I will now turn to a discussion of the activist practices of girl feminist bloggers, drawing connections between their feminist and activist identities and activism. I understand girls' activism as consisting of three key practices: (1) education; (2) community-building; and (3) the production of feminist visibility. Although I take up each of these practices separately for the purpose of a clear analysis, it is significant to recognize that these practices are interrelated and often used in tandem by girl bloggers. Additionally, I will return to these practices throughout the book, because they serve as important foundational concepts to understand girls' feminist blogging.

Education

One of the most important activist practices in which girl bloggers engage is what they describe as "education," specifically the practice of educating their peers about feminist issues and feminism itself. "There's a lot of kinds of activism that goes on online, like online protests, signing petitions, organizing, but I think if we were going to look at the number one thing that comes out of online activism, it would be education," Madison maintains. Other participants echo Madison's insistence on the importance of using blog spaces to educate peers on what feminism is, the history of the movement and the benefits of feminism in order to debunk the harmful stereotypes and misconceptions about feminism. Education, in this sense, is understood by bloggers as necessary for feminist social change and best practiced through blogging and other online platforms.

Courtney was one of the bloggers more outspoken about the importance of education as an activist practice. She has been active for the past two years on her Blogspot and Tumblr blogs and views her ability to spread information via her participation on these platforms, as well as Facebook, as a significant part of her activism. Although it is easy to assume that feminist bloggers are merely 'preaching to the converted,' an issue I will address in the following chapter, Courtney maintains that this is not the case, especially since her friends who do not identify as feminists often follow her Tumblr or view Courtney's status updates on their Facebook feed. Courtney explains that she believes that sharing feminist information online is activism because "I hear back from a lot of my friends who do get involved or do learn something from what I write and share. It makes me feel that even though I'm just doing something simple that I'm getting other people involved and interested and hopefully they'll go out and do the same – spread the good word of feminism!"

Likewise, Madison views her Tumblr blog as a tool to educate people who are just learning about feminism. "That's who I try to hit, people who are hesitant – I don't try and water things down because I don't believe in watering things down for people who are hesitant – but [I try to keep the blog] sort of informational." For example, Madison's blog has recently been an excellent source for information on reproductive rights legislation, especially in her home state of Michigan. She also offers useful information about feminism more generally, such as an extensive listing of feminist women throughout history, a topic I will address in more detail in chapter four. Madison's idea of teaching readers about feminism implies that many girl bloggers aim to educate other young people specifically, rather than adults. And indeed, most girl bloggers tell me that this is who they are speaking to when they blog. For example, Renee says, "I imagine that 99% of the people that are coming to my blog are going to be girls … so I imagine that I'm talking to that teenage girl, or that tween girl who is on her laptop at midnight just browsing around and she's heard about this feminism thing, but she doesn't know what it is and she's trying to do a little research."

Education for girl bloggers, however, isn't necessarily a one-way flow of 'correct' information, but instead is characterized by the "participatory" nature of the web, where users can both consume and produce cultural texts (Jenkins 2006). For example, instead of posting what she herself deems important, Madison utilizes the question function on her blog to encourage questions from readers, which she then answers. She receives as many as fifteen questions a day about everything from white privilege to how to deal with sexist messages online. And while Madison has the power to not respond to certain questions, the question function allows readers to engage with the content in an immediate way that is impossible to do with most other media forms.

Girl bloggers' desire to educate their peers must also be viewed in relation to the absence of feminism in most high school curricula. The majority of my study participants claimed that they did not learn about feminism or women's rights in their high school classes. When feminism was mentioned, it was primarily framed as a historical movement in a U.S. History class, rather than an active movement in the present. Even in these cases, feminism is often relegated to sidebars in textbooks, and bloggers reported relatively little class time spent analyzing the topic. In this sense, girl bloggers' educational activism can be seen as filling an important void in girls' knowledge of history, a topic I'll discuss in chapter four.

In her ethnographic research on girl anti-globalization activists, Taft (2011) found that education was also a significant part of girls' political practices, and girls often designed events and activities with this goal in mind. However, Taft maintains that education involves "not only creating spaces for sharing facts, discussing solutions to problems, and developing philosophies, theories, and vocabularies but also developing dissident feelings, intuitions, and desires" (115). According to Taft, this "feeling production" is a significant, yet often overlooked goal of education as an activist practice, and must be acknowledged as legitimate. Indeed, "feeling production" is certainly evident in many of the images and much of the information circulated by girl bloggers.

For example, about a month before the U.S. presidential election in November 2012, Kat circulated an image on her Facebook profile that reads

"92 Years Ago, Women Gained the Right to Vote. This Year, Make Sure You Use It. GOTTAREGISTER.COM." The accompanying images show a black and white photo of suffragettes protesting and then a color photo of contemporary women cheering at what looks like an Obama political rally. Not only does the image educate Kat's Facebook friends about suffrage and the fact that women have had voting rights in the United States for a relatively short time, but the image calls upon the viewer to act by registering to vote and then getting out to the ballot box. Perhaps most importantly, though, the image circulates feelings of power, strength, progress, and even excitement, suggesting that women have political agency and an important responsibility to participate in this election. It is this "feeling production" that arguably makes the act of circulating this image on one's Facebook profile educational. An image such as this posted to one's Facebook wall may or may not lead someone to actually act (in this case, vote); however, it generates important feelings that benefit young women – such as a sense of political agency and community – and points to the need to take the circulation of digital images seriously (see Shifman 2014). Seeking a direct tangible and measurable "effect" of activism ignores results like the production of feeling. That it is women and girls whose activism often involves this emotional labor is not a coincidence, and again reveals the gendered way that we often talk about activism (Taft 2011).

Community-building

Although I am focusing on issues of community in the following chapter, it is necessary to briefly discuss here how bloggers conceptualize the community building that occurs through their blogging as a form of activism. This is particularly important to emphasize within the context of neoliberalism and the ways in which activism is being increasingly understood as an individualistic endeavor (Hearn 2012; Kennelly 2011; Harris 2008a). As a result, I was struck by the ways in which girl bloggers described how fostering a coalition of young feminist bloggers was viewed as activist, in part because it resists dominant discourses of individualism.

When I ask Renee why she thinks that it's important to view blogging as a form of activism, she says, "I think everybody's voice is important. If you can go online and find this mass of feminist bloggers, it's inspiring to the next generation – it just shows you're not alone." To Renee, finding a community is necessary in order to sustain feminism. Participating in this community then ensures its continuation, functioning as activism by motivating oneself and others to continue the struggle. Similarly, Courtney says that being part of a larger feminist community and actively maintaining these ties allow her to be an activist because she feels supported and knows that there are others to back her up if she needs it. She tells me that it is probably possible to be an "individual activist," although she doesn't see how feminism can achieve anything without "women and girls coming together as a community."

The girl bloggers that participated in this study spend a lot of time building community via their blogs. This work takes various forms; however, it is important to note that while all of the bloggers spoke about engaging in such community-building practices, most described this as happening "unconsciously." In other words, community-building work was viewed by the bloggers as *just a part of having a feminist blog*, rather than an additional voluntary task. This may be due to the participatory culture fostered by web 2.0 platforms, which functions through the sharing and circulation of content via community networks (Jenkins 2006). Additionally, the assumed 'common sense' of this practice may help to obscure the ways in which community-building functions as activism among feminist bloggers.

For example, to celebrate the first birthday of her blog, Amandine hosted an essay contest where participants were asked to answer the question "How has feminism changed your life?" Although Amandine tells me that she received many entries – including several international entries – she didn't immediately describe the contest as facilitating community, even though the contest allowed contestants to share their personal experiences with a wider audience, giving their own blogs exposure. The contest also generated a conversation about the role of feminism in girls' and women's lives and made visible the vast networks that Amandine had cultivated after only one year of blogging.

In addition to Amandine's essay contest, bloggers mobilize a number of practices to build community between their blogs. These include: sharing other girls' stories through 're-blogging' or 'reposting,' promoting other girls' blogs through feature stories or on the blogroll, inviting contributions from other girl bloggers, sharing personal experiences, leaving comments on other girls' blogs and allowing comments on one's blog. For example, when another girl starts a feminist blog, Renee will often promote it on her own site, sometimes including a short interview with the new blogger. To wit: In a May 19, 2011 post, Renee introduces a new feminist blog to her readers and interviews the blog's author about being a teenage feminist. She is constantly adding these new blogs to her blogroll so that her readers can easily navigate to other feminist blogs they may not be familiar with. Thus, the blogroll works to maintain connections and community between blogs, an example I'll return to in the following chapter.

Similar to Amandine's essay contest, Renee frequently poses a question or issue and invites responses from her readers. In an August 6, 2011 post called "5 Perspective on the Recent Birth Control Ruling," Renee writes, "It feels like we're a part of history here, doesn't it? This ruling is a huge, exciting deal, and it's been fun to see the feminist community alive with celebration these past few days ... Since the 'birth control conversation' is often restricted to the twenties-and-older sphere, I wanted to get some younger perspectives on this momentous ruling. Naturally, I turned to my feminist blogger friends!" The post goes on to include responses from five teenage bloggers about the no co-pay birth control ruling as part of the Affordable Care Act. This is an interesting example because it not only makes visible the importance of dialogue *between blogs*, but it also privileges the voices of teenage feminists who are often problematically excluded from conversations about birth control because of their age. Having these conversations then invites girls to take action on issues in which they may have felt excluded, and points to the ways in which these community-building practices function as activism for girls.

To bloggers, community-building and education are not isolated, but related practices that mutually reinforce one another. Courtney explains that sharing feminist information through social media "makes the [feminist] community stronger because there's more people involved and invested." She gives the example of the 2011 SlutWalk phenomenon, which she claims never would have happened without the social media to connect women and girls all over the world. SlutWalks educated the public about rape culture both through online conversations as well as the walks themselves, but the online discourse also built new feminist communities through this education, motivating a diversity of girls and women (and their allies) to organize.

Similarly, we can see how education and community-building function together in the way that Madison uses the question function on her Tumblr, as I previously described. For example, when a reader asks Madison how she deals with sexist backlash from her activist efforts, Madison responds by giving the reader advice, including making use of supportive feminist networks. She writes, "I typed [support] three times because in my opinion having support is the most important part of dealing with backlash. Make sure that you have a solid group of people that have your back. If you don't have those people in real life, make Internet friends!" Here Madison is not only emphasizing the importance of supportive communities, but is engaged in building one by answering this question, legitimating her readers' experience as well as engaging in a form of education by passing on a set of strategies to deal with backlash that worked for her (Figure 2.1).

My participants' commitment to community-building continues a lengthy tradition of this practice within feminist movements, including through the use of digital media technologies. Doreen Piano (2002) describes how online feminist distros in the late 1990s "create[d] feminist pockets or zones in cyberspace," serving to connect feminist zine producers and consumers and build communities based on an alternative economic model antithetical to commercial, male-dominated and for-profit spaces.[5] This type of community-building then serves as an activist practice by challenging dominant capitalist logic and extending a gendered, racial, and class-based critique to economics. I will be further developing this discussion throughout the next chapter.

> Hi :) I recently posted on a supermarket's facebook wall asking why they sold Zoo magazine as it degrades and objectifies women. Of course, got the stock standard auto response back form the supermarket and now getting lots of really nasty comments from guys e.g. 'you're just jealous cause you're way too ugly to be on there', tits or gtfo, you're (insert expletive here). I'm a shy sort of person and not used to speaking out, so not sure how to handle this. How do you handle backlash from guys?

 aussieshadowhunter

Whooo, good question!

Backlash can be hard to deal with. It's important to find ways to cope, I tend to use three strategies when dealing from backlash.

1. Ignore- Don't be afraid to ignore backlash. Block people on facebook, tumblr, or twitter Walk out of the room, put headphones on, hang up the phone. You are under no obligation to read or listen to people saying nasty things to you. I use this a lot with family and with the internet. It's gotten to the point where if someone says something nasty to me on facebook, it's an automatic unfriend. I just don't want to deal!

2. Humor- I use this tactic a lot on tumblr. If I get a nasty message, I'll answer it with a funny gif. Sometimes the only thing you can do about a situation is laugh. If someone is making fun of me, I try to find a way to turn it around and make fun of them. Even if I'm the only one laughing, it helps.

3. Support, support, support- I typed it 3 times because in my opinion having support is the most important part of dealing with backlash. Make sure that you have a solid group of people that have your back. If you don't have those people in real life, make internet friends! I'm serious, having someone that you can vent to is important. It's also important that at the end of your venting, that person agrees with you. When you're dealing with backlash, it's important to have people on your side.

Figure 2.1 Madison's Tumblr Q&A, author screen shot. Used with permission of blog owner.

Producing Feminist Visibility

I was surprised to discover how invested my participants are in making feminists and feminism visible online in order to challenge stereotypes of feminists, an issue that I discuss in the previous chapter. In this sense, bloggers alluded to the idea that *being a feminist publicly* was in itself an activist strategy, a type of public relations mission with the goal of getting more young people involved in a movement often characterized as dead or redundant (McRobbie 2009). For example, Renee says,

> By simply calling yourself a feminist you get others into the conversation. Kids at school, people who read your blog (if you have one), friends and family members … once you're a feminist, you're like a little stone that upsets everything around you with a ripple effect. First, it's little ripples. But over time they get bigger and bigger and people start recognizing you for your strong beliefs.

This strategy can be seen in Renee's "Faces of Feminism" project that I describe in detail in chapter one, whereby Renee invited self-identified feminists to send in pictures of themselves, which she then posted on her blog. By making a diversity of feminists *literally* visible on her blog, Renee positions a feminist identity as something desirable and accessible to everyone, inviting others to identify with the movement with the hopes of it growing.

In her book, *A Little F'ed Up: Why Feminism Is Not a Dirty Word,* Julie Zeilinger, (2012) founder and editor of the *FBomb*, and a participant in this study puts forth a similar argument suggesting that publicly living as a self-identified young feminist is a necessary strategy to keep the movement growing. In her book chapter titled "Please Stop Calling Me a Feminazi (Or Houston, We Have a PR Problem)" she argues,

> Feminists have been so preoccupied with trying to make the world a better place (silly us) that we've kind of forgotten about effectively combating negative stereotypes and projecting positive images of ourselves, in the media and in the world at large. And the thing is that while we can tell ourselves that the way other people view us doesn't matter, it really does. I'm not saying we should change what we are as a movement because some people reject it. I'm not saying we should let those negative stereotypes impact us, or that we should bend over backward to make people like us. No, I'm saying we need to better package and present who we *are* and who we have *always* been. The product is there. (Hello, worldwide equality? Who wouldn't buy that?) We just need to sell it better (79).

I quote from Julie's book at length because I find the language she uses to be fascinating: "images" of feminism, feminism as a "product," and feminists needing to "sell" it to a mainstream crowd relies on the neoliberal language of branding and marketing consultants to promote a complex, collectivist social movement. I want to be critical of this neoliberal discourse, as I believe it potentially frames feminism to become a series of easily digestible images, dangerously close to the ways in which postfeminism privileges empowered feminine visibility, display, and a circulation of images (McRobbie 2009; Harris 2004). Thus, the language of neoliberalism risks emptying the politics out of Zeilinger's feminism with the hopes of making it easily digestible to a mainstream public.

It is not surprising that girl activists may construct feminism in such terms. The young feminists I discuss here have grown up in a neoliberal cultural climate that emphasizes social change and resistance within the confines of a commercial consumer culture (Mukherjee and Banet-Weiser 2012). A key part of this neoliberal culture is the branding practices that "produce sets of images and immaterial symbolic values in and through which individuals negotiate the world *at the same time* as they work to contain and direct the expressive, meaning-making capacities of social actors in definite self-advantaging way, shaping markets and controlling competition" (Hearn 2012, 27). Furthermore, feminist scholars have argued that the emergence of a "neoliberal feminism" (Rottenberg 2013) premised on the recognition of inequality between men and women, yet prescribing individual solutions to this inequality, have become increasingly prevalent within mainstream American culture, further entrenching neoliberal logic within everyday life (see Fraser 2013a).

Let me be clear: I am not suggesting that Julie is promoting a form of neoliberal feminism or is advocating for the shiny, media-friendly feminism promoted by such recent media campaigns as #ELLEfeminism.[6] In fact, her keen awareness of the importance of collectivity, acknowledgment of structural inequalities, and mobilization of intersectional critique point to her understanding of feminism as a movement that is much more complex than her earlier quote may suggest. Yet, I'm fascinated by this seeming contradiction; her use of marketing discourse produces a discursive slippage that suggests an ambiguity about the ideal positioning of feminism within contemporary commercial popular culture that continues to be a point of disagreement among feminists.

The strategy of producing feminist visibility that I've been discussing relies less on mobilizing for specific, tangible changes on particular issues as emblematic of the women's liberation movement, and instead focuses on what Nancy Fraser (1997, 2013b) describes as a "recognition" feminism that emphasizes the cultural and symbolic as sites of social change, an argument I referred to in the previous chapter. Third wave feminists have been particularly invested in "recognition" feminism through their attention to representations, communication, fluid shifting identities, and cultural production (Zaslow 2009; Harris 2008a). As a result it makes sense for bloggers like Renee and Julie to be thinking about how feminism is perceived in popular culture and how they may intervene to change feminism's cultural status, as the cultural arena is a significant space for their own performances of feminism.

However, it is necessary to recognize that this practice did not originate in the third wave and that feminists have always been interested in making their movement visible within the public sphere. In fact, Fraser (2013b) suggests that it was the second wave's attention to issues of recognition, such as identity claims, over a redistributive approach that positioned contemporary feminism to be subsumed within neoliberalism. Whereas it is not my intention to engage with this causal claim here, Fraser's historical analysis is significant to consider. For example, some feminists in the women's liberation movement emphasized the importance of participating in mainstream commercial culture in order to broaden the appeal of feminism to a diversity of women, some of whom may not consider themselves feminist or even political. Amy Erdman Farrell (1998) documents how Ms. magazine was developed in the early 1970s with this mission in mind by promoting what she calls a "popular feminism" (5). This popular feminism, according to Farrell, refers to a "shared, widely held cultural and political commitment to improving women's lives and to ending gender domination that is both articulated and represented within popular culture" (196). Because popular culture often intersects with commercial culture, *Ms'* founders envisioned popular feminism as reaching a wide audience through the commercial women's magazine industry (Farrell 1998).

In part, feminist's desire to ensure their public visibility is related to women's historical exclusion from the public sphere and relegation to the private sphere of the home. In this sense, making feminism visible is a necessary feminist strategy to secure a public voice. Additionally, Farrell emphasizes that many feminists envisioned a commercial feminist magazine as potentially "weaken[ing] women's resistance to feminism and make[ing] them rethink the stereotypical images they had previously known in mainstream media" (16). Interestingly, this goal is markedly similar to Julie's investment in improving feminism's "PR problem" and Renee's desire to "get others' into the conversation." While different language may be employed by contemporary bloggers, the goal remains the same: to make feminism appealing to more girls and women in order to spark a feminist consciousness.

It is important to recognize that this strategy of mainstreaming has always been controversial among activists. Indeed, Farrell notes how not all feminists in the 1970s endorsed the commercial strategy that Ms magazine embraced. Similarly, I have offered a critique of this strategy in relation to contemporary bloggers, warning that their rhetoric of "selling" feminism is informed by neoliberal discourses. Consequently, it is imperative to recognize both the opportunities and limitations of producing feminist visibility with a critical lens to the cultural context and movement goals. Moreover, we can see that while girl feminist bloggers' strategy of producing feminist visibility within the mainstream media appears new, it actually has a lengthy history within feminism that may provide important lessons for today's girl bloggers.

Blogging as an Accessible Feminist Activist Practice

If blogging plays such a central role in many girl feminists' lives today, it is important to ask *why* girls choose *blogging* specifically as a way to practice feminist activism. Several of my participants described blogging as an activist practice that is accessible to them in their everyday lives, making it a desirable way to participate in feminism. Renee explains:

> For those of us who can't drive two hours to protest an anti-choice bill or whip out $100 whenever a worthy feminist charity comes along, blogging is the next best thing. Specifically, blogging about feminism shows that the movement is still alive and kicking, and gives hope to those who may feel alone in their struggle. I can only hope that *my* blog reaches other young people and shows them that feminism is important, that feminism is empowering, and that feminism is *certainly* not dead.

Likewise, Kat tells me that blogging is "the only kind of activism I've had access to over the past three years … Hopefully you can do outreach in person at some point but [blogging] is good for those of us that … live in communities where there is no other way to participate." Kat has wanted to volunteer at Planned Parenthood because of her interest in reproductive rights and sex education, however, the closest clinic to her family's home in rural Indiana is a half hour away, preventing Kat from volunteering due to a lack of transportation to and from the clinic. This has been frustrating to her because she wants to expand her feminist activism, but is limited by her rural location and positioning as a young person with a lack of financial resources. "I see all these protests happening all over the country and I'm like, 'I wish I could go!'" She is excited for next fall, when she will move to a larger urban center to attend university and plans to participate in feminist groups on campus.

Renee and Kat's comments highlight how important blogging is as an accessible way for girls with limited resources – often due to age, but also perhaps gender, class, race, location, and ability – to participate in activism. This point is crucial and is often overlooked by adults who have significantly more freedom and personal income than girls, allowing them to participate in a wider variety of activist practices that may not be accessible to girls still living with parents and often with limited finances and transportation. Girls' activist practices, in other words, are shaped by their social location as girls.

But while blogging is an accessible activist strategy for many girls, it is not accessible to everyone. For example, the ability to blog requires regular access to not only a computer, but also expensive broadband or DSL Internet access. Additionally, girls must also have some disposable leisure time to create and maintain a blog, which can be a time consuming process; the bloggers I interviewed reported spending between five and fourteen hours a week researching, writing, and editing posts. Because many working-class and poor girls work part-time jobs to help support their families or care for younger siblings while their parents work, some girls may lack the leisure time needed to blog in addition to computer/Internet access. Consequently, while I am framing blogging as an accessible activist practice for girls, it is imperative to remember that some girls remain excluded from this activist practice.

I am suggesting that both feminist media scholars and activists must understand girls' feminist blogging practices as activism that is related to their own social context and *positioning as girls*. For example, instead of suggesting that educating their peers about abortion regulations through Twitter is not sufficiently activist, we must understand that education is particularly relevant to young people's lives as *students*. As Taft (2011, 115) argues, "Given their location as students, it is not surprising that teenagers would place a particular emphasis on education and learning within social movements. To a certain extent, this identity position partially explains why they prioritize this social change strategy." Thus, my argument requires that we theorize activism from a girl-centered perspective, as Taft does here and as I aim to do in this chapter.

Blogging as an activist strategy can also be considered in relation to the lengthy history of writing in girls' culture, which I briefly outlined in the introduction to this book. The practice of *writing* a blog can be seen as continuing longstanding writing practices, such as keeping a diary, having a pen pal, and writing fan letters, that girls have engaged in for many years. Many of these writing practices have provided a space for girls to perform and explore their identities, such as the feminist riot grrrl identities performed by girl zinesters in the 1990s (Crowther 1999; Hunter 2002; Kearney 2006). Hunter (2002) also notes how girls in the early 1900s often acted as political activists through their roles as editors on their school newspapers, advocating for women's suffrage in their weekly columns. When viewed in relation to this history, it makes sense that contemporary girls are choosing to write blogs as a way to perform their feminist and activist identities, as writing is a central part of girls' culture both historically and contemporarily.

But understanding the ways that digital culture has fostered girls' feminist activism requires us to reassess the assumption that a practice such as blogging, for example, only functions as 'online activism.' With this in mind, I want to turn to a brief discussion of how we must understand girls' activist identities as beyond the 'online/offline' binary.

"One of the Best Things of My Life": Activism On and Off the Screen

While I am arguing that the practice of blogging itself is a legitimate form of feminist activism, it is also necessary to highlight how feminist blogging serves as a gateway to other kinds of activism for several of the bloggers. Courtney describes her feminist blogging as a "catalyst" for deciding to volunteer at Planned Parenthood and has strengthened her commitment to the Pride Alliance, an organization she was involved with prior to the development of her blog. Similarly, Madison maintains that her feminist blogging has encouraged her to take on other feminist activist practices outside the blogosphere. She explains, "I started blogging and then Walk for Choice happened and that was organized through Tumblr and was the first outside feminist thing I've ever done, as far as black and white activism ... My parents are conservative so I was always nervous to go to these things, but I had a cousin drive me down to Ann Arbor [for Walk for Choice] and it was one of the best things of my life ..."

These accounts reveal a connection between blogging and 'offline' activist practices that must be better articulated by new media scholars. In fact, it may be harder than expected to classify what is 'online' activism in many of the examples of activism that bloggers described to me. For example, the Walk for Choice event that Madison discusses happened only because of its organization through the blogging platform Tumblr. In turn, Madison heard about the event and decided to attend only based on her online participation.

Indeed, as Mary Gray (2009) claims, "'online' and 'offline' experiences of media constitute one another," and this is increasingly important for girls, who have less access to the public sphere than boys. Consequently, as I continue to discuss bloggers' activism throughout this book I aim to complicate further the activist practices I introduce here by demonstrating the ways in which they are constitutive of the everyday lives of girl bloggers.

Conclusion: Blogging as Girl-Centered Activism

In chapter one I argued that the performance of feminist identities are a significant precursor to girl feminist bloggers' ability to understand themselves as political agents in the present. In many ways, this second chapter provides evidence of the resulting action – how girl feminist bloggers mobilize their feminist identities into activist identities and practices of activism via blogging. I describe how an activist identity is made intelligible for girls via their blogging practices, allowing girls to imagine activism in ways that often challenged their early conceptions of both activists and activism. This is a significant point, and thus, I argue that feminist scholars must more rigorously analyze what I describe as gendered and aged cultural narratives about activism in order to better understand how activist identities are discursively produced in opposition to dominant norms of girlhood. A girl-centered approach to activism allows us to see how education, community-building, and making feminism visible function as key activist practices that girls engage in through blogging. In doing so, I argue that blogging must be understood as an *accessible* activist practice in itself, related to girl bloggers' own social context and positioning as *girls*.

More broadly, this chapter also suggests the need for rethinking both public and scholarly conversations we are having about the opportunities and limitations of using digital media technologies to engage in political activism. I argue that we must consider how the dismissal of online activism as not 'authentic' or 'change-producing' is not only shaped by gendered and ageist discourses that I outline here, but problematically relies on a rigid distinction between 'online' and 'offline' spaces – a divide often challenged by the bloggers I spoke to. I continue to problematize the online/offline binary in the following chapter, which examines girls' blogging communities as networked counterpublics.

Notes

1. Despite girls' participation in punk, they often remain marginalized within historical accounts of the subculture. As Helen Reddington (2003) notes, it is those who left recorded music that become regarded as punk pioneers, earning a place in punk's history while constructing a narrative that often excluded the participation of women and girls, who may not have recorded songs or achieved mainstream fame. This is a telling example of how the activist practices of girls' are often erased from history, contributing to the dominant understanding of girls as apolitical.

2. See Nancy Guevara (1987) for a discussion of how hip hop girls utilized 'girl' signifiers as part of their cultural expression, such as graffiti tags with big lips, roses, and other 'feminine' landscape themes.
3. The Westboro Baptist Church is an American unaffiliated Baptist church that has gained widespread attention in the U.S. for its members' extreme ideologies and public picketing of the funerals of LGBTQ people, military personnel, and victims of gun violence. The group has also been known to protest outside of Jewish institutions, churches supportive of gay marriage, abortion clinics, and even pop concerts.
4. While the gendering of contemporary girls' activism problematically reinforces gender binaries, women activists have often foregrounded their gendered identities (for example, mother identities) in order to engage in activism publicly. See Bell and Braun 2010; Rome 2006; Naples 1992, 1998 for a discussion of these politics.
5. A "distro" is an independent store that distributes often handmade or DIY-produced goods and originated within subcultures such as punk.
6. In fall 2013 women's fashion magazine *ELLE UK* launched a campaign to "rebrand" feminism using the Twitter hashtag #ELLEfeminism. This campaign is exemplary of the "neoliberal feminism" described by Rottenberg (2013) as it interpellates a specifically neoliberal (white, middle-class, straight, and cis-gendered) feminist subject who aims to make individual changes in order to challenge gender inequalities (primarily in relation to the white-collar employment opportunities and work/life balance).

References

Aapola, Sinikka, Marnina Gonick, and Anita Harris. 2005. *Young Femininity: Girlhood, Power, and Social Change.* New York: Palgrave MacMillan.

Bell, Shannon Elizabeth, and Yvonne Braun. 2010. "Coal, Identity, and the Gendering of Environmental Justice Activism in Central Appalachia." *Gender & Society* 24(6): 794–813.

Chaney, David. 2004. "Fragmented Culture and Subcultures." In *After Subculture: Critical Studies in Contemporary Youth Subculture*, edited by Andy Bennett and Keith Kahn-Harris. New York: Palgrave MacMillan, 36–50.

Chattopadhyay, Saayan. 2011. "Online Activism for a Heterogeneous Time: The Pink Chaddi Campaign and the Social Media in India." *Proteus*, 27(1): 63–67.

Christensen, Henrik. 2011. "Political Activities on the Internet: Slacktivism or Political Participation By Other Means?" *First Monday* 16(2). http://firstmonday.org/htbin/cgiwrap/bin/ojs/index.php/fm/article/view/3336/276.

Corning, Alexandra, and Daniel Myers. 2002. "Individual Orientation Toward Engagement in Social Action." *Political Psychology* 23(4): 703–729.

Crowther, Barbara. 1999. "Writing as Performance: Young Girls' Diaries." In *Making Meaning of Narratives*, edited by Ruthellen H. Josselson, and Amia Lieblich, 197–220. Thousand Oaks: Sage.

Currie, Dawn, Deirdre Kelly, and Shauna Pomerantz. 2009. *'Girl Power:' Girls Reinventing Girlhood.* New York: Peter Lang.

Farrell, Amy. 1998. *Yours In Sisterhood: Ms. Magazine and the Promise of Popular Feminism.* Chapel Hill: The University of North Carolina Press.

Fraser, Nancy. 1997. *Justice Interruptus: Critical Reflections on "Postsocialist" Condition.* New York: Routledge.

Fraser, Nancy. 2013a. "How feminism became capitalism's handmaiden – and how to reclaim it." *The Guardian,* October 14. http://www.theguardian.com/commentisfree/2013/oct/14/feminism-capitalist-handmaiden-neoliberal.

Fraser, Nancy, 2013b. *Fortunes of Feminism: From State-Managed Capitalism to Neoliberal Crisis.* London: Verso.

Garrison, Ednie Kaeh. 2000. "U.S. Feminism-Grrrl Style! Youth (Sub)Cultures and the Technologics of the Third Wave." *Feminist Studies* 26 (1): 141–170.

Garrison, Ednie Kaeh. 2010. "U.S. Feminism-Grrrl Style! Youth (Sub)Cultures and the Technologies of the Third Wave (updated)." In *No Permanent Waves: Recasting Histories of U.S. Feminism,* edited by Nancy Hewitt, 379–402. New Brunswick, NJ: Rutgers University Press.

Gerbaudo, Paolo. 2012. *Tweets and the Streets: Social Media and Contemporary Activism.* London: Pluto Press.

Gladwell, Malcolm. 2010. "Small Change: Why the Revolution Will Not Be Tweeted." *The New Yorker,* October 4. http://www.newyorker.com/reporting/2010/10/04/101004fa_fact_gladwell?currentPage=1.

Gray, Mary. 2009. *Out in the Country: Youth, Media, and Visibility in Rural America.* New York: New York University Press.

Guevara, Nancy. 1987. "Women Writin' Rappin' Breakin'." In *The Year Left 2, an American Socialist Yearbook,* edited by Mike Davis, Manning Marable, Fred Pfeil and Michael Sprinker, 160–175. London: Verso.

Hains, Rebecca. 2012. *Growing Up With Girl Power: Girlhood on Screen and In Everyday Life.* New York: Peter Lang.

Hall, Stuart, and Tony Jefferson. 1976. *Resistance Through Rituals: Youth Subcultures in Post-War Britain.* New York: Holmes & Meier.

Hands, Joss. 2011. *@ is for Activism: Dissent, Resistance and Rebellion in a Digital Culture.* London, UK: Pluto Press.

Harris, Anita. 2004. *Future Girl: Young Women in the Twenty-first Century.* New York: Routledge.

Harris, Anita. 2008a. "Introduction: Youth Cultures and Feminist Politics." In *Next Wave Cultures: Feminism, Subcultures, Activism,* edited by Anita Harris, 1–13. New York: Routledge.

Harris, Anita. 2008b. "Young Women, Late Modern Politics, and the Participatory Possibilities of Online Cultures." *Journal of Youth Studies* 11(5): 481–495.

Hearn, Alison. 2012. "Brand Me 'Activist.'" In *Commodity Activism: Cultural Resistance in Neoliberal Times,* edited by Roopali Mukherjee and Sarah Banet-Weiser, 23–38. New York: New York University Press.

Hebdige, Dick. 1979. *Subculture: The Meaning of Style.* New York: Routledge.

Hunter, Jane. 2002. *How Young Ladies Became Girls: The Victorian Origins of Girlhood.* New Haven: Yale University.

Inglehart, Ronald, and Pippa Norris. 2003. *Rising Tide: Gender Equality and Cultural Change Around the World.* Cambridge: Cambridge University Press.

Jenkins, Henry. 2006. *Convergence Culture: Where Old and New Media Collide.* New York: New York University Press.

Kearney, Mary Celeste. 2006. *Girls Make Media.* New York: Routledge.

Kennelly, Jacqueline. 2011. *Citizen Youth: Culture, Activism, and Agency in a Neoliberal Era.* New York: Palgrave MacMillan.

Kahn, Richard, and Douglas Kellner. 2004. "New Media and Internet Activism: From the 'Battle of Seattle' to Blogging." *New Media and Society* 6 (1): 87–95.

Klar, Malte, and Tim Kasser. 2009. "Some Benefits of Being an Activist: Measuring Activism and Its Role in Psychological Well-Being." *Political Psychology* 30 (5): 755–777.

LeBlanc, Lauraine. 1999. *Pretty In Punk: Girls' Gender Resistance in a Boys' Subculture.* New Brunswick, NJ: Rutgers University Press.

McRobbie, Angela. 1991. *Feminism and Youth Culture.* London: Palgrave MacMillan.

McRobbie, Angela. 2009. *The Aftermath of Feminism: Gender, Culture and Social Change.* Thousand Oaks: Sage.

Muggleton, David, and Rupert Weinzierl. 2003. *Post-subcultures Reader.* Oxford: Berg.

Mukherjee Roopali, and Sarah Banet-Weiser (Eds). 2012. *Commodity Activism: Cultural Resistance in Neoliberal Times.* New York: New York University Press.

Naples, Nancy. 1992. "Activist Mothering: Cross-generational Continuity in the Community Work of Women from Low-Income Urban Neighborhoods." *Gender & Society* 6: 441–463.

Naples, Nancy. 1998. *Grassroots Warriors: Activist Mothering, Community Work and the War on Poverty.* New York: Routledge.

Norris, Pippa. 2009. "Political Activism: New Challenges, New Opportunities." In *The Oxford Handbook of Comparative Politics*, edited by Carles Boix and Susan C. Stokes, 628–652. Oxford: Oxford University Press.

O'Brien, Lucy. 1999. "The Woman Punk Made Me." In *Punk Rock: So What?: The Cultural Legacy of Punk*, edited by Roger Sabin, 186–198. New York: Routledge.

Piano, Doreen. 2002. "Congregating Women: Reading 3rd Wave Feminist Practices in Subcultural Production." *Rhizomes* 4. http://www.rhizomes.net/issue4/piano.html.

Reddington, Helen. 2003. "Lady Punks in Bands: A Subculturette?" In *The Post-Subcultures Reader*, edited by David Muggleton and Rupert Weinzierl, 239–252 Oxford: Berg.

Rentschler, Carrie. 2014. "Rape Culture and the Feminist Politics of Social Media." *Girlhood Studies* 7 (1): 65–82.

Rome, Adam. 2006. " 'Political hermaphrodites:' Gender and Environmental Reform in Progressive America." *Environmental History* 11: 440–463.

Rose, Tricia. 1994. *Black Noise: Rap Music and Black Culture in Contemporary America.* Middletown, CT: Wesleyan.

Rottenberg, Catherine. 2013. "The Rise of Neoliberal Feminism." *Cultural Studies* 28 (3): 418–437.

Shade, Leslie. 2002. *Gender & Community in the Social Construction of the Internet.* New York: Peter Lang.

Shifman, Limor. 2014. *Memes in Digital Culture.* Cambridge: MIT Press.

Taft, Jessica. 2011. *Rebel Girls: Youth Activism & Social Change Across the Americas.* New York: New York University Press.

Watkins, S. Craig. 2005. *Hip Hop Matters: Politics, Pop Culture, and the Struggle for the Soul of a Movement.* Boston: Beacon Press.

Willis, Paul. 1977. *Learning to Labor: How Working Class Kids Get Working Class Jobs.* New York: Columbia University Press.

Zaslow, Emilie. 2009. *Feminism INC: Coming of Age in a Girl Power Media Culture.* New York: Palgrave MacMillan.

Zeilinger, Julie. 2012. *A Little F' d Up: Why Feminism Is Not a Dirty Word.* Berkeley: Seal Press.

3   "Loud, Proud, and Sarcastic"

Young Feminist Internet Communities as Networked Counterpublics

"I can't see any movement going anywhere without a sense of community. Like, we would have never gotten to where we are today without women coming together as a community."

—Courtney, *phone interview*

In July 2009 a new website caught the attention of the feminist blogosphere. The *FBomb* (http://thefbomb.org) appeared similar to existing feminist blogs; it had a snarky name, a blogroll filled with feminist titles, and postings that tackled issues like rape culture and representations of women in the media. However, it differed from popular sites like *Feministing, Feministe,* and *Racialicious* in one important way: The founder of the *FBomb* was still in high school, living with her parents in suburban Ohio. Hardly the archetype of a feminist blogger – often assumed to be an urban-dwelling, college educated progressive twenty-something – sixteen-year-old Julie Zeilinger wanted to create a space for the peers she knew existed, but often had trouble finding in the halls of her high school ... other teenage girl feminists.

Upon announcing the *FBomb* through a press release to both mainstream media outlets and feminist media organizations, Julie became the topic du jour in the feminist blogosphere, in part because the *FBomb* contradicted dominant postfeminist logic that girls are not interested in feminism. The *FBomb* was dubbed "the blog we wished we had as teens" by feminist pop culture blog *Jezebel* and *Feministing* reported the launch as something "very cool" (Kelleher 2009; Perez 2009). The *FBomb*'s manifesto was forthright:

> In this case the "F Bomb" stands for "feminist." However, it also pokes fun at the idea that the term "feminist" is so stigmatized – it is our way of proudly reclaiming the word. The fact that the "F Bomb" usually refers to a certain swear word in popular culture is also not coincidental. The *FBomb.org* is for girls who have enough social awareness to be angry and who want to verbalize that feeling. The *FBomb.org* is loud, proud, sarcastic ... everything teenage feminists are today.

The website was unique in that it made visible a group of girls often assumed to be nonexistent.[1] And girls were clearly excited about it.

After being online for only a couple of months, the *FBomb* was receiving over 13,000 hits monthly and currently exceeds 35,000 unique visitors a month. Julie continues to edit the site as a college student and has become a 'public voice' for young feminists, regularly appearing in the mainstream media and authoring two books at the time of this writing. Six years after its launch, the *FBomb* remains one of the most popular feminist blogs and continues to be an important online space for young feminists.

I open this chapter by focusing on the *FBomb* because of the significant role that the website has played in creating young feminist communities within the feminist blogosphere. In part, this has been due to both the attention that the *FBomb* has received within feminist and mainstream media as well as because of the way the website is structured as a community space. While Julie began writing most of the posts when the site launched in late February 2009, she invited other girls to contribute their own posts in order to facilitate a diversity of young feminist voices on the website. In an interview she told me, "Beyond anything else, what I really hoped to accomplish by starting the *FBomb* was to create community. I didn't want the *FBomb* to solely reflect my feminist beliefs but to create a comprehensive, inclusive picture of what feminism looks like and what it can be for my generation."

The *FBomb* publishes posts by contributors from diverse countries such as Jordan, India, France, Iraq, and England, and several of my study participants have written for the site. Consequently, the *FBomb* serves as a fascinating example of how girl bloggers work collectively, which informs the guiding questions of this chapter: What specific practices do girls utilize to foster community through their blogs? How can we better theorize the connections girls are making through feminist blogging in order to recognize their political potential? Finally, how might we regard the collective nature of girls' feminist blogging as challenging the models of individualized social action promoted by postfeminist and neoliberal discourses?

I begin this chapter by framing girls' feminist blogging communities as networked counterpublics, building on foundational scholarship on publics in order to more accurately account for the fluidity and mutability of online communities. I then map specific issues that girl bloggers view as being particularly pertinent to them as young feminists based upon my interviews, focus group data, and textual analysis of their sites. I demonstrate how discussions of teenage feminist identities, reproductive rights and rape culture facilitate networked counterpublics that often move seamlessly between online and offline spaces. Next, I focus on the comment section found on most blogs as a productive example of a strategy that girls use to build connections, followed by a discussion of the often-overlooked issue of girls' friendships as a significant part of their organizing. This analysis attempts to narrow in on some of the intimate connections established through common participation in a networked counterpublic, something that is often glossed over in both the theoretical discussions of the concept and the literature on online communities. In the following section I offer an in-depth critique of racial diversity in young feminist online communities, suggesting that cultural capital (Bourdieu 1984) problematically limits *which* girls have the ability to access, participate in, and gain visibility within in the young feminist blogosphere.

I conclude by arguing that understanding these communities as networked counterpublics disrupt neoliberal and postfeminist discourses that privilege individual action rather than collective social change. I suggest that the concept of networked counterpublics allows us to privilege the modes of collective organizing facilitated via digital media technologies and platforms, while recognizing that these connections are fluid, traversing online and offline spaces. In doing so, I constructively intervene in digital media, girls', and feminist studies literature by making visible the *collective aspect* of feminist blogging that sustains the practice as a viable activist strategy.

From Community to Counterpublics: Theorizing Digital Connections

One of the interventions I make in this chapter is to suggest that the theoretical concept of the "counterpublic" (Fraser 1992) will help us to better understand the way in which girl feminist bloggers function as a collective, rather than an assortment of individual bloggers. I planned to use the word 'community' to describe these connections, a term I used in my interviews with bloggers. While this move made sense initially, in part due to the attention that both new media and feminist scholars have given to community as a important concept, I realized that 'community' provided little traction to analyze the multiple connections and associations I saw as important to understanding girl feminist bloggers. The concept of community remains somewhat stuck within debates about the authenticity of online communities (see Baym 2010; Fernback 2007; Turkle 2011; Yuan 2013), with many of these arguments reifying an assumed divide between 'online' and 'offline' life – a binary that I am suggesting is negated by the networked counterpublic concept.

I am not the first to use the concept of "publics" to explore digital life (see Gray 2009; boyd 2008, 2014; Papacharissi 2002). Yet I believe that the concept is not exhausted in terms of its useful application to new media – especially in relation to *girls*, a social group often marginalized from analyses of the public sphere. Thus, I draw on existing scholarship (Fraser 1992; Warner 2005; boyd 2008, 2014) to argue that the collectives of girl feminists formed through blogging are best understood as what I'm calling "networked counterpublics."[2] This concept is derived from Fraser's (1992, 123) well-known theorization of "subaltern counterpublics" as a "parallel discursive arenas where members of subordinated social groups invent and circulate counterdiscourses to formulate oppositional interpretations of their identities, interests, and needs." It also takes into account Fraser's recognition of the operation of multiple counterpublics, which "better promote the ideal of participatory parity than does a single, comprehensive, overarching public" (127).

I have previously utilized Fraser's work to conceptualize girl feminist bloggers (Keller 2012). However, here I supplement Fraser's analysis with Michael Warner's (2005) theorization of a public as coming into being through the circulation of discourses, or "the social space created by the reflexive circulation of discourse" (90). He elaborates: "Publics are essentially intertextual frameworks for understanding texts against an organized background of the circulation of other texts, all interwoven not just by citational references but by the incorporation of a reflexive circulatory field in the mode of address and consumption" (16). In this sense, publics are not about externally organized activity such as voting, or personal identity such as being a member of a racial group; instead, publics are produced through discourse circulated among strangers that demonstrate at least minimal participation, even if this is "merely paying attention" (71). Consequently, Warner differentiates publics from the crowds, audiences, and communities with which they're often confused.

Warner's conceptualization of publics is particularly useful for my analysis because of his emphasis on identity and transformation, drawing on Fraser's work to argue that counterpublics are publics that maintain an awareness of their subordinate status in relation to a dominant public. Identity is entwined with this process, as Warner argues, "The subordinate status of a counterpublic does not simply reflect identities formed elsewhere; participation in such a public is one of the ways by which its members' identities are formed and transformed. A hierarchy of stigma is the assumed background of practice. One enters at one's own risk" (121). In this sense, Warner's attention to the connection between identity and the workings of a counterpublic illuminates the ways in which the teenage feminist identities of my participants are intricately related to their collective participation in the blogosphere.

Additionally, Warner suggests that social transformation is a significant part of the formation of a counterpublic, which creates a space for a "new sociability and solidarity" (14). He writes that counterpublics "are testing our understanding of how private life can be made publicly relevant. And they are elaborating not only new shared worlds and critical languages but also new privacies, new individuals, new bodies, new intimacies, and new citizenships. … Publicness itself has a visceral resonance" (62–63). Warner's argument aligns with the history of feminist thought, which has paid particular attention to the ways in which patriarchal power structures women's exclusion from the public sphere. While an in-depth discussion of feminist theorizing of the public/private binary is beyond the scope of this chapter, it nonetheless serves as a significant context for which to understand girl feminist bloggers as a networked counterpublic.

I include "networked" in the concept of counterpublics, drawing on danah boyd's (2008, 2014) understanding of networked publics being "the spaces and audiences that are bound together through technological networks" (2008, 125). According to boyd, networked publics have key architectural differences from other kinds of publics that affect social interaction, including persistence, replicability, invisible audiences, and searchability. Yet the notion of networking extends beyond the digital realm; Mary Celeste Kearney (2006) reminds us that the term refers to both a coming together and extension of a group outwards.[3] This dual functioning of networking is also emphasized by Fraser (1992, 124) who writes that counterpublics, "function as spaces of withdrawal and regroupment; on the other hand, they also function as bases and training grounds for agitational activities directed toward wider publics. It is precisely in the dialectic between these two functions that their emancipatory potential resides." I want to highlight this aspect of a counterpublic as it is not only crucial to how girl feminist bloggers operate, but why I chose to discuss them as such, rather than a community. This is primarily because the language of networked counterpublics recognizes power inequalities that motivate counterpublics to intervene into hegemonic publics, a relationship that is not necessarily part of every community.

Thus, I argue that girl bloggers are best understood as networked counterpublics, forming networks around particular discursive feminist identities and issues, coming together, dissolving, mutating, and reconvening in a fluid manner. This is markedly different from how we usually imagine a community, often as a homogenous group with an agreed-upon list of goals and aims. Of course, this does not mean that there aren't communities present within the feminist blogosphere or that there aren't important affective connections generated between bloggers; both community and affective relationships (particularly friendships) are a part of girl bloggers' networked counterpublics. However, understanding girl feminist bloggers as networked counterpublics both allows us to better understand how contemporary feminism is being practiced, as well as provides a politicized language with which to talk about girl bloggers. This politicized language is a necessary step to recognizing girl feminists' blogging as a political practice.

A conversation I had with Kat demonstrates how these networks appear to the bloggers themselves. I ask Kat if the feminist blogosphere is best understood as a community or as communities.[4] Kat, who primarily blogs about sex education and reproductive rights, responds: "Communities is [a] better [way to describe the feminist blogosphere] because there are different groupings of blogs that blog about different [feminist topics] but they all relate to each other. Usually the people that blog communicate with each other, so I think that for each topic there's a different community but they also form an overall [feminist] community." Kat describes how she considers herself to be particularly connected with bloggers interested in sex education, but that these connections often lead her to other feminist conversations about a range of other topics.

Nonetheless, I want to caution against representing feminism online as completely amorphous. Thus, I am suggesting that several popular blogs (often written by a collective of bloggers rather than a single author) function as the "hubs" of feminist networked counterpublics. The *FBomb*, for example, is one of these, along with other blogs, such as *Feministing*, *Racialicious*, and *Jezebel*. These hubs often serve as a collection space for reports and commentary on a variety of feminist issues (as well as some original content) that link to other feminist blogs and/or online resources. According to Kat, these feminist hubs "pull from everyone," thereby serving as an aggregate of feminist information and perspectives online.

Consequently, many feminists new to the blogosphere often 'enter' through one of the more popular hub sites, as several of my participants discussed. For example, Kat explains, "I had been doing random research on the Internet when I was a [high school] sophomore I think, and I came across an article on [Jessica Valenti's book] *The Purity Myth*, and I clicked on a link and it took me to *Feministing*, which kind of showed me everything else." Kat's comment reflects how hubs like *Feministing* serve as an easy-to-locate introduction to the feminist blogosphere, particularly those sites which may be more difficult to find via Google searches. It should also be noted that many of the bloggers on these hub sites will often serve as public commentators about feminist issues for the mainstream press, and thus, their blogs also gain new readers through their participation in traditional media, a topic I'll elaborate on in chapter five.

Once acquainted with one feminist blog, readers often discover other blogs through the blogroll function. A blogroll is merely a list of other websites, often grouped by theme and hyperlinked to the site itself. As a hub for teenage feminists, the *Fbomb*'s blogroll is an important part of the site and is divided into "Advocacy" and "Feminist" blogs listed in red alongside the right side of the blog (Figure 3.1). However, the blogroll is not just a list, but a way to make visible the connections that comprise feminist networked counterpublics. *FBomb* readers need only click any of the links to discover a new online feminist space that may take up one or several feminist issues. Indeed, I used the *FBomb*'s blogroll as a way to find feminist blogs written by teenagers for my research and regularly check it as a quick way to find out about new feminist blogs. Consequently, the blogroll function serves as an important tool for building and maintaining the networks needed to circulate girls' feminist content.

I now turn to my ethnographic data and textual analysis in order to illustrate how feminist girl bloggers operate as part of networked counterpublics.

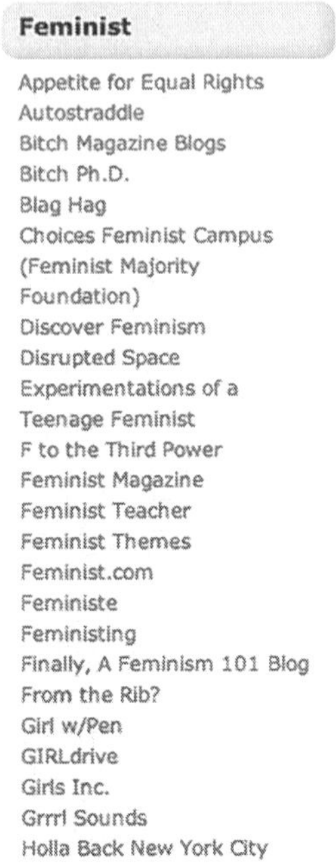

Feminist

Appetite for Equal Rights
Autostraddle
Bitch Magazine Blogs
Bitch Ph.D.
Blag Hag
Choices Feminist Campus
(Feminist Majority
Foundation)
Discover Feminism
Disrupted Space
Experimentations of a
Teenage Feminist
F to the Third Power
Feminist Magazine
Feminist Teacher
Feminist Themes
Feminist.com
Feministe
Feministing
Finally, A Feminism 101 Blog
From the Rib?
Girl w/Pen
GIRLdrive
Girls Inc.
Grrrl Sounds
Holla Back New York City

Figure 3.1   FBomb blogroll, author screen shot. Used with permission of Julie
         Zeilinger.

Being a Teenage Feminist: Identity and Counterpublic Formation

As I examined in chapter one, girl bloggers' identities as teenage feminists
are central to their blogging practices and significantly shape the ways in
which they enact feminist activism. This teenage feminist identity is also
intimately linked with the ways in which young bloggers organize as a counterpublic. In other words, a teenage feminist identity was one of the primary ways that girl bloggers coalesce online. For example, blog names often
incorporate the identity of a "teenage feminist" into the title, privileging this
particular identity in order to attract other young feminists. Renee explains:

> Just because I'm a high schooler, I'm thinking about feminism from a
> young person's point of view, so my primary focus right now is femi-
> nism as it relates to young people – like, getting the word out. A lot of
> those issues that have to deal with equal pay, for example, they're kind
> of adult issues, that I haven't experienced first hand yet … but right
> now I would say that feminism for me is advocacy for young people,
> telling them what it is … it's a scary word to a lot of people. Just trying
> to dispel those stereotypes is what I'm focusing on.

Renee privileges her identity as a teenage feminist as a way to reach out to
other teens, particularly girls. In addition to maintaining her blog, she has

blogged for the *FBomb*, and her blog is featured on the *FBomb*'s blogroll. Although Renee reads a variety of feminist blogs and lists a couple of adult-written blogs (primarily some of the larger hub sites I mention earlier) as some of her favorites, she is most invested in blogs written by other teenage feminists. Consequently, Renee has primarily developed networks with other young bloggers, rather than adults.

This connection between identity and community is important to consider, especially in relation to my discussions of feminist and activist identities in the previous two chapters. I highlighted how this latter relationship is confirmed though my participants' experiences. Recall how Courtney comments that her blogging practices allowed her to understand her feminist identity in relation to a larger community, her feminism becoming "a lot more about community issues than just about myself." Warner (2005) reminds us that participation in a counterpublic is "one of the ways by which its members' identities are formed and transformed" (57). Thus, whereas young bloggers may be drawn to participate in a community like the *FBomb* because of their teenage identity, the *FBomb* simultaneously functions as a space where this identity will likely transform, particularly due to interactions with other young feminists.

Facilitating connections between individual identity and community is a longstanding feminist practice, what has been termed "consciousness-raising" by feminists active in the women's liberation movement. In this sense, feminist blogging communities share many similarities to the consciousness-raising of the women's liberation movement and the early third wave and riot grrrl movements that produced zines for this purpose in the 1990s (Kearney 2006; Piepmeier 2009; Schilt 2003). Madison even uses the term "consciousness-raising" to describe the online activities she and other young feminists engage in. She says, "[Young feminists] spend the majority of our time online organizing and consciousness-raising. Especially with consciousness-raising – that's a big one. Older feminists are still in favor of getting in a room together and talking about sexism and patriarchy, but that's not how young feminists do it anymore – they do it online, through blogs and Facebook."

Madison's comments are significant to consider, as they problematize some of the dominant discourses about young feminists' digital media practices that continue to be circulated by some feminist scholars. For example, Linda Steiner (2012) argues:

> The blogosphere does not offer the shared identity or nurturing enjoyed by second wave feminist communities, nor do they provide a specifically feminist structure. Producing online content facilitates self-expression in the moment but neither requires nor encourages group interaction or ongoing loyalty to a shared 'cause.' Feminists' new online social interactivity and networking is largely virtual, anonymous, and accomplished by individuals. In particular, personal blogs (essentially online diaries) have a libertarian essence that is arguably at odds with the feminism of the older generation (190).

Steiner's argument is troubling for several reasons. Not only does her analysis of 'third wave' feminist blogs lack methodological rigor, her problematic generalization of feminists into neatly contained 'third wave' and 'second wave' camps simplifies the complexities of feminist movements, an issue I will address in the next chapter. Furthermore, her critique of a lack of a shared identity, nurturing personal relationships, and feminist structure contradicts Courtney and Madison's experiences I describe earlier in this chapter, as well as those of other scholars who have studied girls' and women's online practices (Piano 2002; Kearney 2006; Polack 2007; Driver 2007).

Yet Steiner's argument is indicative of a viewpoint that, according to the bloggers I interviewed, remains common in the feminist community – especially among older feminists. Madison reports, "Older feminists do not understand online activism, therefore they don't think that online activism is true activism … And that just pushes young feminists away because that's where we spend the majority of our time, our organizing, and our consciousness raising." Contrary to Steiner's comments, young bloggers recognize the importance of transforming critical consciousness and producing political identities through community in ways similar to past generations of feminists, and this remains a central way that bloggers build the solidarity needed for social action. Participation in networked counterpublics is a fundamental part of how girl feminist bloggers continually perform identity and vice versa. However, the networked counterpublic created by teenage feminist bloggers is not merely a meeting place for young feminists, but also functions to produce and circulate particular discourses about teenage feminists to the wider publics of the (adult-dominated) feminist blogosphere and mainstream society.

One of these discourses produced by these young bloggers is the claim that teenage feminists are in the process of still learning about feminism. This discourse was reflected by many of my participants who emphasized during interviews and on the focus group discussion blog that they don't view themselves as 'experts' and they still have to learn through life experiences. Websites like the *FBomb* then serve as a space to talk among one's peers rather than seek 'correct' answers or impart 'facts' to others. Renee explains: "Calling myself a teenage feminist gives myself the permission to make mistakes because I'm not claiming to be an expert. I've always had this idea, at least I did at first, like I'm a newbie, this is something I'm exploring, so I might make mistakes."

Renee discusses how she once posted an article about "20 Ways to Lesson Your Risk of Sexual Assault" that focused on things girls can do to prevent sexual assault. However, upon reading another blog post by a fellow teenage blogger that "really touched [her]," Renee added an update to the bottom of the post clarifying the need to address men's role in ending violence against women. Renee tells me that this post has stuck with her as an example of how she's embraced the opportunity to learn through blogging, especially from other teens. While adult-oriented blogs are written by bloggers who are often expected to be confident in their feminist position, teenage feminist networks seem to offer their participants more leeway to, as Renee suggests, "explore."

An early incident on the *FBomb* suggests that girl bloggers have had to use this discourse to protect their discursive space in the wake of adult *FBomb* commenters. A July 14, 2009 tweet from Julie's *FBomb* twitter account indicates this tension: "older feminist readers I'm a teen its for teens can't be perfect don't have a degree. Get some perspective plz & stop writing mean comments!" (Figure 3.2). The tweet implies a tension between younger feminist bloggers and their older counterparts who may not understand and/or respect the discourses underpinning the girls' networked counterpublic.

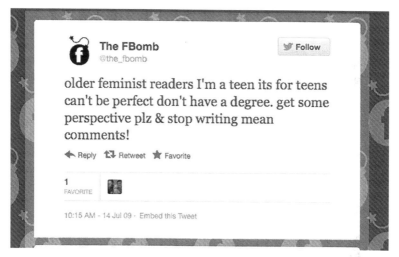

Figure 3.2 Tweet from the *FBomb*, author screen shot. Used with permission from Julie Zeilinger.

Although Julie is significantly more experienced with speaking to the public today and describes her tweet somewhat "cringe-worthy," she remains cautious about her positioning as a "young feminist voice" that's often called on by mainstream media. In other words, like Renee, she attempts to avoid presenting herself as an authority on young feminist issues. However, this is significantly more difficult to do as a guest on the *Melissa Harris-Perry Show*, for example, than it is when you're writing a blog post. Mainstream journalists will call Julie because they want an 'expert' to comment on a particular young feminist issue. In an email, Julie tells me that this has been a challenging experience for her to navigate. She explains, "It's difficult to feel like as an individual you're representing an entire generation of feminists. While on the one hand I can't qualify everything I say with a phrase like 'this is my experience' because in a lot of ways it undermines the ultimate message, on the other I feel compelled to because it's ultimately the truth." Julie's experience sheds light on the tension between the persistent construction of some individual girl bloggers as cultural authorities and the collectivist, "newbie" friendly ethos of the counterpublic, a tension I will further analyze in chapter five.

The findings I discuss here are similar to Jessica Taft's (2011) analysis of girl activists as performing activist identities that she describes as "in process" (60). Rather than claim authority of certain political issues in which they're active, Taft discovered that her study participants would instead describe themselves as activists that are "still learning" (116). According to her participants, this learning often occurred within the space of activist peer groups, which – like the feminist girl counterpublics I analyze here – emphasize the importance of conversation and dialogue. Taft recognizes the girl activists' emphasis on an "open-ended approach to pedagogy" and listening to their peers as clearly gendered, framing these strategies within a history of women's activism that utilizes this non hierarchal organizational strategy (118). Although I agree with Taft, I'd also like to suggest that this hesitancy to claim an expert status and shy away from being viewed as an authority may be related to persistent gender and generational norms that discourage girls from comfortably accepting themselves as an expert. Consequently, whereas this practice highlights the important role of dialogue, debate, and growth within girl feminist bloggers' networked counterpublics, it also reminds us that these counterpublics are situated amidst cultural constraints that must be acknowledged.

The teenage feminist blogging community can certainly be considered a networked counterpublic; however, girl bloggers also simultaneously participate in other networked counterpublics that form around particular feminist issues, such as reproductive rights and rape culture. I now turn to examine these two issues more closely in order to demonstrate how they have become focal points for the formation of feminist networked counterpublics of which girls are a part.

Uncovering Young Feminist Issues: Reproductive Rights and the "War on Women"

In chapter one I outlined how girls broadly define feminism. I'd like to continue that discussion here by analyzing the specific feminist issues girl bloggers are passionate about in order to understand how communities are built around these issues, rather than 'feminism' or 'teenagedom' in general. In this section and the following one I will focus on reproductive rights and rape culture as two significant examples of girl bloggers' activism. I chose these issues as case studies based on the frequency of these issues being mentioned as important to young feminists in interviews with bloggers, as well as the frequency with which these topics were discussed in girl feminists' blogs. It is important to reiterate that these issues are something of a non-comprehensive 'snapshot' of key issues among U.S.-based bloggers during the time of this study and must be examined within the cultural context in which they are situated.

Several of the bloggers spoke to me about reproductive rights as a topic that was particularly important to them. A longstanding feminist issue, reproductive rights acquired new significance in the United States during the time of my research in the wake of several events, including: the introduction of a slate of new Republican-sponsored bills restricting abortion in several states over 2011 and 2012; the Susan G. Komen Foundation's decision to cut funding to Planned Parenthood in late January 2012; and the ongoing controversy over free contraception that is a part of President Obama's Affordable Care Act. While many issues fall into the category of reproductive rights, the bloggers I interviewed were particularly interested in sexuality education, the accessibility of Plan B (the 'morning after' pill), and Republican-initiated bills restricting abortion, such as Virginia's law requiring a transvaginal ultrasound before a woman can obtain an abortion. Several of the bloggers mentioned these issues as being of particular significance due to their age. For example, Madison describes the availability of Plan B over the counter as an important concern for many girls and younger women, yet notes that older feminists often overlook this issue.

Several of my study participants discussed their participation in the feminist blogosphere as facilitating their involvement in reproductive rights activism. For example, Madison discusses how her participation on Tumblr has inspired her interest in reproductive rights. "Tumblr is a very pro-choice feminist space, so that would probably be my number one issue. My problem is that I care about so many feminist issues ... and because I'm so young I haven't really found one that I'm super passionate about. But definitely reproductive rights is up there." This is clearly evident from Madison's blog, where information about reproductive rights has dominated her postings throughout the eight-month period in which I am focusing my analysis. In this sense, Madison's surrounding community – what I'm arguing functions as a counterpublic – is instrumental in both educating and motivating Madison. Madison is not an individual blogger who happens to blog about reproductive rights – she is part of an extensive network of bloggers producing and circulating particular discourses about the importance of reproductive rights for American women. It is these discourses, as I demonstrate later in this chapter, that are crucial in the development of a counterpublic (Warner 2005; Shaw 2012a, 2012b).

Consequently, Madison's use of Tumblr to actively spread awareness about reproductive rights issues, like abortion laws, is intricately tied to a larger network of bloggers that function between online and offline spaces. Madison's participation in the mobilization of Michigan women and girls in opposition to new abortion restrictions in summer 2012 serves as a useful example that showcases the way in which a networked counterpublic formed around this important issue. In early June 2012 Michigan State Representative Bruce Rendon (R-Lake City) sponsored a 60-page bill that would criminalize all abortions after twenty weeks of pregnancy, with a narrow exception when a physician determines the mother's life is at risk. The bill was heard quickly by lawmakers after its introduction and was rushed through to a vote in the Michigan State House of Representatives within a few days. The situation prompted panic among prochoice activists and quick organizing among feminist bloggers, including Madison.

A June 2012 posting from Madison titled, "I'll be in Lansing Thursday, will you?" gives details about an upcoming protest of the bill and encourages her Tumblr followers to spread the word ("Please Signal Boost This") and come out to the demonstration. To accompany her post, Madison includes a video from another protest a few days prior, depicting hundreds of pink-clad women and men infiltrating the state Capitol shouting, "This is our house!" in protest of the bill. The video provides a powerful visual and aural representation of a counterpublic that creates an affective response in Madison's followers. "Lipstickfeminist" reblogged the video, commenting "THIS IS OUR HOUSE. These are … Michigan. What an incredible sound." The ability for this short video to be re-circulated among Tumblr users allows people who may not have been able to physically attend the demonstration to experience the 'feel' of the room. In her doctoral dissertation examining an Australian feminist blogging network, Frances Shaw (2012a) argues that these affective connections are a crucial part of creating and maintaining feminist blogging communities and they, therefore, must be understood as politically important. Thus, the video that I describe does not merely document an event, but produces and circulates affect among fellow feminist bloggers that binds people together as a counterpublic.

Similarly, Alison Piepmeier (2009) describes zine communities as creating a "currency of intimacy" whereby zinesters foster connections through the exchange and/or gifting of zines (75). By sharing personal feelings, secrets, and (sometimes painful) experiences, girl zine makers generate affective attachments with one another, creating 'support group' communities that Kristen Schilt (2003) recognizes as a form of resistance (80). Thus, we can understand the affective connection that sustain girl feminist bloggers' networked counterpublics as a politically significant part of girls' media making practices, an issue I'll return to when discussing the comment sections of blogs.

A few days later Lisa Brown, a Democratic representative in the Michigan legislature, was banned from the Capitol floor for using the word 'vagina' when criticizing the abortion legislation. Madison documents the reactions to Brown's banning on Tumblr and encourages her readers to attend the "Vaginas Take Back the Capitol" event planned in protest of Brown's banning. After attending the event, which attracted over 5,000 people, Madison posted pictures on her blog, depicting a range of women, men, and girls participating in the protest [Figure 3.3]. She writes: "It was the most amazing experience I have ever had. … It brought me to tears knowing that all of those people showed up for choice. I am in serious awe of the women of Michigan."

We went down to Lansing to protest house bills 3711-3713 which would have taken abortion rights away from Michigan women. The House was supposed to vote on them today, but decided to delay the vote. My theory is that they were too cowardly to vote on them while 400 people protested in the Capital building.

Figure 3.3 "Vaginas Take Back the Capitol" blog post, author screen shot. Used with permission of blog owner.

Later that day, in a post titled, "I Met Women Who Talked About Protesting in the 60s, 70s, and 80s," Madison continues recounting her experience: "I met women who talked about remembering when Roe was announced. I met women who remembered when it was illegal. I met women who fought for the ERA. I met 15-year-old girls with braces. I met 10-year-old girls who made their own signs. All those women. All together for the same purpose. It's overwhelming." Madison's posting clearly emphasizes the importance of solidarity between generations of women and girls as a necessity to success-fully challenge the threat to reproductive rights in Michigan. She most likely would not have encountered these girls and women outside of the context of protesting reproductive rights legislation in Lansing, and she may never cross paths with some of them online or in person again. Nonetheless, Madison is clearly inspired by the women she met that day at the Capitol, and these con-nections remain an important part of how a counterpublic operates.

I want to clarify that I am not implying that girl feminist bloggers use online media simply to organize or publicize in-person community events. While this does happen, my analysis reveals a more complex circulation of connections indicative of a counterpublic. For example, Madison not only attended the "Vaginas Take Back the Capitol" event, but she returned to her Tumblr after the protest, posting not only the 'facts' of the dem-onstration (in this case, for example, that Eve Ensler attended), but also her feelings about being in attendance ("in awe of Michigan women"), as well as photos and videos she took. As I discuss earlier in this chapter, these posts (particularly the photos and videos) create affective attach-ments that can be 'liked,' 'reblogged,' and/or commented on (called 'notes' on the Tumblr platform) by her many followers, who in doing so recirculate Madison's experiences among their Tumblr followers. Madison received 499 notes on one of her vagina protest posts, and these notes became a part of the discourses circulating the networked counterpublic built upon the threat to reproductive rights in Michigan.

Finally, these networked counterpublics also help to create and circulate particular discourses that enable participants to communicate with one another and make sense of certain issues. For example, making visible and combating the "War on Women" became a central discourse for the counterpublic I've been discussing, and almost all of the bloggers I interviewed listed the "War on Women" as a major issue of concern.[5] Consequently, it is not surprising that the phrase frequently appeared in their blog posts as a way to speak about contemporary sexism. To wit: A June 2012 post by Amandine titled, "What War on Women?" contained an infographic detailing the number of American women killed by their male partners in relation to Americans killed in terror attacks and U.S. troops killed in Afghanistan and Iraq (Figure 3.3). Using an infographic rather than merely descriptive text, Amandine's post makes visible the war on women as a serious problem that requires her readers' attention.

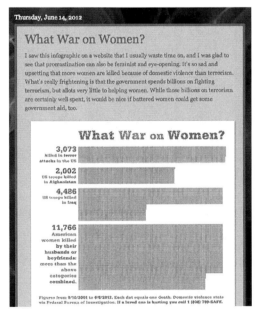

Figure 3.4 "What War on Women?" infographic, author screen shot. Used with permission of blog owner.

However, not only do discourses like the "War on Women" create discursive space to address reproductive rights and highlight misogyny, but these discourses are also affect-laden, fostering connections, or "attachments"

(Ahmed 2004) between girls and women that mobilize (at least in this case) anger, urgency, vulnerability, fear, and determination (Piepmeier 2009). Thus, much like Madison's posts that I discuss earlier, the "War on Women" serves a political function that creates solidarity among a group of girls and women that may never meet in person.

Rape Culture: SlutWalk and 'Slut Shaming'

Rape culture is another key issue that the bloggers discussed at length. Whereas adult women are certainly not excluded from experiences with rape culture, Courtney believes this issue is particularly pertinent to teen-age girls and college students because of their active social lives. "As a college student I go out a lot and cat-calling, touching women at parties, these are things that I experience," Courtney says.[6] When the bloggers discuss rape culture, they include various issues under this term: 'slut-shaming,' cat-calling, sexual assault, sexual harassment, and representations of these behaviors in media, are all part of the rape culture girl feminist bloggers are concerned about. In particular, Julie notes that 'slut-shaming,' when a girl is publicly shamed for her sexual activity, is an issue that many girls feel strongly about, but with which older feminists seem less concerned. Julie explains, "The reactions around SlutWalk are a good example of this. Granted, a lot of older feminists were really supportive of our mobilization around an issue we believe in, but there were definitely some who felt 'slut-shaming' is a trivial issue compared to issues like equal pay." I will return to Julie's comment later in this section.

The 2011 SlutWalk mass demonstrations are a recent response to the prevalence of rape culture, and serve as a visible example of the ways in which networked counterpublics are mobilized in the digital age (see Mendes 2015). Largely organized online by girls and young women, participants marched through cities around the world to express their disapproval with rape culture logic that suggests women 'ask for' rape if they wear certain clothing, such as a short skirt or a low-cut blouse. While SlutWalk was first organized by a group of young women in Toronto in response to a police officer telling a group of college students that they could avoid sexual assault by not dressing like "sluts," the marches quickly spread to other cities across the world, including New York City, New Delhi, London, Dallas, and Cape Town, gaining widespread global media attention. For the most part, SlutWalks attracted a diversity of participants and cannot be regarded as solely a young feminist phenomenon. Nonetheless, in many places girls and college-aged women organized and promoted the marches through social media and blogs and did appear to dominate many of the rallies. For example, the organizer of the Chicago SlutWalk was Jamie Keiles, an 18-year-old freshman at the University of Chicago who had become interested in feminism after she began blogging.

Several of the bloggers I spoke to attended SlutWalks near to their homes and blogged about their experience. For example, Renee's experience at a SlutWalk on the U.S. west coast is worthwhile to consider in full:

> This was my first real 'protest.' I probably saw more skin that day than I've seen in my entire life, but the fact that people could be so bold in order to make a point was truly inspiring ... For me, the most surreal and passionate and amazing part of the protest was when everybody chanted together. Hundreds of voices tangled to create a gigantic, powerful echo; we rattled the entire city with sayings like "Wherever we go, however we dress, no means no, and yes means yes!" and "When women's rights are under attack, what we do? Stand up! Fight back!"
>
> If you can imagine the strangest collection of people ever—men, women, children, the elderly—of every orientation, color, body shape, and style of dress—all united by a common cause, that's what SlutWalk felt like. Being a feminist can feel lonely and alienating when it seems like the world is against you, but last Sunday I was embraced by an entire community of people who were willing to risk anything to fight for women's rights.

Similar to Madison's experience at the "Vaginas Take Back the Capitol" demonstration, Renee's blog post highlights an intense affective attachment to her experience of SlutWalk (words such as "surreal," "passionate," and "amazing") and emphasizes the importance of collectivity in order to challenge rape culture. The images and video that she posts extend this sentiment. Renee posts photographs she took at the demonstration with girls, women, and men holding signs with sayings like "Consent is Sexy," "My Dress is Not a Yes," and the cheeky "God Loves Sluts!" Farther down in the entry Renee also posts a sixteen-minute video of a rape survivor addressing the SlutWalk crowd where she details the lengthy process of convicting her attacker. Serena comments on Renee's post, writing, "I have tears in my eyes right now. It's sad and wonderful to see SlutWalk. Wonderful to know that people won't take that s*** anymore and sad that we have to have a SlutWalk. Thank you for sharing this video!"

Whereas scholars such as Sherrie Turkle (2011) may understand Renee's post as evidence that she had to participate in this community 'in real life' in order to truly feel a part of a collective, I am arguing that we need to understand Renee's experience with SlutWalk as extending before and after her actual attendance at the event. The networks she has cultivated through blogging not only informed her desire to attend SlutWalk, but also provided an avenue to share her feelings about it afterwards, again circulating and stimulating particular discourses and affects produced by this networked counterpublic. People like Serena become part of Renee's experience of SlutWalk, as she shares an affective connection with her through the video she posts. Renee's commitment to end rape culture can also be seen beyond her SlutWalk commentary. Several weeks later she posts a guest entry from a fellow teenage feminist who writes about the prevalence of date rape and victim blaming in American culture. The conversation about rape culture thus continues beyond Renee's initial entry and is linked to the guest blogger's own blog as well as any other blogs that may choose to circulate the posting via social media.

It is not my purpose to weigh in on the debates about SlutWalks here (for example, if the word 'slut' can ever really be recuperated by women), as I am most interested in how SlutWalk became a visible symbol of a feminist networked counterpublic that can become obscured if we do not analyze online spaces carefully enough. In other words, I discuss SlutWalk at length here because it is emblematic of how I am arguing feminist networked counterpublics operate today: as interconnected networks held together by particular, pertinent issues that are often responding to public conversations and debates. Girl bloggers such as Renee strengthen these networks through not only showing up to participate in the SlutWalk march, but also through producing and circulating discourse about SlutWalk, such as the language of 'slut shaming.'

Similar to the "War on Women" discourse I discussed in the previous section, the discourse of 'slut shaming' was mobilized and circulated by bloggers active in this networked counterpublic. The phrase became popularized alongside the SlutWalk marches and functions similarly to the "War on Women," producing affective connections while additionally working to reclaim the word 'slut' as a source of power and agency for girls and women. However, the phrase has caused controversy among feminists, highlighting the way in which the phrase carries generational tensions as Julie mentioned. For example, in an editorial published in *The Guardian,* adult feminists Gail Dines and Wendy J. Murphy (2011) assert, "Women need to find ways to create their own authentic sexuality, outside of male-defined terms like slut ... While the organizers of the Slutwalk might think that proudly calling themselves 'sluts' is a way to empower women, they are in fact making life harder for girls who are trying to navigate their way through the tricky terrain of adolescence. Women need to take to the streets – but not for the right to be called 'slut.'" Not only does this comment implicitly suggest that girls are not participating in the SlutWalk movement, it highlights how those outside of this networked counterpublic may lack the connections that allow 'slut shaming' to make sense to a particular group of girls and women. I will return to the issue of SlutWalk later in this chapter to demonstrate how bloggers used the issue to support one another and open up space for conversation about sexual assault.

In concluding this section I want to highlight that while reproductive rights and rape culture are central issues for young feminists, they are certainly not the only feminist issues girls care about. I have outlined two issues here that have received a lot of attention from young bloggers over the past couple of years, in part due to both the age of the bloggers as well as our contemporary cultural context. However, there are many more issues that concern the bloggers I interviewed, including body image/beauty norms and media representations of girls and women. While the bloggers I interviewed recognize that certain topics such as rape culture do get more attention from young feminist bloggers, they will often attempt to address less-discussed issues, such as the intersection of feminism with religion, on their own blog by inviting a guest blogger to write a post on a topic they might be particularly knowledgeable about, an activist strategy of community-building I discussed in the previous chapter. I now turn my analysis to another one of these practices that facilitate connections among girl feminist bloggers – participation in the comments section.

Connecting Through Comments

In chapter two I analyzed the ways in which community-building practices function as activism for the bloggers I interviewed; I want to now return to this discussion in order to focus on how one particular strategy – the employment and use of the comments section – illustrates the ways in which these multiple strategies of facilitating connections become crucial to the formation of feminist girl bloggers' networked counterpublics. Unlike many popular websites' comments section, which often can be dominated by negative and derogatory "feedback" (Banet-Weiser 2011), the comment section in many teen feminists' blogs serve as a space for productive conversation, education, and sometimes even the sharing of personal stories about sensitive topics like sexual assault, eating disorders, or the death of a family member. For example, in an August 2011 *Fbomb* post titled "Thank You, Slutwalk" Kelsie M. details her rape the year before, writing, "You will never understand that feeling of being completely alone. That feeling that even your own body has betrayed you, and is no longer your own. That feeling of hating yourself more than you've ever hated any other human being. You will never understand … and if you do, I am so sorry." The post is powerful and difficult to read, laying bare the emotions of denial, hatred, loneliness, anger, and eventually, relief.

The twenty-one comments that follow this post reveal how girl bloggers' counterpublics are strengthened through this type of emotional sharing, again revealing an affective dimension to the connections they create. In addition to showing their support for the writer, commenters shared their own stories of sexual violence. For example, Connie writes,

> Thank you! I went through something similar two years ago (raped by a friend of a friend at a party) and it has taken me until very recently to confront the scars it has left me with – I felt exactly that same as you did, disgusted and repulsed by what had happened and so isolated in the knowledge that no one would ever believe me. I missed the London Slutwalk … but I can't tell you how comforting it has been to read your post, now I don't feel quite as alone. I admire your bravery very much.

Similarly, Alyson responds, "I understand what you are saying completely. I was raped six years ago by a boy who was about to join the air force, who I had been consensually intimate with prior to the rape, who my own 'best friend' didn't believe raped me. I am also participating in the Slutwalk in my city in a few weeks."

The community space of the *FBomb* provides discursive space for this conversation and is simultaneously strengthened by it, as members become increasingly emotionally invested in the space, something that Susan Driver (2007) also found in her study of queer girls' online communities. Likewise, Kristen Schilt (2003, 80) argues that "emotional validation" is crucial to the formation and maintenance of girl zines communities that often serve as "support groups" to deal with topics like sexual abuse, self-mutilation, puberty, and sexual harassment. This example also reveals the ways in which a counterpublic is formed around the important issue of rape culture, connecting people in this case from places that include London, Berlin, Philadelphia, and Cleveland. Even if these connections are fleeting, the production of what Driver (2007) calls "community as healing and hope" allows "girls to help each other feel better and move on" (182).

Because the majority of teenage feminist blogs are single-authored (unlike the *FBomb*), the strategies I outline here function as a type of *dialogue between blogs*, demonstrating the connective nature of blogs as a medium. Yet, unlike the recent focus of new media scholars (see van Dijck 2011, 2013) on the ways in which technological networks produce connectivity via algorithmic data, I am arguing for the need to conceptualize the connections and counterpublics I describe as part of a lengthy history of feminist media production and activism. In this sense, I echo Carrie Rentchler's (2014, 79) call to understand these young feminist online counterpublics as indicative of "networks of feminist affinity and young women's collectivity" that offer the affective glue that holds girls' feminist networked counterpublics together.

These digital practices I describe also challenge dominant discourses that characterize girls as relationally aggressive and in competition with one another, rather than working together as friends and allies (Ringrose 2006, 2012; Gonick 2004). Jessica Ringrose (2006, 414) argues that the 'mean girl' is a postfeminist discourse that "construct[s] a universal, pathological feminine culture of meanness with massive reach" which often equates girl power with girl meanness. In these accounts, feminism is often blamed for the supposed crisis of the mean girl and is "held accountable for the fostering of girls' aggression" (Ringrose 2006, 415). The girl bloggers I spoke to are aware of this problematic discourse; Renee tells me, "I think women in general are taught to be competitors, to be enemies, we're taught to want to be better than all the other girls. [But] women in general, we need to unite!"

Consequently, we see a different story emerge in girls' feminist blogs, one that shows how girl bloggers are not competitors for the most popular blog or "frenemies"[7] looking to take each other down, but are resisting the 'mean girl' by investing in each other's voices and thriving off of the connections they make. As Renee tells me, "I started to get emails from other girls who were also finding feminism for the first time, and that feedback was really validating and empowering – I would say that that's what I like most about blogging."

Forming Friendships

Girls in my study report that they perceive several positive benefits from their participation in online feminist communities, and I am arguing that one of these benefits is the formation of positive female friendships. For example, when I ask Renee about the friendships she's made online, she can't hide her enthusiasm:

> The friendships that I've made have been one of the best things about starting a blog overall … The girls … that I meet online … we just seem so similar that it's so easy to start a friendship. In real life, talking to someone the first time can be awkward, but online, from the first email, you feel like you're friends already. It becomes this amazingly comfortable friendship that if you ever met in real life you'd be best friends.

Renee clearly regards the friends that she's met through feminist blogging as a significant part of her experience blogging. And while she uses language like 'real life,' which implies a separation between online and offline life, further discussion reveals that this binary does not structure Renee's understanding of friendship at all. In fact, the friends that Renee has met blogging are very much part of her daily life away from the keyboard. To wit: Renee has made two very close friends through her experience as a feminist blogger, and both have stayed at her home when traveling in her state. Renee describes how one has chosen to go to college only a few hours away from her and that she's excited that they'll be able to hang out frequently.

Renee explains how she's been in close frequent contact with nine other young feminist bloggers in order to plan a new feminist site that they'd like to launch as a collective. She details how the participants have been using voting and consensus models to determine the site's name, mission, and plans for peer editing. Indeed, the project she describes sounds very much like the media production collectives that have long history within feminism such as the London-based feminist print shop collectives active in the 1970s and 1980s (Bains 2012). Again, we can see how feminist blogging continue practices that have been used by feminists of other generations. Renee is clearly excited about this new project and tells me that she believes it will showcase the ways in which she's grown as a blogger and will be a great way to talk about the new challenges she's anticipating as she begins college.

Because I was expecting that email and online social networking sites like Facebook and Skype would be the primary mode of communication between this collective of bloggers that are dispersed internationally, I was surprised to hear from Renee that several of the girls had begun to exchange handwritten letters and small gifts through snail mail. When I ask Renee how this ritual developed she explains how one of the girls was bored over the summer at her parent's home and sent Renee a surprise via the mail on a whim. They continued the exchange and now regularly correspond this way (in addition to email, of course). This type of exchange between girls has long been a part of girls' friendship cultures, which includes practices such as pen pals, chain letters, and the exchange of self-produced goods such as friendship bracelets and zines (Kearney 2006; Piepmeier 2009). Consequently, this example reveals a link between girls' feminist blogging and girls' culture, something that neither girls' studies nor digital media studies researchers have explored in detail. Yet, this linkage may help to explain the large numbers of American girls who have a blog or social networking site (Lenhardt et al 2008).

Other study participants have also discussed female friendships as being a very positive part of their experience online. For example, Madison tells me, "I've met one of my best friends through Tumblr's 'ask' feature. I wrote her, she wrote me back, and we went from there. Now we're Facebook friends and we talk on the phone. I've never met her in person, but we're close because we bonded over Tumblr." Similarly, Amandine says, "I think blogging has made me more feminist. I never would have made such amazing feminist friends if it weren't for my blog, and they've helped me stay very much into women's rights advocacy."

Amandine's comment is particularly interesting because it suggests the political potential that girls' friendships can have. According to Amandine, it is her feminist friends that have encouraged her to continue her activism and have made her become 'more feminist.' This idea is significant because it points to the importance of friends – and community – for sustaining feminism as a movement. Blogging becomes a key practice through which young feminists are fostering these friendships. Amandine continues, "Blogging definitely helps link individual feminists to the larger feminist community. I said it before, I never would have made so many feminist friends, especially those my age, if it wasn't for blogging. I actually recently received an email from a girl saying that she likes my blog, and it made me so happy! Positive feedback is always appreciated."

The idea that friendship and community is necessary to sustain feminism as a movement is important to recognize in light of frequent critiques that marginalized communities are merely 'preaching to the converted.' Tim Miller and David Roman (1995) describe how queer theatre is often dismissed using this logic, which assumes that community practices like queer theatre, or in my case, girl feminists' networked counterpublics, hold little political weight or initiative for broad social change. More recently, this critique of 'preaching to the converted' has been levied at online communities, which have been assumed to attract small groups of likeminded individuals that "affirm one another's perspective and lead people away from political action" (Baym 2010, 96). However, Miller and Roman argue that this critique ultimately ignores the political value in connecting with those who may share a marginalized status or political stance. They write,

> Regardless of how [preaching to the converted] is employed ... the uncontested phrase shuts down discussions around the important cultural work that queer artists perform for their queer audiences. The result is yet another occasion of queer disempowerment, one which undermines the idea of building a community culture around an ongoing series of events and gatherings (173).

I am most interested in Miller and Roman's insistence on the significance of producing and maintaining a community culture among marginalized groups and the ways in which these communities sustain community member's investment. Thus, their assertion that the critique of 'preaching to the converted' "dismisses the emotional and political benefits of queer people's gathering together in a shared public space" is particularly relevant for theorizing the political significance of girl feminist bloggers' networked counterpublics (177). Similarly, Stephen Duncombe (1997) describes how zinesters' webs of communication provide "the support and the feeling of connection that are so important for dissent and creativity" (55). Taking this scholarship into consideration, we can understand how girl bloggers' networked counterpublics are both continually produced through these instances of friendships/interpersonal relationships and are sustained by the emotional connections that foster political motivation. Consequently, the friendships and relationships girl feminist bloggers form through their blogging become a political resource that is both personally meaningful and essential for understanding girls' feminist blogging communities as networked counterpublics.

In addition to keeping bloggers motivated and in touch with feminist issues, friendships with other girl feminist bloggers function as a much-needed support system for girls. This was mentioned by all of my study participants as a key reason why they understand the feminist blogosphere as shaped by the notion of community. For example, Abby says that, "I have found that simply the existence of the feminist blogosphere is supportive ... simply know[ing] that there are girls who think and feel like you, who you can relate to." This issue of support is especially important in relation to online harassment and 'trolling' that many feminist bloggers regularly experience. Madison explains:

> Since I use Tumblr for blogging, I think it makes it easier to support other girl bloggers. The ask feature draws out some really nasty people. I have gotten some terrible comments, but at the same time it allows for people to talk and interact with one another in a positive way ... Everytime I get a nasty or disturbing ask, and I publish it or

write about it, I always get an outpouring of support. The support always outweighs the negative. I think there is this feeling that we need to watch out for one another.

Thus, rather than keep nasty comments private, Madison publicizes these insults in order to draw on the support of a larger community of girl bloggers.

In a focus group conversation, other bloggers also discuss this issue. Kat says, "All the feminist blogs [on Tumblr] help each other out by reblogging each other's posts and by supporting each other when we get nasty Anons.[8] I help by reblogging from other feminist blogs and adding positive comments." Courtney responds: "I definitely feel you on the Anons, I am pretty sure that I've turned off Anon for now but I've gotten and seen some terrible things written. It doesn't take a lot to see the support that comes around when something like that happens. So many people will leave nice notes, or if someone wrote a post, it's so easy to see the positive reblogs." This exchange points to one of the reason that several bloggers I spoke to prefer Tumblr, because they can visually see community through 'reblogs' (Figure 3.5). Thus, rather than wonder who has seen your blog posting, bloggers see who has reblogged their post and who then reblogs the post from the reblogger. In some ways it is this visual representation of the networked counterpublic that encourages girls to keep blogging despite their critics.

Figure 3.5 Reblogs on Madison's Tumblr, author screen shot. Used with permission of blog owner.

Whereas a perfect world would be without sexism on the Internet, online harassment may work to foster stronger feminist communities. For example, in a January 20, 2012 posting on the *FBomb* called "Countering Hatred on the Internet," Gina S. recommends connecting with feminist communities online as a way to deal with what she calls "Internet haters." She suggests: "Surround yourself with likeminded individuals! Using feminist-friendly sites and participating in discussions with fellow feminists is a great way to ensure you feel part of a community who hold similar beliefs and values as you do yourself. Not only is this a way to meet new people, it's reassuring to use these sites." Gina S.'s post emphasizes the supportive qualities of feminist online communities and presents the troubling phenomenon of online harassment to *FBomb* readers as an important issue that can be overcome not by individual feminists, but *feminist networked counterpublics*.

Despite the importance that friendship plays in girls' blogging practices, literature examining girls' online practices has largely ignored the ways in which girls are forming friendships online with other girls. Most digital media scholarship addresses pre-existing friendships with peers (see Schofield Clark 2005; Baker 2011; and boyd 2008, 2014) or suggests the impossibility of authentic friendships formed online. To wit: In her recent book *Alone Together*, Sherrie Turkle (2011, 153) argues, "Virtual places offer connection with uncertain claims to commitment. We don't count on cyberfriends to come by if we are ill, to celebrate our children's successes, or to help mourn the death of our parents. People know this, and yet the emotional charge on cyberspace is high." Turkle's assessment may be true in some instances, but her claims do not match the experiences of friendship that I describe in this chapter.

For example, when Renee's father passed away unexpectedly in 2011, she posted about her experiences several times online and tells me in an interview that these posts remain most important to her. Renee says, "I was just kind of talking about what goes on after you lose somebody … I just told it how it is, how exactly I was feeling. That was my first major loss and for someone who was going through the same thing to read that, I'd hope they could get some solace from that." In a touching tribute to her father posted on the day of his funeral, Renee received several messages of support from readers, including invites to get in touch if she wanted to talk. These notes may not be substitute for a hug and a batch of homemade muffins, however, they reveal affective attachments that are not adequately represented by Turkle's characterization of "cyberfriends."

Girls do not understand the friendships they form through blogging as 'Internet friends' that are different from their 'real friends.' This lack of distinction can be seen through Madison's discussion of her friend Sarah, whom she met online. Madison explains, "She was one of the first people to follow me and she was a teenager too, so we bonded over that. Sarah is definitely one of my best friends." Madison does not qualify her friendship with Sarah as her 'best Internet friend' or the 'best friend she's met online,' but describes her merely as a best friend, regardless of the fact that they've never met in person. Thus, while research such as Turkle's suggests that 'online friendships' do not require the same time commitments and notions of reciprocity as those friendships formed through more traditional face-to-face interactions, my research suggests this is not always the case.

For example, I describe how reciprocity is an important part of girl feminist bloggers' interactions, and note how bloggers support one another in the case of trolling and harassment. Furthermore, bloggers spoke of the commitment they feel toward the friends they know are following their blogs, often feeling guilty if they get busy and can't follow their regular posting schedule. Of course, not every blogger will necessarily build the friendships I describe here. I am suggesting, however, that these friendships serve an important function within girl feminists' networked counterpublics, providing the close connections that motivate bloggers to continue their activism.

White Unless Proven Otherwise? The Struggle for Inclusive Counterpublics

Thus far I have discussed the variety of connections that girl bloggers form as part of their participation in the feminist blogosphere. I now turn my attention to focus more specifically on who is participating in these networked counterpublics. Which girls are a part of these networks? Who is excluded? And how do girls think about inclusivity when it comes to communities that appear to form 'naturally?' I will take up these questions in this section, focusing specifically on race as an identity that highlights some of the limitations of networked counterpublics to connect a diversity of voices.

I have previously discussed how girl bloggers are aware of the importance of diversity in the feminist communities, and that some even draw on the language of intersectionality to express their understandings of how power operates to create multiple oppressions in the lives of women. However, this desire to facilitate diverse communities is held in tension with the fact that there are few visible girls of color participating in teenage feminist blogging communities. All eight of the bloggers that participated in the online focus group identify as white, although two claim ethnic Jewish identities. While I made a conscious effort to recruit girls of color to participate in this study, I was unfortunately not able to find anyone of such identity that was able to commit to the project.[9]

I want to emphasize that I claim there are few *visible* girls of color who are feminist bloggers because it is nearly impossible to discern the actual number of minority girls participating in various feminist blogging counterpublics. Indeed, part of the reason for this is because we do not know what many bloggers look like – the problematic way in which we often determine race – unless they choose to make themselves physically visible through posting a photo of themselves or specifically writing about their appearance and/or body. Julie discusses this as an issue that she struggles with as an editor of a teenage blogging site. She tells me,

> My blog is based on submissions that are almost entirely anonymous in that I have no idea what the race/sexual orientation/age/class/etc.

of my submitters are unless it's part of what they've written. But I recently got an email from a reader asking why there weren't more women of color featured on my blog. I found that email to be really interesting because, as I just stated, I have no idea how many women of color have written for my blog and it was interesting to me that that person would assume that just because I'm white and I run the blog that everybody that writes for it is white. It's almost like on the blogosphere, *you're white unless proven otherwise*.

So, I don't want to make any assumptions about who is involved with the teen feminist blogosphere solely based on the most prominent faces out there. That being said, I think our generation of feminism kind of has the responsibility to work on diversifying this movement and it's something we definitely need to be aware of (italics not in original).

I quote Julie at length because I find her comments especially pertinent to dominant discourses about race and the Internet.

The discourse of the "digital divide" has framed much of the public conversation and academic analysis of inequality online. The digital divide posits that there is a large disparity between socioeconomic groups' access to and knowledge of new information and communication technologies. As Janell Hobson (2008) notes, digital divide discourse is also racialized and gendered, positioning people of color, women, and communities from the Global South as failing at technological literacy. In doing so, the digital divide often erases the knowledge that these groups contribute to technological advances. Hobson thus contends that hegemonic discourses that inform the digital divide problematically position people of color "outside of technology," reproducing associations of whiteness with progress, technology, and civilizations and blackness within a discourse of nature, primitivism, and pre-modernity. Other scholars (boyd 2011; Watkins 2009) have challenged notions of the digital divide (specifically related to the Internet) by demonstrating how mobile devices, platform preferences, taste and aesthetic cultures, and the diffusion of cheaper technology have debunked the notion of a simple divide between middle and upper class technological haves and lower and working class have-nots.

However, these scholars recognize that despite the fact that a diversity of people may now have access to the Internet and other communication technologies, online spaces continue to be structured by the power dynamics present in social life. Thus, social inequalities are often reproduced in new media spaces, and that identities such as race and gender can often be 'read' in these spaces in particular ways (Nakamura 2002, 2013; Nakamura and Chow-White 2011; boyd, 2011). Lisa Nakamura (2002, 32) asserts, "The celebration of the Internet as a democratic, 'raceless' place needs to be interrogated, both to put pressure on the assumption that race is something that ought to be left behind, in the best of all possible cyberworlds, and to examine the prevalence of racial representation in this supposedly unraced form of social and cultural interaction." While Nakamura (2002) made this argument over a decade ago, the issue of how race works online continues to be of central importance, particularly for feminists.

The bloggers I interviewed were aware that racial diversity is a problem within the teenage feminist blogosphere. Amandine says, "I never actually really found the teen feminist blogosphere terribly diverse. In my experience, of the teen bloggers, it's mostly white middle class females. Off the top of my head I can only think of one teen feminist blog run by a guy, and I can't think of any run by non-whites. The non-teen feminist blogosphere is much more diverse." Renee agrees, commenting in this same focus group discussion,

> I think Amandine really hit the nail on the head. The adult feminist community seems to be much more diverse than the teen feminist community. When I stop and think about it, most of the teen bloggers I know are white, middle-class females. That's something we should really be exploring – why people of different ethnicities aren't joining in the conversation … I wonder if there's something we're not doing to make the movement more inclusive, because all of these issues – equal pay, reproductive rights, body image, gender stereotypes – span all races and ethnicities.

While Amandine and Renee clearly understand the importance in fostering diverse feminist communities, they lack the language to unravel the complex ways that identities like race and class operate to exclude certain voices from "joining in the conversation." This is illustrated more clearly when I ask Amandine why she thinks that more girls of color are not participating in the feminist blogosphere. She replies,

> I think that black culture doesn't emphasize education so much, and to have a blog and write on a regular basis you need to be relatively educated, so I guess that may be one factor. (I'm sorry if that sounded not so pc). If this is true, then it makes sense that the blogosphere gets diverse as people get older, because those non-whites who have managed to get educated get inspired to start blogs … Also, white people are much more economically secure, I attended a NOW webinar a while ago and they said that unmarried African-American women's median wealth is $100, unmarried Latinas' wealth is $125, and unmarried white women's wealth is $41,500. So non-whites have better things to worry about than feminist theory.[10]

Amandine makes several problematic statements here. Most obvious, she draws on troubling and incorrect stereotypes of 'black culture' and uses this to assume that many black people are poor and uneducated, preventing many from starting blogs due to limited technological and literacy skills. In this sense, she conflates race with class, connecting black people, low educational attainment, and a low class status. In doing so, she seems to imply that it is actually one's class status that prevents one from blogging, although her idea of class is clearly racialized. Whereas she grapples with intersectionality when she mentions the statistics on women's incomes she was provided by the National Organization for Women (NOW), she fails to link her own feminist activism to the issues affecting women and girls of color. Thus, instead of using these statistics as incentive to question larger power structures that often position women and girls of color in lower class positions, she seems to understand this economic discrepancy as connected to cultural values of education and success.

Additionally, Amandine reproduces the 'black-white' binary to talk about race more generally. While this is common in the United States, it obscures the actual racial makeup of the country and fails to take into account the experiences of girls and women who may not identify with the narrow categories of either black or white. It is also interesting to note that while my initial question that sparked this conversation was about diversity – not specifically race – the conversation quickly became centered on race. This points to the bloggers' recognition of race as an issue of ongoing importance in the United States. However, it also risks obscuring the experiences of other girls who may be prevented from blogging due to a range of inequalities. For example, these may include: white girls who may be poor or working class, girls who live in rural areas lacking reliable high speed Internet signals, and girls who may have a physical or learning disability that make blogging difficult. Although it is not possible here to interrogate each of these particular issues in the depth they deserve, it is nonetheless important to recognize how a multitude of structural factors can impede a girls' ability to participate in the feminist blogosphere.

Of course, part of what Amandine is saying makes sense. If a woman has to work multiple jobs in order to put food on the table she most likely does not have the leisure time or resources to blog. Similarly, a girl from a poor family may have to work a part time job or look after younger siblings after school, taking up leisure time that wealthier girls may use to blog. Nonetheless, Amandine's response seems to absolve her from responsibility to change the situation, which is troubling. Her comments also reaffirm notions of technological whiteness as critiqued by Hobson (2008), which prevents a more comprehensive analysis that would allow us to better understand how power inequalities are enacted online in ways beyond the digital divide.

It is not my intention to imply that Amandine is 'racist' or 'failing' at the feminist goal of fostering diverse blogging networks and recognizing intersectional oppressions. The young feminists I discuss must be acknowledged as still learning about feminism, as I discussed in chapter two. However, I am suggesting that the bloggers may lack the discursive resources to talk about issues of race, class, and other intersecting oppressions in ways that challenge the status quo. It is not surprising that Amandine adopts dominant discourses that position people of color as responsible for their own failure to attain economic prosperity, as this is the neoliberal story that we often hear in public discourse. It is also important for me to stress that Amandine's neoliberal perspective on racial diversity was not expressed by all bloggers.[11]

When I ask Renee to suggest reasons why there are not more girls of color blogging on feminist sites, she draws on her own experience growing up in a very racially diverse, working-class neighborhood in a small west coast city. She describes how her two best friends, one of whom is first generation Filipino-American and the other who is first generation Korean-American, have not been interested in getting involved in feminist activism in the way that she has. She explains this difference not in terms of race, but in terms of ethnic identity and the communities that these identities foster. Renee says, "They are so much more connected to their cultures than I am as a white person. I have always been so jealous of people that have any connections to their heritage, to where their families came from." When I ask her to clarify what she means by this, Renee suggests that her friends' participation in their ethnic communities provide a sense of community and belonging that she has not experienced as a "white person." Renee's turn to feminism then, implies that feminism has offered her a way to connect her identity to a larger community in the same way that her friends can do this with the Filipino and Korean communities in their city. Whereas the idea that white people have no culture problematically reproduces notions of the exotic Other, Renee's explanation highlights the importance of a feeling of belonging produced through her blogging.

Although Renee's explanation is a somewhat apolitical understanding of community and identity, it nonetheless points to the issue of conflicting identities that Mary Celeste Kearney (2006) discusses in her analysis of girls' participation in hip hop and punk cultures in the 1980s. Kearney argues that punk girls, who were predominantly white, had more leeway in experimenting with gender identity and performances because their "femininity was already affirmed as a result of their dominant racial identity and its associated privileged class status" (57). In contrast, hip hop girls were constrained in the ways that they could perform femininity because of their deprivileged racial, and often class, status (Kearney 2006). Additionally, Tricia Rose (1994) reminds us that many black girls and women who participated in hip hop chose not to identify as feminist because of the history of racism within mainstream feminisms and a lack of a "concrete link to black women or the black community" (Rose 1994, 177). These analyses affirm that girls of color do not merely lack resistance (their resistance is often made invisible because it occurs outside of white culture), but social inequalities like racism can prevent girls of color from participating in feminist activism.

Considering this scholarship, I am suggesting that something similar is happening with regard to girls' participation in the feminist blogosphere. As Christina Scharff (2012) convincingly argues, the feminist identity challenges conventional notions of femininity, as well as destabilizes the heteronormative order. White girls may then more easily be able to adopt a feminist identity with less of a social penalty than girls of color, as their whiteness aligns with privileged femininity (see Wald 1998). Thus, adopting a feminist identity appears to be less risky for white girls, although class status, ethnicity, ability, and sexuality may complicate this claim. If girls' adoption of a feminist identity serves in part as a form of resistance to normative femininity, as I suggest in the first chapter, girls of color may be less invested in the need for a feminist identity, as they already possess non-normative identities on which to draw.

The history of racism in feminist movements may also discourage girls of color from participating in feminist blogging. Whereas intersectionality and difference have been important parts of the feminist lexicon for close to thirty years, lingering stereotypes about feminists as white, middle-class women (note, not girls!) remain. Scharff (2012) found that many of her participants, a racially and sexually diverse group of young women in their twenties and early thirties living in England and Germany, disassociated with feminism in part because of the raced and classed connotations they perceived feminism as carrying. Renee also acknowledges this during our conversation when she suggests that girls who are not white or middle class may choose not to participate in feminism because of these associations.

Sociologist Jacqueline Kennelly's (2011, 117) research on youth activism in Canada helps us further consider diversity within the young feminist blogosphere. Drawing on Pierre Bourdieu's conception of social capital and habitus (see Bourdieu 1984), she coins the concept of "relational agency" to analyze how race and class function in the anti-globalization activist communities she studied. Kennelly defines relational agency as "the contingent and situated intersection between an individual's social position within a field of interactions, and the means by which the relationships within that field permit that individual to take actions that might otherwise be inconceivable – or, in other words, permit them to achieve a habitus shift" (117). According to Kennelly, one's personal relationships can give one the "knowledge, capacity, and resources" to engage in activism. Agency then is not only an individual attribute, but connected to a larger network of relationships that makes possible for some people to be excluded from activism because of their lack of particular social relationships.

Kennelly (2011, 270) writes, "Since friendships often emerge unconsciously along class, gender, and race lines – because the people with whom we feel 'at ease' often share these characteristics with us – they can also serve to perpetuate class, gender- and race-based exclusions also identified by participants throughout the ethnography." Consequently, existing social relationships may allow some girls to take up feminist activism more easily than others who come from communities where feminism is not a part of the social and cultural context. While Kennelly's research did not examine how relational agency may function in online spaces, I suggest this may not be problematic because girls' online practices are very much related to their lived experiences offline, as I've demonstrated throughout this book. Kennelly's insights suggest the importance of examining social relationships to better understand why some girls may be more comfortable Googling 'feminism' and then participating in the movement than others.

Sarah Thornton's (1996) concept of subcultural capital is relevant here, because it highlights how 'hipness' circulates as a form of capital within youth cultures. Subcultural capital is an accrued knowledge of the norms of a subculture, or in this case, the networked counterpublic. Thornton (1996, 14) emphasizes how media are "a network crucial to the definition and distribution of cultural knowledge" necessary for subcultural capital, a distinguishing factor from Bourdieu's cultural capital and a point that's particularly salient for my study. While being a teenage feminist blogger may not be 'cool' within high school environments (as I discussed in chapter one), being a feminist blogger does require the development of a particular knowledge that functions as subcultural capital with feminist blogging counterpublics. For example, bloggers must not only understand and utilize language like 'slut shaming,' which requires a certain amount of intellectual theorization, but must also often be versed in popular media culture and cultural happenings, which often informs blog posts and sustains conversations. While this knowledge is most likely connected to Bourdieu's social and cultural capital (such as being educated about feminism by one's parents), it is something that bloggers can accrue through their interaction as consumers and producers of media, and then from a continued participation in the blogosphere.

We can see the development of subcultural capital in Amandine's experience that I described in chapter one. By discovering and reading Jewish feminist blogs Amandine became familiar with the language and norms of the community and was able to identify with members due to shared identities and beliefs. This subcultural capital fosters social capital, or a certain relational agency that Kennelly describes, giving Amandine the confidence to start her own blog and a network of connected bloggers that were eager to read it. Amandine's commitment to blogging meant that she was continually building social and subcultural capital by posting on her blog regularly as well as commenting on the blogs of others. In turn, this practice provides publicity for her blog. Amandine's visibility in the networked counterpublic of the teenage blogosphere allows her to garner subcultural capital in ways that exclude those girls who are online irregularly and therefore lack the knowledge of cultural events and popular media culture to contribute to discussions.

Amandine's offline positioning may also assist her in accruing this capital. Amandine comes from a middle-class single-parent household, has no self-identified feminist friends (outside of the friends she's met online), and attends a conservative, religious private school. However, Amandine lives in a large urban center on the east coast, meaning that she has access to cultural events, feminist politics, and a variety of (feminist) media that generates subcultural capital – that of which a blogger in rural Indiana may not be able to access. I raise this example to demonstrate that we cannot make simplistic generalizations about the young feminist blogosphere based solely on class, race, or location, but must recognize the complex ways in which these identities and the social, cultural, and subcultural capitals they generate may position some girls more likely to become feminist bloggers. Thus, contrary to what neoliberal logic may suggest, a lack of agency or interest among individual girls does not tell the whole story as to why some girls are not feminist bloggers.

Whereas it is impossible to definitively conclude why the networked counterpublics formed by girl feminist bloggers do not reflect the diversity of the American public, my discussion emphasizes that social and cultural contexts and capital make a feminist identity more accessible and socially desirable to some girls. This does not mean that there are no girls of color participating in the young feminist blogging networks; indeed, as Julie suggests, they may not be as visible as their white counterparts, a topic I return to in chapter five.

Conclusions: Networked Counterpublics as Disrupting Neoliberal Individualism

In this chapter I suggest that girl bloggers are best understood as participating in networked counterpublics, forming networks around particular discursive feminist identities and issues, coming together, dissolving, and reconvening in a fluid manner. I demonstrate this through three case studies that examined how girl bloggers have formed networked counterpublics in relation to a teenage feminist identity, reproductive rights, and rape culture. Although girls' networked counterpublics include 'strangers' and see participants come and go, I contend that affective relationships and friendships are an important part of the functioning of these counterpublics and often serve to sustain girls' activism. These findings challenge much of the scholarly literature that continues to compare 'online communities' with those 'offline,' failing to take into account the fluidity across online and offline spaces that these networked counterpublics exhibit.

I argue then, that girl feminist bloggers are challenging postfeminist and neoliberal discourses through collective organizing via networked counterpublics. The language of networked counterpublics not only suggests a collective strategy, but one that also contains transformative and emancipatory potential (Warner 2005; Fraser 1992). Thus, networked counterpublics generate new opportunities to engage in activist practices that attempt to intervene in changing public discourse. SlutWalk is an example of how this works, producing and circulating discourses about 'slut shaming' that aim to change cultural common sense. Therefore, understanding girl bloggers as participating in networked counterpublics provides us with a model to think about the opportunities for communal action via digital technologies in ways that complicate the emphasis on individual social change embedded within neoliberal and postfeminist discourses.

Yet, I also suggest that we must be critical of the ways in which networked counterpublics do not necessarily foster diversity among participants. Moving beyond narratives of the digital divide, I propose the need to employ alternative concepts, such as relational agency and subcultural capital, in order to better understand how social inequalities are reproduced online – even within communities that are attuned to these inequalities in everyday life, with the hopes of producing more inclusive networked counterpublics in the future.

Notes

1. Whereas the *FBomb* certainly isn't the only feminist blog for girls today, it was the first website of its kind to be widely discussed in both the blogosphere and mainstream press when it launched in 2009. Indeed, several of my respondents mentioned that the *FBomb* inspired them to start their own blogs.
2. Yochai Benkler (2007) utilizes the related term "networked public sphere" in his book, *The Wealth of Networks: How Social Production Transforms Markets and Freedom* however, his macro-level analysis centers on shifting communication policy to account for the Internet as a "networked public sphere." My own use of term departs from Benkler's, as I aim to understand the meanings of bloggers' networked connections rather than attempting to make claims about how the Internet as a network functions in relation to commercial mass media, the focus on Benkler's book.
3. The term "networked" also can be referred back to Ednie Kaeh Garrison's (2000, 2010) description of third wave feminism, as well as Stephen Duncombe's (1997) discussion of zine cultures. This connection is not a coincidence, as I position girls' feminist blogging in relation to both third wave feminism and zine culture throughout this book. There is also a rich body of scholarship on "network theory" and "network society," however this "macro" sociological work exists alongside my own analysis, rather than directly informing my ethnographic-influenced approach (see Castells 1996, 2012).
4. One of the challenges in conducting personal interviews is the language one uses to communicate with interviewees. In this case I used the term 'community' with my participants, although I knew that I wanted to frame the collectivities that girl bloggers are forming online in slightly different terms (eventually choosing "networked counterpublic"). Due to the theoretical nature of "networked counterpublic" I did not use this term in interviews, as most subjects would not be familiar with it. This issue means that quoting participants often means slipping back into the language of community, which I recognize may be awkward.
5. While the "War on Women" as a phrase has been used sporadically for over two decades, it gained prominence most recently after the 2010 U.S. midterm elections. Today, the phrase primarily refers to the Republican initiatives in federal and state legislatures aimed to curb reproductive rights, although other related issues have been discussed using this discourse, including the prosecution of violence against women (including rape), access to birth control and abortions services, the defunding of women's health organizations such as Planned Parenthood, and the treatment of women's discrimination in the workplace.
6. Since the completion of this research, this issue has gained even more prominence, especially on U.S. college campuses where there has been increased activism around sexual assault. See Grigoriadis 2014.

7. The term 'frenemy' is a popular culture term that combines the words 'friend' and 'enemy' to refer to a (usually female) person who acts both as one's friend and enemy.
8. The Internet slang term 'Anon' refers to an anonymous commenter.
9. I contacted bloggers based upon their inclusion in the *Fbomb*'s blogroll, and then using the email addresses they provided on their blog. I then used a snowball sampling method, asking these bloggers for referrals to other teenage bloggers that may be interested in participating in the study, as well as asking them to post my call for participants on their blog. I asked all participants to confirm their racial identification upon start of the project. After I discovered all of my participants were white, I searched through the blogs listed on the *FBomb* blogroll, but was unable to find any blogs that were written by teenage girls of color. This does not mean that none exist, however, at the time of research there were none listed on the *FBomb* blogroll. One African American girl feminist blogger did contact me after seeing my call for participants listed on one of the other bloggers' sites, however, while expressing initial interest she did not return any of my follow-up emails and I noticed that she had taken down her blog shortly after contacting me.
10. I confirmed that these statistics are correct, according to a study release in spring 2010 by Insight Center for Community Economic Development. The report can be accessed at: http://www.insightcced.org/uploads/CRWG/LiftingAsWeClimb-WomenWealth-Report-InsightCenter-Spring2010.pdf.
11. During my follow-up interviews with the bloggers almost two years later I discovered that several had developed much more sophisticated understandings of intersectionality upon entering college. See chapter six for further discussion.

References

Ahmed, Sara. 2004. *The Cultural Politics of Emotion*. Edinburgh: Edinburgh University Press.

Bains, Jess. 2012. "Experiments in Democratic Participation: Feminist Printshop Collectives." *Cultural Policy, Criticism and Management Research* 6: 29–51.

Baker, Sarah. 2011. "Playing Online: Pre-Teen Girls' Negotiations of Pop and Porn in Cyberspace." In *Mediated Girlhoods: New Explorations of Girls' Media Culture*, edited by Mary Celeste Kearney, 171–187. New York: Peter Lang.

Baym, Nancy. 2010. *Personal Connections in the Digital Age*. Malden: Polity Press.

Benkler, Yochai. 2007. *The Wealth of Networks: How Social Production Transforms Markets and Freedom*. New Haven: Yale University Press.

Bourdieu, Pierre. 1984. *Distinction: A Social Critique of the Judgment of Taste*. Cambridge: Harvard University Press.

boyd, danah. 2008. "Why Youth [Heart] Social Network Sites: The Role of Networked Publics in Teenage Social Life." In *Youth, Identity, and Digital Media*, edited by David Buckingham, 119–142. Cambridge: The MIT Press.

boyd, danah. 2011. "White Flight in Networked Publics: How Race & Class Shaped American Teen Engagement with MySpace and Facebook." In *Race After the Internet*, edited by Lisa Nakamura and Peter Chow-White, 203–222. New York: Routledge.

boyd, danah. 2014. *It's Complicated: The Social Life of Networked Teens*. New Haven: Yale University Press.

Castells, Manuel. 1996. *The Rise of Network Society*. Cambridge: Blackwell.

Castells, Manuel. 2012. *Networks of Outrage and Hope: Social Movements in the Internet Age*. Cambridge: Polity.

Dines, Gail, and Wendy Murphy. 2011. "Slutwalk is not sexual liberation." *The Guardian*, May 8. Accessed October 12, 2012. http://www.guardian.co.uk/commentisfree/2011/may/08/slutwalk-not-sexual-liberation.

Driver, Susan. 2007. *Queer Girls and Popular Culture: Reading, Resisting, and Creating Media*. New York: Peter Lang.

Duncombe, Stephen. 1997. *Notes From the Underground*. New York: Verso.

Faludi, Susan. 1992. *Backlash: The Undeclared War Against American Women*. New York: Anchor Books.

Fernback, Jan. 2007. "Beyond the Diluted Community Concept: A Symbolic Interactionist Perspective on Online Social Relations." *New Media & Society* 9 (1): 49–69.

Fraser, Nancy. 1992. "Rethinking the Public Sphere: A Contribution to the Critique of Actually Existing Democracy." *Social Text* 25/26: 56–80.

Garrison, Ednie Kaeh. 2000. "U.S. Feminism-Grrrl Style! Youth (Sub)Cultures and the Technologics of the Third Wave." *Feminist Studies* 26 (1): 141–170.

Garrison, Ednie Kaeh. 2010. "U.S. Feminism-Grrrl Style! Youth (Sub)Cultures and the Technologies of the Third Wave (updated)." In *No Permanent Waves: Recasting Histories of U.S. Feminism*, edited by Nancy Hewitt, 379–402. New Brunswick: Rutgers University Press.

Gonick, Marnina. 2004. "The 'Mean Girl' Crisis: Problematizing Representations of Girls' Friendships." *Feminism & Psychology* 14 (3): 395–400.

Gray, Mary. 2009. *Out in the Country: Youth, Media, and Visibility in Rural America*. New York: New York University Press.

Grigoriadis, Vanessa. 2014. "How to Start a Revolution." *New York*, September 22.

Harris, Anita. 2004. *Future Girl: Young Women in the Twenty-first Century*. New York: Routledge.

Hobson, Janell. 2008. "Digital Whiteness, Primitive Blackness." *Feminist Media Studies* 8 2: 111–126.

Joannou, Maroula. 1995. "'She Who Would Be Politically Free Herself Must Strike the Blow:' Suffragette Autobiography and Suffragette Militancy." In *The Uses of Autobiography*, edited by Julia Swindells, 31–44. London: Routledge.

Kearney, Mary Celeste. 2006. *Girls Make Media*. New York: Routledge.

Kelleher, Katy. 2009. "Teen Feminists Drop 'F-Bomb.'" *Jezebel*, July 14. http://jezebel.com/5314187/teen-feminists-drop-f+bomb.

Keller, Jessalynn. 2012. "Virtual Feminisms: Girls' Blogging Communities, Feminist Activism and Participatory Politics." *Information, Communication & Society* 15(3): 429–447.

Kennelly, Jacqueline. 2011. *Citizen Youth: Culture, Activism, and Agency in a Neoliberal Era*. New York: Palgrave MacMillan.

Lenhardt, Amanda, Sousan Arafeh, Aaron Smith, and Alexandra Macgill. 2008. "Writing, Technology, and Teens." Pew Internet and American Life Project, Washington, DC. http://www.pewinternet.org/ Reports/2008/Writing-Technology-and-Teens/06-Electronic-Communication/04-Blogging-and-social-networking-are-dominated-by-girls.aspx.

M, Kelsie. 2011. "Thank You, Slutwalk." *FBomb*, August 5. http://thefbomb.org/2011/08/thank-you-slutwalk/.

McRobbie, Angela. 2009. *The Aftermath of Feminism: Gender, Culture and Social Change*. Thousand Oaks: Sage.

Mendes, Kaitlynn. 2015. *Slutwalk: Feminism, Activism & Media*. Basingstoke: Palgrave MacMillan.

Miller, Tim, and David Roman. 1995. "Preaching to the Converted." *Theatre Journal* 47(2): 169–188.

Nakamura, Lisa. 2002. *Cybertypes: Race, Ethnicity, and Identity on the Internet*. New York: Routledge.

Nakamura, Lisa. 2013. " 'It's a Nigger in Here! Kill the Nigger!': User-Generated Media Campaigns Against Racism, Sexism, and Homophobia in Digital Games." In *The International Encyclopedia of Media Studies*, edited by A. Valdivia, 6:5:21. New York: Routledge.

Nakamura, Lisa, and Chow-White, Peter. 2011. *Race After the Internet*. New York: Routledge.

Papacharissi, Zizi. 2002. "The Virtual Sphere: The Internet as a Public Sphere." *New Media & Society* 4 (1): 9–27.

Piano, Doreen. 2002. "Congregating Women: Reading 3rd Wave Feminist Practices in Subcultural Production." *Rhizomes*, 4. http://www.rhizomes.net/issue4/ piano. html.

Piepmeier, Alison. 2009. *Girl Zines: Making Media, Doing Feminism*. New York: New York University Press.

Perez, Miriam. 2009. "Quick Hit: A New Blog for Teenage Feminists." *Feministing*, July 13. http://feministing.com/2009/07/13/quick_hit_a_new_blog_for_teena/.

Polak, Michele. 2007. "'I Think We Must be Normal ... There are Too Many of Us for This to be Abnormal!!!': Girls Creating Identity and Forming Community in Pro-Ana/Mia Websites." In *Growing Up Online: Young People and Digital Technologies*, edited by Sandra Weber and Shanly Dixon, 81–94. New York: Palgrave MacMillan.

Rentschler, Carrie. 2014. "Rape Culture and the Feminist Politics of Social Media." *Girlhood Studies* 7 (1): 65–82.

Ringrose, Jessica. 2006. "A New Universal Mean Girl: Examining the Discursive Construction and Social Regulation of a New Feminine Pathology." *Feminism & Psychology* 16(4): 405–424.

Ringrose, Jessica. 2012. *Postfeminist Education? Girls and the Sexual Politics of Schooling*. London: Routledge.

Rose, Tricia. 1994. *Black Noise: Rap Music and Black Culture in Contemporary America*. Middletown: Wesleyan University Press.

S., Gina. 2012. "Countering Hatred on the Internet." *FBomb*, January 1. http:// thefbomb.org/2012/01/countering-hatred-on-the-internet/.

Scharff, Christina. 2012. *Repudiating Feminism: Young Women in a Neoliberal World*. Surry: Ashgate Publications.

Schilt, Kristen. 2003. "'I'll Resist with Every Inch and Every Breath:' Girls and Zine Making as a Form of Resistance." *Youth & Society* 35(1): 71–97.

Shaw, Frances. 2012a. "Discursive Politics Online: Political Creativity and Affective Networking in Australian Feminist Blogs." PhD diss., University of New South Wales, Australia.

Shaw, Frances. 2012b. "Hottest 100 Women: Cross-platform Discursive Activism in Feminist Blogging Networks." *Australian Feminist Studies* 27 (74): 373–387.

Steiner, Linda. 2012. "Using New Technologies to Enter the Public Sphere, Second Wave Style." In *Feminist Media: Participatory Spaces, Networks and Cultural Citizenship*, edited by Elke Zobl and Ricarda Drueke, 182–193. Germany: Transcript.

Schofield Clark, Lynn. 2005. "The Constant Contact Generation: Exploring Teen Friendship Networks Online." In *Girl Wide Web: Girls, the Internet, and the Negotiation of Identity*, edited by Sharon Mazzarella, 203–221. New York: Peter Lang.

Taft, Jessica. 2011. *Rebel Girls: Youth Activism & Social Change Across the Americas.* New York: New York University Press.

Thornton, Sarah. 1996. *Club Cultures: Music, Media and Subcultural Capital.* Middletown: Wesleyan University Press.

Turkle, Sherry. 2011. *Alone Together: Why We Expect More From Technology and Less From Each Other.* New York: Basic Books.

van Dijck, Jose. 2011. "Flickr and the culture of connectivity: Sharing views, experiences, memories." *Memory Studies* 4 (4): 401–415.

van Dijck, Jose. 2013. *The Culture of Connectivity: A Critical History of Social Media.* Oxford: Oxford University Press.

Wald, Gayle. 1998. "Just a Girl? Rock Music, Feminism, and the Cultural Construction of Female Youth." *Signs* 23(3): 585–610.

Warner, Michael. 2005. *Publics and Counterpublics.* Cambridge: Zone Books.

Watkins, S. Craig. 2009. *The Young and the Digital: What the Migration to Social Network Sites, Games, and Anytime, Anywhere Media Means for Our Future.* Boston: Beacon Press.

Yuan, Elaine. 2013. "A Culturalist Critique of 'Online Community' in New Media Studies." *New Media & Society* 15 (5): 665–679.

4 "I've really got a thing for Betty Friedan"

Girl Bloggers and the Production of Feminist History Online

"I always felt more of a connection to the Second Wave, my mom always says that I was born 50 years too late! Doing research led me to read feminist classics like The Feminine Mystique *and* The Dialectic of Sex, *among many others that really affected me. That's when I realized I was a feminist ... I think what really struck me at first, and really continues to hook my interest, is the fact that so many of the Second Wave goals haven't really been met. ..."*
—Amandine, focus group discussion

The opening quote from Amandine contradicts much of what we hear about girls and feminism – that girls don't want to be feminists, and if they do they certainly don't want to be associated with the supposed bra-burning of the second wave. But perhaps more importantly, Amandine refuses to understand herself as distinct from her feminist predecessors that fought for many of the same things she continues to pursue today. In this sense, Amandine challenges hegemonic constructions of youth as ignorant of history, in a constant state of waiting passively for the future. Nancy Lesko (2001, 196) argues that the linear, unidirectional, and cumulative conceptions of growth and change that characterize dominant discourses about adolescence presume "the present always overtakes the past." Consequently, youth are often positioned as either overly invested in the present with little thought to past or future, or in a constant "state of becoming" where teens' agency is understood as located in the future. Neither of these discourses recognizes youth's investment in and connection to the past, something I will explore here in relation to girls' feminist blogging practices.

In this chapter I analyze how girls' feminist blogs fit into feminism as an ongoing, fluid political movement. This requires paying attention not only to how the bloggers understand their own positioning as historical subjects within the contemporary context, but how they relate their activism to the history of feminism. This relationship between the history of feminism and contemporary girl feminist bloggers is particularly significant for several reasons. First, dominant feminist discourses based upon the wave metaphor often characterize younger 'third wave' feminists as being ahistorical, disconnected from how their feminism aligns with past feminism(s). These arguments are further buttressed by postfeminist rhetoric that problematically "generationalizes" feminism (Scharff 2012). Consequently, we must pay attention to how girl feminist bloggers are challenging this argument in complex ways.

Mary Celeste Kearney (2014, 58) argues that scholars of youth media have neglected to "consider the historical contexts of media, focusing instead on contemporary culture with a myopically presentist and ahistorical lens." She notes that this has been especially true for scholars studying youth's Internet practices "no doubt because of the relatively young age of the Web and thus seeming absence of its history." By focusing on both the content of girls' blogs, as well as the productive practice of blogging itself in relation to feminist history, I hope to begin the process of better understanding girls' feminist blogs as continuing a historical legacy of feminist activism, while also adding fresh perspectives and ideas to the movement.

Finally, Red Chidgey (2012) draws on the work of Michel Foucault to argue for the significance in understanding the potential of feminist digital media production to create "counter-memories" of feminism (Foucault 1980). She maintains, "Part of feminism's cultural battle is thus to secure the role of women's movements in popular memory. Feminist media can become discursive 'weapons' in this struggle: to contest hostile framings and to put forward counter-understandings of what feminism is, what feminism can do, and who a feminist can be" (87). Consequently, it is necessary to explore how girls' blogging as a feminist media production practice fulfills this function. The questions that inform this chapter then include: How do girl feminist bloggers view their own feminism as related or not to feminisms from previous decades? In what ways do these girl feminists use their blogs to engage, negotiate, and rewrite feminist histories? And finally, how might girls' engagements with histories of feminism challenge postfeminist narratives of feminism's 'pastness'?

I begin this chapter by outlining the significance of the history of feminism, briefly mapping how writing feminist history has long been a part of women's feminist activism. This discussion sets up my own attention to and analysis of girl bloggers' creative engagement with feminist history, which I argue takes the form of several interrelated practices: (1) by writing about particular historical feminist figures; (2) by connecting present feminist issues with past feminist struggles; (3) by telling history in new ways using the architecture of the web; and (4) by performing as historiographers through rewriting feminist histories. These practices, I maintain, allow the bloggers to complicate the wave metaphor and to understand their own feminist identities in more fluid ways, suggesting that young feminist bloggers have little investment in portraying themselves as a 'fourth wave' of feminism distinct from their predecessors.

Ultimately I argue for understanding girl feminist bloggers as historiographers who not only are learning about feminism online and educating their readers about feminist history, but are actively producing feminist history through their blogging. This argument has three significant implications:

First, we can understand the Internet, including girls' blogs, as a useful alternative space for girls to engage with feminist history. Second, this assertion challenges both the wave metaphor and other postfeminist discourses that "generationalize" feminism (Scharff 2012). And finally, it demonstrates the historical complexity inherent in some girls' feminist blogs, which has been problematically overlooked by feminist scholars. I conclude by contending that this connection to the past allows girl bloggers a feeling of belonging to a movement with both a past and a future; this sense of belonging not only offers an alternative narrative to the "pastness" (McRobbie 2009) of feminism, but an investment in the sustained future of the movement.

"The Badasses Who Came Before Us": Exploring Feminist History

Julie Zeilinger's 2012a book *A Little F'd Up: Why Feminism Is Not A Dirty Word* begins not with a description of the feminist blogosphere or the popularity of SlutWalk, but with a chapter titled, "The Badasses Who Came Before Us: A Brief History of Feminism." Julie opens the chapter by writing,

> I know what you're thinking: History is boring … [But] there are three major reasons I think it's really important to understand the history of the women who came before us before we delve into all the shit we're dealing with right now … Reason #1: Our generation desperately needs some perspective … Reason #2: History repeats itself and all that jazz … Reason #3: It makes sense to start at the beginning … So without further ado, let's talk about the history of feminism!

Julie returns to 1786 BC, when ancient Babylon's Code of Hammerabi legislated women as property of their father or husband. She traces women's position in society through Aristotle's theorizing (dubbing him a "master" of sexism), the development of religion (under the heading "Muhammad Was a Feminist"), the Enlightenment (or, according to Julie, "Not So Enlightened, Actually"), and finally, the first, second, and third 'waves' of feminism of the nineteenth, twentieth, and now twenty-first centuries. Julie includes side-boxes that introduce short bios of prominent feminists, such as Mary Wollstonecraft, Sojourner Truth, Gloria Steinem, and Rebecca Walker, highlighting the specific contributions of a diversity of feminists. While it is of course impossible to tell 'the' history of feminism (more accurately described as histor*ies*), the sixty seven-page chapter does a decent job making feminism's lengthy and complex past accessible to readers who may begin with little or no knowledge of the movement.

Julie's inclusion of feminist history in her book for teenage girls is significant, considering the ways in which postfeminist discourses generationalize feminism as something located in the past, offering little relevance to girls and young women today. Indeed, like Amandine's quote that begins this chapter, it complicates many of the assumptions about young feminists as overly individualistic, ahistorical, and eager to take for granted the rights they enjoy. My goal in this chapter is to move beyond merely demonstrating that young feminist bloggers are interested in feminism's history, although this point remains important. Instead, I argue that their creative engagements with feminist history, particularly as historiographers, is a significant move that establishes a sense of belonging and functions as a political act. Furthermore, this writing of women's history has been a significant part of feminist activism since the nineteenth century. Girl bloggers are contributing to this lengthy history of feminist historiography (Stanford Friedman 1995; Cowman 2009) by continuing this practice on their blogs.

The practice of producing history also continues the work of 1990s grrrl zinesters who often constructed a "female specific history" in their zines that showcased the contributions of older feminists, a practice that acknowledged the lineage between these feminists' work and their own (Kearney 2006). For example, Mary Celeste Kearney (2006) describes how the zine *Ms. America* #2 included a spread on "Riot Grrrandmas" like Harriet Tubman, Virginia Woolf, and Susan B. Anthony, linking past historical feminists with contemporary riot grrrls. As Kearney argues, "This 'herstory' not only reclaims girls and women for feminist history, but also works to position grrrl zinesters within a particular historical trajectory and thus mode of identity" (174). Consequently, zinesters often positioned historical feminists as role models for contemporary girls in much the same way that bloggers do today, something I will discuss further in the next section of this chapter.

Feminists have long valued women's – and feminism's – history as a significant part of feminism's political project. Krista Cowman (2009, 143) writes that in 1707 Mary Astell, a British feminist, acknowledged the writing of history by women as "primarily a political act." More recently, Cowman describes how young British college-educated women in the late nineteenth and early twentieth centuries often worked as amateur historians, using new social science methodologies to conduct both historical and contemporary research to better the lives of women. Cowman notes how much of this research was funded by notable bodies such as the Women's Industrial Council, which "linked feminist activism with historical research" (144). She reports, "Such work, which included Clementina Black's investigations into sweated labor (1907) and married women's work (1915) alongside thorough statistical reports on the conditions of laundresses and homeworkers, was effectively contemporary history" (144).

Similarly, Cowman acknowledges the important, yet often overlooked, contributions of British suffragettes' autobiographies to feminist historiography. Moroula Joannou (1995, 32) describes these works as an "active record of women intervening in history and making history." The autobiographies again challenged dominant structures of history writing, retaining their feminist predecessors' belief that history must be written for a purpose beyond merely creating an objective account of past events (Cowman 2009).

Suffragette autobiographies, in this sense, were activist documents that were written with the political agenda of taking women's rights beyond the right to vote. Unfortunately, Cowman notes, these documents, along with the work of the amateur historians I discuss earlier in this chapter, remained on the margins of the historical record. This was in part due to the belief that these documents were the "product of activism, written for a political purpose or by politically involved individuals," which did not correspond with academic historian's belief that true history was objective, impartial, and detached (146). This unwillingness to accept these forms of 'alternative' histories demonstrate a divide between academic and nonacademic histories that have continued to shape feminist histories even with the development of women's studies and women's history programs.

The institutionalization of feminism in universities through the efforts of the second wave was an important step in legitimizing the history of feminism, documenting women's stories, and archiving women's historical records. While it is not my intention to detail this complex process here, it is important to acknowledge that this institutionalization did not often alter the power structures that privileged men as representing history, change, linear time, and great achievements. As Sylvia Paletschek (2009) notes, women's history that did not mimic the (masculine) form of history as revolving around 'great men' and 'great ideas' remained marginalized as "not truly worthy" and "not important," given sidebar status in history textbooks and passing mention in curricula rather than serious scholarly engagement.

I will return to this issue later in this chapter in relation to my interview data and textual analysis, because it raises the question as to what 'counts' as history. Consequently, the public's knowledge of feminist history is centered on a few 'great women,' like Gloria Steinem, 'great works,' like Betty Friedan's *The Feminine Mystique*, or 'iconic' media images, like suffragettes holding placards. This is not surprising, considering that when feminist history is addressed in high school curricula, it is often presented in such as manner. Thus, while women's and feminism's history may be more prominent within historical records today than in the past, the stories that we do know often fail to account for the diverse and complex movement that feminism was and continues to be.

For example, girls' participation in feminist activism throughout history remains almost invisible in both mainstream and feminist historical accounts. My own literature review of this topic yielded few results, yet the little research available (Hunter 2002; Pike 2011) demonstrates that girls have been passionately engaged with issues of gender inequality since the late nineteenth century. Consequently, there is still much work to be done in terms of both historical research and writing feminism's history, practices that should be viewed as activism. As Susan Stanford Friedman (1995, 29) argues, "The unending, cumulative building of broadly defined histories of women, including histories of feminism, is a critical component of resistance and change." This sentiment can also be seen in the early research of the "amateur historians" I discuss earlier in this chapter, and I will argue, feminist girl bloggers.

It is important to recognize history as not only about the past, but about the present and future as well. Stanford Friedman reminds us: "As a heuristic activity, history writing orders the past in relation to the needs of the present and future. The narrative act of assigning meaning to the past potentially intervenes in the present and future construction of history. For feminists, this means that writing the history of feminism functions as an act in the present that can ... contribute to the shape of feminism's future" (13). Thus, writing feminist history is not just activism, but also a necessary activist strategy needed to give feminism a future. It is this framework that I adopt when analyzing how girl bloggers write and engage with feminist history.

The "Pied Piper of Feminism": Affective Attachments to Feminist Role Models from the Past

In a December 2012 interview on CBC radio's *Q* Kathleen Hanna, prominent riot grrrl and lead singer of the punk band Bikini Kill (1990–1996), admitted, "The whole reason I got on stage was to be the Pied Piper of feminism" (*Q* 2012). Hanna's comment is interesting because it highlights her role in delivering feminism as an accessible discourse to her girl fans, many of whom may not have previously encountered feminist politics in their lives. Hanna's adoption of a girl subjectivity likely contributed to her accessibility for teenage girls and young women who could identify with many of the feminist issues that Hanna raised through her music, live performances, and interviews. It is little surprise then that Hanna continues to be cited, including by several girls in my focus group, as an influential feminist role model.

Feminist role models are significant way for girl bloggers not only to learn about feminism, but to explicitly connect to the history of feminism. In the online focus group the bloggers discussed a wide range of what I'm calling feminist role models, spanning both contemporary and historical figures, pop culture icons, 'professional' feminists and what Renee called "everyday feminists," referring to bloggers and feminist commentators. Several bloggers I interviewed mentioned Jessica Valenti, the founder of influential feminist blog *Feministing*, as a major contemporary feminist influence, along with Hillary Clinton, Tina Fey, Lady Gaga, Eve Ensler and M.I.A. as contemporary feminist role models. Feminist bloggers such as Courtney Martin, Latoya Petersen, and Julie Zeilinger were also well respected among my study participants.

Almost all of the bloggers mentioned at least one historical figure as a major feminist influence in addition to the contemporary role models I list earlier, and spoke about them in passionate ways. "I've really got a thing for Betty Friedan rather than Gloria Steinem," Amandine tells me when I ask about her feminist role models. She also cites "old-school second wave feminists" like Shulamith Firestone, and Letty Cottin Pogrebin as particularly influential to her identity as an Orthodox Jewish feminist. Interestingly, Amandine claims that she's not into "modern feminist authors" and was disappointed by Valenti's 2007 book *Full Frontal Feminism*, which is popular among young feminists. Despite being a feminist blogger, Amandine's feminist role models are not fellow bloggers but women who were most active several decades before she was born.

Abby also tells me that Letty Cottin Pogrebin, a Jewish feminist activist, journalist, and author who co-founded *Ms.* magazine with Gloria Steinem, is her biggest feminist influence: "I read her book *Deborah, Golda, and Me* about six months ago, and there have been few things that have made me feel more secure in myself than reading that book and discovering that my thoughts and fears, hopes and dreams, are shared by such a woman." Similarly, Madison claims, "I learned about feminism through history, so a lot of the feminists I admire come from history. I like Alice Paul, Gloria Steinem, Kathleen Hanna … I'm also a sucker for Jessica Valenti, probably because she's the one who inspired me to start a blog and we now have some personal contact because of it."[1] These conversations revealed the importance that feminist history plays in these bloggers' own conceptions of and feelings about feminism. While Madison does mention some contemporary feminists, such as Valenti, her inclusion of these present-day figures could be seen as a way to link the present to the past and recognize contemporary women as historical subjects.

Girl bloggers often write posts about the historical feminists they admire, a crucial part of how they engage with history and encourage their readers to do the same. For example, a lengthy October 2010 post called "Finally, A Post About Gloria Steinem" by Renee details the life and work of Steinem and what she means for Renee's own relationship to feminism. Renee writes,

> If I've learned anything from Gloria Steinem, it's simply to accept yourself for who you are. I mean, claiming the feminist label a million thoughts ran through my mind: what will people think of me? What will my friends say, or my parents? But after reading about Steinem and her amazing history, I knew she never cared about what people thought about her. Whether they worshipped her, mocked her, exalted her, or despised her, it had absolutely nothing to do with who she was as a person. So, in a way, Gloria Steinem has helped me to accept myself for who I am, and simply be.

In addition to sharing her own feelings about the *Ms.* founder and educating readers about Steinem and her work, Renee's post inspired some interesting comments discussing the merits of Steinem's work in relation to that of Betty Friedan. One commenter also recommends the work of bell hooks, Catherine MacKinnon, and Simone de Beauvoir as other must-reads for feminists. In this sense Renee not only educates but also learns from her readers, assuring them she will check out their recommendations.

Renee is not the only blogger to write about her feminist influences from the past. To wit: Amandine wrote a thoughtful tribute to Shulamith Firestone upon her passing in August 2012, directly relating her own experience as an Orthodox Jewish feminist with that of Firestone. Amandine posts:

> I got into women's rights advocacy when I wrote a paper about second wave feminism. When I did research for the paper and read second wave classics, those books really resonated with me ... It fascinated me that someone with a name as Jewish as Shulamith could be a feminist. I know it sounds a little silly, but when I thought of feminists ... I thought of white bread [sic] American names like Betty and Gloria, not Shulamith. While it wasn't a conscious thought, it struck me as "if she can be so ethnic and such a classic feminist, why can't I?"

Amandine and Renee's postings serve a dual function, allowing the writer to articulate her own feminist narrative in relation to a lengthy history of feminism, while also introducing readers to the work of important historical feminist figures. This connection to one's own feminism is important to consider, as I'm suggesting that bloggers articulate more than an appreciation of these past feminist role models, but an intense affective connection that facilitates a sense of belonging to a larger cause. For example, this can be seen in Abby's comment that "there have been few things that have made me feel more secure in myself than reading that book and discovering that my thoughts and fears, hopes and dreams, are shared by such a woman." Renee's musings about Steinem reveal a similar emotional engagement that credits Steinem with learning to accept herself and "simply be."

In her book *Selenidad: Selena, Latinos, and the Performance of Identity* Deborah Paredez (2009, xv) argues that Selena Quintanilla-Perez's (known as "Selena") performances "document and serve as methods for experiencing latinidad as an affective mode of belonging" for the late Tejana pop singer's fans. Paredez describes how Latina identity is generated as affect through Selena's performances, working "as a sensibility, a shared feeling of placeness, and at times placelessness, within the U.S. national imaginary" (2009, 33). In this sense, Selena's girl fans are not merely enjoying the pleasure of a musical performance (although this is most likely occurring), but are experiencing new agential possibilities of being Latina that is intimately tied to a sense of belonging to a larger community. Perhaps most important though is Paredez's recognition of the political possibilities inherent in this "affective mode" that offers a collective form of resistance and social action to young Latinas.

Paredez's analysis can provide insight into how the act of writing about their feminist role models may function politically for girl feminists. For example, Amandine's written tribute to Firestone attributes her own present feeling of belonging to the feminist movement to Firestone, who demonstrated to Amandine that a Jewish ethnicity was not in conflict with feminist values. Similar to Selena's Latina girl fans that Paredez discusses, Amandine was able to navigate her own sense of marginalization and "placelessness" through her affective attachment to Firestone. The end of Amandine's tribute post reveals some of these sentiments. She writes, "I just feel so bad that Firestone was alone at the end. I would have been there for her faithfully. She truly changed my life, influenced my views on feminism and the world at large; it would have been the least I could do in return."

Nonetheless, as Paredez emphasizes in regards to Selena, it was Firestone's ability to connect Amandine to a larger community of Jewish feminists both past and present (and later teenage feminists as well) that is crucial to Amandine's politicization, a process that I discussed in depth in the previous chapter. Consequently, I am not advocating for the historical feminist role models I discuss here to be viewed as examples of individualism within feminism's history, but instead as figures embedded within larger communities of feminists spanning past, present, and future that are able to generate affect that ultimately holds feminist communities together over periods of time.

Connecting Past to Present: The Case of No-Cost Birth Control

One of the most important ways in which girls incorporate feminist history into their blogs is by demonstrating the similarities between past and present feminist issues. Indeed, this continuity between past and present is what interests many girl bloggers in feminist history. During a focus group discussion about Amandine's interest in the history of feminism, she reports, "I think what really struck me at first, and really continues to hook my interest [in feminist history] is the fact that so many of the second wave goals haven't really been met. We fought for equal pay, we still only make 77 cents (and that's if you have white privilege). We fought for reproductive rights, and so many are being taken away; it's terrifying." Amandine's point is important and reflects the connection between feminism's history, feminism in the present, and feminism's future, as she recognizes how both successful and failed feminist struggles of the past continue to influence present public debates and future policy, as in the case of ongoing reproductive rights legislation at the state level.

As I discussed in chapter three, many girl bloggers are passionate about reproductive rights; therefore, it is not surprising that birth control became an important topic of discussion in relation to feminist history.[2] I was particularly struck by the ways in which bloggers included a historical discussion of birth control (most often, the birth control pill) into their posts. For example, in a July 2011 post titled, "No-Cost Birth Control Matters!" Amandine provides a detailed overview of the history of birth control, starting with mention of it in early Egyptian civilizations (some, according to the post, used "crocodile dung" as a diaphragm!), moving through the work done by twentieth-century activists, like Margaret Sanger, important court cases in the 1960s and 1970s that finally legalized birth control in the United States, and ending with contemporary debates about no-cost birth control that have dominated recent headlines.

Similarly, Kat's blog's focus on sex education has meant that she writes frequently about the history of birth control. In a January 2011 entry titled "History of the Birth Control Pill," Kat posts a short video from Planned Parenthood celebrating the fiftieth anniversary of the birth control pill. On May 9th of that year she published a reblogged Tumblr post that reminds readers that it was on May 9, 1960 that the U.S. Food and Drug Administration approved the world's first commercially available birth control pill. The post acknowledges the long struggle for birth control since Margaret Sanger opened up the first birth control clinic in 1916 and highlights how the legalization of the pill is fundamental victory for women's rights. Kat's brief, to-the-point postings make the history of the birth control pill accessible and digestible to readers.

As Kat's postings demonstrate, images and videos are frequently used by bloggers to incorporate history into their blogs and can easily be reblogged and circulated among readers easier than a lengthy written post. In a posting titled "For Teens: Why Talking About Birth Control Matters" Renee includes a photo that appears to be taken in the 1960s of a woman holding a Planned Parenthood sign reading "You can decide how many children you want … Planned Parenthood can help … with information on birth control and infertility services" (Figure 4.1).

In the 50's and 60's, many women were hearing about their reproductive options for the first time. (Shock!)

The average woman spends three quarters of her reproductive life trying to prevent pregnancy, so yeah, birth control is a big deal. The National Women's Law Center is hopeful that the DHHS will "see the light" on this issue, and ultimately heed the recommendations given by a non-partisan, independent panel of scientific and medical experts at the Institute of Medicine (the panel's recommendations range from providing "yearly well-woman preventative care visits" to "screening and counseling to detect and prevent interpersonal and domestic violence").

For the millions of women who rely on birth control to keep their options open, and for your future and mine, I really hope the DHHS is able to reach a favorable consensus. In teen lingo: I hope they don't screw the heck up.

Figure 4.1 "For Teens" blog post, author screen shot. Used with permission of blog owner.

By choosing to use this historical image rather than a more contemporary one, Renee puts her post in conversation with the past struggles for access to birth control. In another 2011 entry, Renee discusses a paper she wrote for her American History class about the history of the birth control pill. She posts the introduction to her paper along with the PBS Special called "The Pill" (in six parts) that her paper was based upon. Again, Renee privileges the use of video to supplement and enhance her historical post.

By incorporating images and videos (as well as links, memes, infograph-ics, and other visual data) into their historical posts, the bloggers I discuss here are attempting to make history more interesting to their readers by harnessing the affective function of image-based media. Tiziana Terranova (2004, 42) argues that the significance of the image within digital media "is the kind of affect that it packs, the movements that it receives, inhibits, and/ or transmits." Jodi Dean (2010, 115) builds on Terranova's scholarship by arguing that her analysis can be expanded to include the numerous con-tributions to digital networks, "including music, sounds, words, sentences, games, videos, fragments of code, viruses, bots, crawlers, and the flow of interactions themselves as in blogs, Twitter, Facebook, and YouTube." Dean continues, "The most interesting aspect of the image, in other words, is the way that it is not simply itself but itself plus a nugget or shadow or trace of intensity. An image is itself and more" (115).

While Dean goes on to ultimately argue for the constraining and never-quite-satisfying quality of the image's affect, the analysis of my own data departs from Dean's argument to suggest that the affective dimension of images and other modes of online interactions (e.g. links), is viewed posi-tively by the girl bloggers, especially when in relation to topics that, like history, may be considered 'boring.' For example, when I asked Kat during a phone interview why she chose to use so many videos and links in her work, she told me that it's the interactivity that this type of visual data fosters (rather than solely written posts) that makes her so excited about blogging as a media production practice. This desire for interactivity and the affect it creates may be especially pertinent for girls who are often marginal-ized from the production of history, offering up a significant opportunity to actively engage with the past.[3]

A December 2010 post on the *FBomb* by Julie called "Reproductive Rights: The Stuff That Got Left Out In School" also takes a historical approach to thinking about birth control. In the post Julie discusses how teenage girls often know little about the importance of reproductive rights and "don't have respect for or an understanding about the trials our moms and grandmas had to go through so that we have what to us seem like the basic rights of being able to control and make choices about our bodies." She writes,

> Now, I don't think this is entirely the fault of a generation that's being painted as total self-obsessed brats ... I think a lot of the blame can

be put on our schools. When I took AP U.S. History we spent maybe a week total on women's rights and the feminist movement. As far as reproductive rights go, Margaret Sanger was mentioned, and then we moved on … On the *FBomb*, we spend a lot of time talking about feminism as it relates to us personally, in pop culture and in current events, which is awesome. But I think there's probably room to fill in for the education we're apparently not getting in school.

The post goes on to describe some of the major highlights in the fight for reproductive rights in the United States, including the Comstock Laws of the 1870s that made contraception illegal, Sanger's birth control clinics and resulting legal battles in the early twentieth century, the legalization of the pill and abortion in 1960 and 1973 respectively, the changes to reproductive rights laws following the election of Ronald Reagan in 1980 and then Bill Clinton in 1993, and the 2009 murder of Dr. George Tiller, a Kansas doctor who performed late-term abortions.

Julie's post makes evident the clear link that she is attempting to establish between past and present, ending with a sad event that reinforces how divisive reproductive rights are even today. Julie also includes a link to "a more comprehensive timeline" on Planned Parenthood's website, directing readers to find out more if they're keen.[4] I am also interested in this post, however, because of its clear educational mission. Julie recognizes how girls are not getting taught the history of women's rights in high school, and she uses the *FBomb* as an educational tool to "fill in" for the lack of attention to this topic in school curricula. The enthusiastic comments from readers following this post is a testament to Julie's assessment of the high school curriculum.

For example, Katherine C. writes, "YAY!!!!!! *applause* I am a huge fan of women's history and you would not believe (or, actually, you probably would) the crap I take for it in history class. Brava!" Similarly, Marisol reports that, "You know, I've never actually heard of Margaret Sanger before now (yes I stay awake in history class; she's just not in our curricula at all). But she sounds like a badass that I need to find out more about!" Zoe writes, "Cool and informative. Thanks!" And Bri comments, "Wow. It really shows you how recent all of that is. Contraception was illegal is 1936. That wasn't very long ago at all and Roe V Wade was 1973, my mother was already a young girl at that time. In one way it's disturbing how slow the process has been and makes me think of how long a way we have to go, but there is also hope. We may be moving slowly, but we're moving." These comments simultaneously reveal an interest in and lack of basic knowledge of the history of reproductive rights, and emphasize the educational role that posts like these play in the feminist blogosphere. In this sense, girl bloggers often perform as teachers through their discussions about feminism's histories.

The pedagogical function of blog posts such as Julie's, must be viewed as part of a lengthy educational history within feminist media. For example, Linda Steiner (1992) documents how suffrage periodicals were crucial to the movement, explaining and legitimizing their instrumental and expressive purposes to both committed participants and those uninitiated to the suffrage agenda. Publications from the women's liberation period also served a pedagogical function, such as the seminal 1971 book *Our Bodies, Ourselves*, which contained information related to women's health and sexuality from a feminist perspective.[5] Steiner argues that feminist media producers have long been "dedicated to bringing forth knowledge to bring about transformation, not neutral observers distributing information commodities" (124). This is a significant point, in that we must recognize how feminist bloggers such as Julie and her predecessors expect that the information they relay will be used to motivate and politicize their readers. We again see how education functions as an activist strategy that has been important for feminists for over a century.

The examples in this chapter from Amandine, Kat, and Renee's blogs, as well as the *FBomb*, demonstrate a variety of approaches to the inclusion of feminist history in blogging. Amandine's well-researched discussion outlines how seemingly 'current' feminist issues often have historical lineage, drawing detailed links between feminist past and present. Kat's historical infographics are easily reblogged and circulated among readers, providing 'reminders' about important days in history for women's reproductive rights. Renee's uses of videos and images provide visual documentation of the past that she puts in conversation with contemporary concerns, and Julie's timeline of reproductive rights history maps the development of these rights in an easy to read format.

However, all of these examples use feminist history as a lens for the bloggers to better understand their own feminism in the present, mobilizing history as a source to ignite their own and their readers' activism. Education becomes key to this process, as Julie notes, as this knowledge becomes foundational to feminist activism in the present. This process also helps bloggers to understand themselves as historically situated subjects, in that the present is also historical. By sharing her own thoughts on the importance of birth control as a teen, Renee positions herself as a historical subject that is both conscious of the past and aware of the future – a positioning that youth are often assumed to not inhabit (Lesko 2001). Finally, in looking to the past these bloggers acknowledge the ways that feminist history is intricately tied to feminism's present in a way that is often obscured with discourses of postfeminism and the wave metaphor, which I will address later in this chapter.

"We Won't Stop … 'Til We Have Suffrage": Sharing History Creatively

Feminist historians have criticized the ways that mainstream history has been constructed as linear, progressive, objective, and academically situated, a form that often excludes women's experiences and voices because of their positioning outside spheres of power. New forms of history, then, such as oral history, have been important for feminists in order to make visible women's contributions, and as Joan Sangster (1994) argues, contest the reigning definitions of social, economic, and political importance that obscured women's lives. This is not a recent phenomenon as there is a lengthy history of feminists creatively telling their own histories in innovative ways. Krista Cowman (2009) describes how British suffragettes, often restricted from the masculine domains of politics and academic history, recorded and disseminated history through visual forms, such as Cicely Hamilton's Pageant of Great Women, first staged in 1909. She also notes how suffragettes would often adopt historical costumes for suffrage processions as a means of presenting precedence, honoring the past, and creating spectacle that we often forget has a longstanding role in feminist activism.

The feminist blogosphere offers a space that encourages this feminist tradition of challenging masculinist history defined by seemingly objective dates and names, in favor of presenting history in creative and playful ways. This "playful activism" embodies the spirit of many feminist blogs and third wave feminism more broadly (Keller 2012; Heywood and Drake 1997). While third wave feminists, such as media commentators Jennifer Baumgardner and Amy Richards (2000), often claim playful activism as something unique – or at least defining of – the third wave, I maintain that this strategy must be understood as extending from a much longer history going back over at least a century, as I describe earlier.

A video posted by Amandine to her blog in April 2012 is an excellent example of how feminist history is being told in creative new ways online. The video, "We Are Caught in a Bad Romance 'Til We Have Women's Suffrage," a parody of Lady Gaga's "Bad Romance" music video, is about the fight for women's suffrage in the United States and features dancing suffragettes singing about the need to get the vote.[6] The video opens with a sign announcing the "National Women's Party" with the suffragettes singing, "Vo Vo votes ah aah, whoa aa, won't ta aah, stop ha, ooo la la, 'til we have suffrage! It's gotten ugly, they passed the 15th, still women have no right no guarantee to liberty ... child, health, wealth or property!" in the tune of the popular Lady Gaga hit song. Throughout the five-minute video a story of suffrage is depicted, including violent demonstrations, mustached men singing that women, "don't need to vote," and wives dropping children onto husband's laps as they head out the door to protest (Figure 4.2).

This video may not be 'educational' or 'historical' in the traditional sense (it lacks dates, names, and places, for example), but it is nonetheless circulating American feminism's history among a wide audience that may not read a 1,000-word blog post about suffrage. Similar to the British suffragette's plays or costume processions, a video such as this one is meant to attract attention through an unusual display that is playful and fun, yet undeniably political and educational.

Figure 4.2 "We Are Caught in a Bad Romance" video, author screen shot. Used with permission of blog owner.

Nonetheless, it is important to understand why this type of historical engagement is so important to bloggers. Why would a blogger like Amandine post this video to her blog? First, a video can be quickly reblogged and shared, something that my participants stressed as being very important in the online environment. A video can be circulated with the click of a button and can be reposted to personal blogs and social networking pages, functioning as what Henry Jenkins, Sam Ford, and Joshua Green (2013) call "spreadable media." This dispersement of media widely has been crucial to contemporary feminist digital initiatives, such as the "Planned Parenthood Saved Me" campaign and the #YesAllWomen initiative.[7]

Additionally, the video has pop culture cache, drawing on the global popularity of Lady Gaga, her catchy "Bad Romance" song and edgy accompanying music video to draw attention to the importance of suffrage. This tie to Lady Gaga will most likely attract Gaga's younger female (and male) fans, many of whom may not normally come into contact with or watch a feminist video. Finally, the Bad Romance suffragette video has contemporary relevance in this U.S. election year, where there has been increased attention to both voting legislation and the "War on Women" in popular media. These qualities make it ideal for a blog post where image-based, interactive, and easily digestible material can be displayed easily and circulated widely.

Consequently, this video must be viewed as more than just a fun post, but as a strategy that employs new media production and circulation to put feminist past in conversation with present.

Carrie's blog also provides an interesting example of how feminist history is being told in creative ways online. In late summer and fall 2012, guest blogger Alanna wrote as series of posts about zines, detailing how girls can make their own.[8] This blog series is interesting to think about in relation to history because it calls upon girls to take up the creation of a historical document via a new media platform (a blog). As numerous scholars (Duncombe 1997; Schilt 2003; Kearney 2006; Piepmeier 2009) note, zines and other handmade pamphlets have been an important medium for earlier generations of feminists, produced since the 1850s. Piepmeier (2009, 29) argues that these feminist participatory media productions "have offered a snapshot of their own cultural moment's take on issues [such as gender, identity, community, and resistance]." Within this context, zines function as historical documents that not only capture moments of feminist history, but also incorporate scrapbook skills traditionally privileged in girls' and women's culture, including collage-making, drawing, and personal writing.

Piepmeier describes how, as the Internet became increasingly accessible to more people in the late 1990s and early 2000s, both scholars and popular commentators began to assume that blogs would replace zines. She explains, "Zines, then, can be seen as a sort of nostalgic medium, harking back to a punk or grunge era that no longer exists" (14). While Piepmeier goes on to argue that zines continue to be produced within the age of digital culture, it is interesting to note that it is the history of the medium that seems to fascinate Alanna and other bloggers. For example, the second entry of Alanna's three-part series, "Zines: A History Lesson," documents the history of zine culture, beginning with the science fiction fanzines of the 1930s. She goes on to describe the evolution of the subculture through 1960s counterculture publications, punks' use of the do-it-yourself (DIY) medium in the 1970s, and the feminist riot grrrl zines of the 1990s. While Alanna does not explicitly state why we should care about the lengthy history of zines as a political medium, I understand this detailed entry as suggesting that part of producing a zine requires a historical knowledge of the medium, often in the form of aesthetics, tone, and politics. For example, Alanna describes how the punk aesthetic and DIY philosophy is "crucial" to the development of zines and she includes photos to give the reader a feel for the unique aesthetics often found in zines.

Posts such as these take a unique approach to feminist history, simultaneously educating readers about the history of zinemaking as a feminist activist practice, while encouraging them to participate in the process of producing history through the creation of their own zines, something that I'll discuss in more detail in the next section. Rather than merely produce blog posts that discuss feminist history for others to read, posts like Alanna's promote an active engagement with history through a medium that has a lengthy legacy within feminism dating back over 150 years. Consequently, the use of 'new' media to deliver 'old' media to readers demonstrates the potential of blog spaces to be used for engaging with feminist history in unique and exciting ways and challenges the assumption that new media is replacing mediums often considered outdated.

Rewriting Feminism? Girl Bloggers as Historiographers

In addition to using their blogs to tell women's stories in new ways, girls are also challenging dominant histories of feminism, encouraging their readers to rethink what Chela Sandoval (2000) calls "hegemonic feminism." These bloggers are not the first to critique the privileged and published versions of feminist history as reproducing social hierarchies through excluding the voices of women of color, lower-class women, lesbian women, Third World women, and girls. Yet it is important to consider how the girl bloggers I discuss both attempt to challenge dominant portrayals of feminist history while also sometimes problematically reproducing these social hierarchies.

In the introduction to *Make Your Own History: Documenting Feminist and Queer Activism in the 21st Century*, Lyz Bly (2012, 2) writes how her own archival research made it clear to her "how much media images shaped [her] generation's image and understanding of the women's liberation movement of the 1970s." Interestingly, this sentiment was also echoed by one of my participants as well who claims that her knowledge of feminist history had come solely from mainstream media images, primarily images of women at mass rallies and protests, prior to her engagement with feminist blogging. This suggests the importance for feminists both to produce their own media and to ensure its documentation as a necessary strategy to guarantee the survival of feminist *histories*, rather than *history*.

Deborah L. Siegel (1997) cautions feminists to avoid reproducing historical accounts that obscure the heterogeneity of feminisms at any given moment. However, she argues that historiography can nonetheless be an important tool for challenging limited historical narratives. She writes, "Inasmuch as we need to problematize the writing of history so as to avoid the re-creation of master narratives, we must nevertheless continue to make history through the very act of making historiography" (62). Siegel advocates for young feminists to "read, write, and make feminist history as process ... [to] understand feminist history as perpetually in motion" (60). Her poststructuralist framework is useful for understanding history as discursively formulated narrative that can never adequately reflect an objective 'truth' about any iteration of feminism. In a similar vein, Stanford Friedman (1995) advocates for "constructing histories in the plural," suggesting that the need to make history as a political act must exist simultaneously with problematizing the practice in order to avoid the creation of grand narratives.

Based upon this literature, I am suggesting that the girl feminist bloggers I spoke to act as historiographers through the practice of blogging about feminist history. Drawing upon Stanford Friedman's excellent discussion of what a historiography of feminism might look like, I am defining the act of feminist historiography as the writing of histories that construct stories of girls and women's experiences using a feminist perspective with attention to one's own position of power within the historical narrative and the goal of social transformation or, an "oppositional bite" (Stanford Friedman 1995, 25).[9] Kearney's (2006) discussion of grrrl zinester's rewriting of feminist history reminds us that this practice must be again understood in relation to an important tradition of feminist intervention into dominant histories. For example, Kearney (2006, 177) notes how zinesters often attempted to write the contributions of women of color into their zines, as well as pop culture icons that push the boundaries of "traditional standards for female and feminist identity." Consequently, the examples I discuss here should be understood as part of this important history.

Madison is one of the bloggers who performs as a historiographer through blogging. In a July 2012 post called, "I'm Over Rosie," Madison discusses her frustration with Rosie the Riveter as one of the only visible symbols of women history and encourages her readers to embrace the history of, what she calls, "real women." She suggests that feminists have "clung on to [Rosie] so tightly" in part because "we are so desperate for some recognition of our accomplishments and our history that we took the first thing we got and ran with it." Madison's critique is smart and challenges dominant representations of feminist history by suggesting that we must make more of an effort to celebrate a range of women, such as the Women's Air Service Pilots who flew during WWII or the Air Service Nurses who played key roles in WWII and Vietnam, in order to understand the diversity of women's historical experiences. She writes,

> I say, we give up Rosie. I'm not going to take her down from my wall, or throw away my t-shirts, but I am going to stop collecting things with her face on it just because it's the only thing I can find that's women history related. Instead of dressing up as Rosie for Halloween, maybe I'll dress up as Alice Paul (the founder of the National Women's Party) or Marie Currie (who won two noble prizes). I'll celebrate the accomplishments of those women, real women.

In such a posting Madison challenges her readers to think about feminist history in new ways and even provides a lengthy list of "badass women in history" where readers can educate themselves further on women's and feminist histories. Madison's list contains a diversity of women, including lesser-known activists such as Yuri Kochiyama and Sacagawea, as well as more prominent women such as Maya Angelou, Mary Wollstonecraft, and Susan B. Anthony.

Madison's commitment to expanding her reader's knowledge of feminists throughout history can again be seen in a July 2012 posting where she re-blogs a tweet from Think Progress, a politically liberal blog, that reads: "TODAY in 1848, pioneers including Susan B. Anthony & Elizabeth Cady Stanton, met in Seneca Falls, NY and founded the Women's Movement." Madison begins her post by writing, "Oops! Historical slip-up of the day" and proceeds to explain that Think Progress' tweet is incorrect, as Anthony did not attend Seneca Falls and didn't meet Stanton until 1851. Madison corrects that it was actually Lucretia Mott who helped organize the conference. The second part of Madison's post is worth citing at length:

> Why does this matter? Women's history is not very well known as it is, most people can only name the big names: Stanton, Anthony, and Paul. It's important that we get history right so that all women can get the recognition that they deserve. Anthony, Paul, and Stanton didn't do it alone, and it's our job as progressives and feminists to make that clear. Women are routinely erased from history as it is, we shouldn't erase them further by getting our facts wrong when we talk about them. When I tweeted at Think Progress to correct them they didn't respond. I'm disappointed, you would think a progressive organization would care about getting the facts right.

Madison's entry reminds us that the contributions of many women are routinely erased from the history of feminism, which has consequences for the ways in which later generations of people understand the movement. Specifically, she implies that (masculinist) historical records often privilege the contributions of a few selected 'stars' while obscuring the important contributions of many others. I would argue that this dominant approach to history reflects a neoliberal individualist ethos at odds with how feminism (and other progressive political movements) actually came to be. While Madison says that she's disappointed that Think Progress didn't seem to care about "getting the facts right," her explanation suggests that this issue is about much more than 'correct facts,' but about a politics of history. By arguing that it's our job as feminists and progressives to 'correct' the record, Madison maintains that history remains a contentious space in which feminists have a responsibility to pay attention.

Nonetheless, despite her interest in honoring and celebrating "real women" and her acknowledgement of women's erasure from dominant histories, Madison still focuses her discussions of feminist women's history on prominent women that have been heavily celebrated, such as Alice Paul and Marie Curie. In doing so, she problematically reproduces a historical narrative centered on 'great women,' of the past in much the same way that hegemonic history has celebrated 'great men.' Madison isn't the only blogger to do this, though; indeed, I was surprised by the fact that none of the bloggers mentioned their moms or other 'everyday' women/girls they know as feminist role models and worthy of historicizing. This oversight points to the ways in which the lives of everyday women are often overlooked as being historically irrelevant, and how even well-intentioned feminists can reproduce this assumption.

Likewise, Amandine's blog reveals her interest in intervening in dominant historical narratives of feminism, especially those that assume Western religions to be only patriarchal. Amandine, who identifies as Jewish Orthodox, frequently posts about historical Jewish women (in addition to non-Jewish women) whom she argues have made important feminist contributions to the religion, yet often remain absent in both Jewish and feminist history. For example, one of her first posts explores the figure of Deborah, the Wet Nurse of Rebecca, as a woman deserving of more attention for her potentially important role in Jewish history. Another one of Amandine's early posts discusses Belva Lockwood, who she claims has "fallen into obscurity." Amandine goes on to talk about Lockwood's many accomplishments as a lawyer and her important role in feminist history, writing Lockwood back in to feminism through introducing her story to blog readers. Amandine also regularly posts feminist analyses of Jewish prayers and songs, challenging her readers to rethink some of their assumptions about religion and feminism. These types of postings demonstrate extensive research, and Amandine claims that she spends many hours researching these types of posts. In other words, this information does not just appear, but requires significant labor to unearth from online archives and other sources that can be difficult to navigate – a skill Amandine has developed as a historiographer.

Finally, the *FBomb* offers another model as to how girl bloggers are rewriting history. Every Sunday since the site's inception Julie has posted a feature on a woman or girl artist under the heading, "Support Women Artists Sunday." The weekly feature aims to recognize the contributions of women and girls to the arts, contributions that are often not publicly acknowledged or recorded in dominant histories, such as syllabi for history of film classes. While Julie does write about contemporary artists also, her inclusion of women artists from the past (both recent and more distant past) is what I'll focus on primarily here. By including contemporary artists, Julie is placing them within history, creating an archive where future readers may be able to read about them. While "Support Women Artists Sunday" is not explicitly focusing on feminist artists, many of the artists featured are indeed presented as feminist and are often positioned within their historical and cultural context, reflecting their struggle within a patriarchal culture. Thus, I am arguing that although the "Support Women Artist Sunday" feature is not explicitly promoted as an exploration of feminist history, it often functions as such, demonstrating the fluidity needed to understand the ways in which history is threaded through girls' feminist blogs.

For example, on January 1, 2012, Julie writes about Vera Chytilova, a Czech filmmaker who was influential in the Czech New Wave movement in the 1960s. A female filmmaker in an industry that continues to be male-dominated, Chytilova's films often dealt with critical social issues and were consequently censored by the communist government. The *FBomb* post introduces Chytilova to readers while writing her into feminist cultural history. Similarly, the 1980s new-wave group The Go-Go's was the topic of a September 2011 post where Julie notes how the group was "one of the first commercially successful female groups that wasn't controlled by male producers or managers." She also notes how their style, influenced by both the new wave and punk movements in the late 1970s and early 1980s "was raw and rocking; it may not have directly inspired the female alternative rockers and riot grrrls of the '90s, but it certainly foreshadowed it." Another post covers Ani DiFranco, whose most prolific time as a songwriter was around the time that many FBombers were still in diapers in the mid-1990s. The article emphasizes DiFranco's DIY (do-it-yourself) feminist roots that informed her decision to remain an independent artist throughout the entirety of her career, and again introduces an influential feminist artist to young readers.

Other bloggers have also intervened as historiographers to feminist cultural history. For example, in a November 2011 post titled "The Women *Rolling Stone* Forgot," Carrie writes,

> This week, *Rolling Stone Magazine* published a list of the 100 greatest guitarists of all time – and only two of them are women. ... I can't help but feel that some serious oversights have been made, not only by the voters (made up of mostly famous male guitarists), but by the music world at large. So, without further ado, here are just some of the many fabulous ladies who I think should have been on *Rolling Stone*'s list and who should be recognized and respected as the incredible guitarists that they are. Comment with your favorite female guitarists!

Carrie goes on to feature Carrie Brownstein (Excuse 17, Heavens to Betsy, Sleater-Kinney, Wild Flag), Lita Ford (the Runaways), Sister Rosetta Tharpe ("original soul sister" of the 1930s and 1940s), and Allison Robertson (the Donnas) as female guitarists worthy of attention. In doing so, Carrie intervenes in the hegemonic historical record legitimated through *Rolling Stone*, using the space of her blog to write her own history and inviting others to do the same through the comments section.

It is significant to note how women in popular culture, especially female musicians, serve as feminist role models for my study participants and their peers. This is not surprising, considering how popular music has been and continues to be one of the primary spaces for feminist expression, communication, and networking (Kearney 2006). For example, Kearney (2006, 177) outlines the ways in which grrrl zinesters frequently wrote about female musicians, often "resurrect[ing] and reclaim[ing] female performers who have been disparaged or silenced as a result of their radical, eccentric, or perverse ideas or behavior, thereby refusing simultaneously both male history and traditional standards for female and feminist identity." Kearney suggests that this may be due to the ability of popular musicians to speak to young people who may be alienated by academic feminist rhetoric, and I would add, adult feminists who may disregard girls' experiences and ideas.

By re-writing feminist musicians and other popular culture figures into history, girl feminist bloggers are challenging not only a masculinist history of popular culture, but also an adult-centered feminist history that tends to omit/disregard women and girls who have performed feminism primarily within popular culture spaces. In doing so, girl feminist bloggers produce and circulate new feminist "counter-memories" (Foucault 1980) that highlight girls' interest in and commitment to feminism. However, I do want to acknowledge how many of the women that girl feminist bloggers are writing about in their historical posts are white and American, with only the odd exception (Carrie's mentioning of Sister Rosetta Tharpe, for example). Consequently, whereas the girl bloggers I spoke to verbalize their commitment to democratizing history, their postings again only represent a partial history where the voices of women of color, non-American, and lesbian women remain somewhat marginal. When women of color are discussed, for example, it is often already celebrated women that receive mention, such as bell hooks or Maya Angelou.

I was also surprised to see that the bloggers did not attempt to highlight *girls'* contributions to feminist history. Considering the importance that my study participants place on age within their own feminist practices, the invisibility of girl feminists as historical role models on girls' feminist blogs suggests a significant dissonance. This lack of attention to girl feminists' positioning in history is likely due to the paucity of information on such girls. Indeed, my own research into the history of girls' feminist activism has revealed little scholarship or popular press about the topic. This significant historical gap is easily reproduced, and problematically renders feminist girls' historical record invisible on contemporary feminist girls' blogs.[10]

Researching Women's History: The Case for Online Networks

It is probably not surprising that few bloggers I interviewed claim to have learned about feminist history in school, with the exception of a few girls lucky enough to have a rare feminist teacher in (an often private) middle or high school. Where then can girls learn about feminist history? In the third chapter of this book I argue for understanding girl feminist bloggers as part of networked counterpublics whose sustained connections are valuable and vital to sustaining the feminist blogosphere. Through my interviews, I discovered that it is these networks that also provide resources for girls' historical research on feminism, and in turn, girl bloggers aim to 'pass on the favor' through serving as a resource for feminist history for their readers. In this sense, girls can be historiographers in part because of their participation in networks that provide them access to a variety of online resources where they can conduct their own research on feminist history.

Almost all of the bloggers participating in the focus group spoke of various blogs, websites, and other online resources that serve as their primary resources for learning about the feminist history included in their own blogs. For example, Kat tells me, "I honestly think I've learned the most from Tumblr. I owe it all to the blog *Historical Slut*. She is always posting about the history of feminism and female issues. I found this blog from following other feminist Tumblrs. It is one of my favorites." Likewise, Courtney explains,

> I feel like I learned the most [about feminist history] from blogs on Tumblr … *Lipstick Feminists* is probably where I have learned the most. They're usually super good about reblogging/making posts about important days for feminism or leaders in the movement. [Amandine's blog] is also one of my favorites, very insightful and easy to read … I've definitely come across a LOT more names, women like Marie Curie and Rosalind Franklin. Just a lot of stuff I never got the chance to learn in school.

Amandine often uses online sources like the *New York Times* archive and is also "particularly fond of using videos of interviews or events as sources, it's actually how I made a really cool feminist second waver friend!" These responses remind us how feminist blogs (as well as other online resources) are serving an educational function that is a crucial part of circulating feminist knowledge among a diversity of readers.

In this sense, girl feminist bloggers use the Internet as an archive, "poaching" (de Certeau 1984) from various sites in order to write their own feminist histories. Internet scholars have discussed the web in such a way, highlighting how web 2.0 sites like YouTube, for example, serve as what Jean Burgess and Joshua Green (2009, 88) call a "living archive of contemporary culture from a large and diverse range of sources." Similarly, Jodi Dean (2006, n.p.) argues that blogs "are archives, specific accountings of the passage of time that can then be explored, returned to, dug up." Based on my conversations with the bloggers, it seems as though the girls are indeed using online sources in such a way and incorporating their findings into their own posts.

This practice then also points to the bloggers' role as archivists, creating their own "mini-archives" of feminist content that circulates among their networks. For example, Amandine's entry about Belva Lockwood involved using the online *New York Times* archive to research the post, which then circulated via Amandine's various feminist counterpublic networks, such as those focusing on teenage and Jewish feminist issues. Many of Amandine's readers would not have read the original *New York Times* articles, and thus Amandine's decision to circulate such as history becomes fundamental to the inclusion of women like Lockwood within the young feminist blogosphere and the creation of counter-memories. Through the use of feminist zines, blogs, and other digital grassroots projects, Chidgey (2012, 95–96) argues that

> tentative counter-memories are therefore produced, cited, and cir-
> culated, creating new archives of meaning whilst also revisiting
> residual investments. These counter-memories draw on mainstream
> media accounts, challenge them, and further appropriate commercial
> platforms such as YouTube and Issuu to popularize and disseminate
> personal narratives held in a collectivity ... An uneven terrain, feminist
> cultural memory embraces the experiences, artefacts, stories and also
> silences – from the personal to the institutional, and always mediated –
> that shape identities, structures of belonging, and affective economies.
> As such, memories have political consequences.

I cite Chidgey at length because she makes two key points relevant to my own analysis. First, her recognition of the intertwining of mainstream media and commercial platforms with girls' feminist blogs demonstrates how "participatory culture," what Jenkins (2006) describes as a culture where consumers also produce cultural texts, functions as a significant aspect of girls' practice of historiography. We can see this in many of the examples I've discussed, such as the Lady Gaga video posted by Amandine, or Carrie's critique of *Rolling Stone Magazine*. Thus, the "mini-archives" produced and circulated by girl feminist bloggers must be viewed as part of a wider, contemporary participatory media culture that they're contrib-uting to through their own labor of researching, writing, and circulating their historical posts.

Second, I want to highlight Chidgey's acknowledgment of the connection between feminist cultural memory and structures of belonging, something I've emphasized throughout this chapter. By performing as historiographers and creating "mini-archives" girl feminist bloggers are producing links to the past that allow them to imagine themselves as belonging to a larger movement of women and girls beyond their current historical positioning, challenging the "pastness" of feminism promoted by postfeminist discourses (McRobbie 2009). The "mini-archives" they create extend this structure of belonging into the future, where other girls may discover them and learn about feminist history from the stories they tell.

What Fourth Wave? Moving Beyond the Wave Metaphor

Thus far I have outlined the various ways that girl bloggers have been engag-ing with feminist history on their blogs. But how do bloggers view their own positioning in feminist history, particularly in relation to the dominant wave metaphor used to describe such history and feminists' place in it? I conclude this chapter by considering this question, drawing on the discussions I had with my participants about the wave metaphor in order to better understand the usefulness of labels like the 'fourth wave' within a digitally mediated cultural context.

In November 2009 the *New York Times Magazine* published a question and answer interview with feminist blogger/author/public speaker Jessica Valenti titled "Fourth-Wave Feminism." The article generated speculation about this supposed 'fourth wave' based on Valenti's response to the question posed by Deborah Solomon if she considered herself a third wave feminist: "I don't much like the terminology, because it never seems very accurate to me. I know people who are considered third-wave feminists who are 20 years older than me." When Solomon followed up by asking, "maybe we're onto the fourth wave now?" Valenti responded with, "Maybe the fourth wave is online." Valenti later commented on her personal blog that when she found out the title of the interview, she "instinctively made a face" (Valenti 2009). She writes that while she's never been a fan of the wave model because it contributes to generational tension, she nonetheless believes that "feminists today do things differently than feminists in the 60s, or the 90s, or shit, even two or three years ago." She explains,

> That's the incredible thing about feminism; it's constantly evolving. After all, we kind of have to; the world and sexism and patriarchy aren't stagnant things, so we can't be either. I also think there's something to the idea that there's a new model for feminism being built online. For better or worse, the Internet has changed feminist organizing, writing and networking *forever* …
>
> So maybe the work we're doing *is* the fourth wave. But it's probably more accurate to describe what's going on online as fourth *waves*. Because there's no one cohesive movement, or one feminist platform, or one feminist leader. There are multiple online feminisms and feminist communities. To some, those who feel a social justice movement needs a monolithic center, the ideas of 'waves' may seem disorganized or odd. But really, it's perfect …
>
> So perhaps I was wrong; maybe the wave model is useful after all – *if* we use it to honor the complexity and nuance that is feminism, instead of relying on a strict framework that homogenizes what is, in its essence, wonderfully complicated (emphasis in original).

Valenti's response illustrates the complex ways that feminist bloggers are grappling with the wave metaphor, yet she is not prescriptive to her readers. Instead, she leaves the possibility of fourth waves open for others to adopt or not.[11]

Before I began my interviews I expected the bloggers to identify with this supposed emerging fourth wave, considering their use of the Internet in their own feminist activism as bloggers. Indeed, Julie's personal website claims that she's "one of the leaders of the fourth wave feminist movement"

(Zeilinger 2012b). However, I was surprised to discover that none of my study participants identified as fourth wave, and several had never heard of the term. Amandine tells me,

> I've heard of the fourth wave and I think it's stupid. I like the wave metaphor because historically, it's very accurate: very active, not so active, very active, no so active, very active. From the 90s until now, there hasn't really been a period of 'not so active,' so I don't see why there has to be a fourth wave just yet. I understand that people could argue that there have been two halves to the third wave, since the age of the Internet heralded Feminism 2.0 mid-wave, but to argue for a fourth wave IMHO [in my humble opinion] is jumping the gun.

Similarly, Renee argues that, "I don't think we're ready to move on [to a new wave] just yet. If the third wave has been ushered in with the advent of technology and various communication methods, I think the fourth wave should coincide with the 'next big breakthrough,' though I don't know what that will be." Even Julie tells me that, "I personally don't identify with the third wave … but I don't really think we're in a fourth wave either. If the fourth wave is defined by use of the Internet, I know women in their 30s who are still considered 'young' bloggers and who really pioneered feminism on the Internet so it doesn't seem right for my generation of teens/20-somethings to claim this movement as solely our own." Julie's comment again points to the complicated intersection between waves and generations, revealing uncertainty about the start and end of particular generations and waves.[12]

Despite having reservations about simplistic relationships between generations and waves, some bloggers ultimately understood their own wave positioning in relation to when they were born, but even this marker remained somewhat murky for the bloggers. For example, while Julie, who was born in 1993, does not identify as third wave, Amandine, who was born in 1995, reluctantly considers herself a third wave. She tells me, "I do consider myself part of the third wave because time-wise that's how it worked out for me. However, in general I don't really like third wave feminists, and I think the issues they spend so much time and effort on are such an embarrassingly large waste." In addition to finding the third wave "trying too hard to be politically correct," Amandine dislikes what she perceives as the third wave obsession with sex to the detriment of other issues. She elaborates,

> I'm not trying to say that sex and all the related issues (pregnancy and abortion, bullying based on perceived promiscuity or lack thereof, pornography and sex work, etc.) isn't important, since it is, but many younger feminists only pay attention to sex-related issues and abandon other ones. For example, childcare. This is a women's issue that has yet to be solved, but it's absolutely critical to women's equality in the workplace and economy. And yet feminists pay little attention to it.

Amandine's comment surprised me because I assumed that if girl bloggers were not identifying as fourth wave, that the third wave would then
serve as a primary identity for the bloggers. However, as Amandine suggests, third wave identification is complicated for the bloggers. Amandine
considers herself a part of the third wave, but she does not necessarily
consider herself a third wave feminist. Carrie, on the other hand, views
the third wave not as Amandine describes it, but more centered on the
riot grrrl movement, which was her entry into feminism as a musician.
Amandine and Carrie's view of the third wave reveal how people experience the waves in different ways depending on personal experiences. In
other words, the 'third wave' can't mean only one thing, but can be viewed
as a historical period, an ideological perspective, and/or a collection of
multiple issues and strategies.

Renee also echoes these ideas when she claims, "I thought of myself as
a feminist before I thought of myself as a third waver … Honestly, I think
I'm more connected to my identity as a feminist than I am as a third waver,
because … it does kind of divide you from the older generation. I think feminist is just good because it unites everybody." Renee's comments are interesting because they depart from feminist writing in the mid-1990s to the early
2000s, when a third wave feminist identity seemed to be a significant identi-
fier that was mobilized to indicate third wavers as distinct from their predecessors.[13] Although it is impossible to definitely conclude why this shift
seems to be occurring among some young bloggers, the cultural context that
bloggers grew up in may suggest some possible answers. In an era characterized by disintegrating coalitional organizing and collective politics, bloggers
seem to be eager to articulate themselves as part of a movement that has a
sense of historical lineage. This is evident from Renee's comment that she
gets a "proud feeling" not from forging a new feminist politics different
from past feminisms, but from being a part of a larger feminist continuum.

I argue that the feminist history lessons that happen in the blogosphere
contribute to encouraging girls to think more critically about the wave metaphor, leading to more ambivalent identifications with the third wave than
I expected. This does not mean that all bloggers reject the wave metaphor,
although some, like Madison, do. Madison tells me that while she used to
like the wave metaphor, her experience as a blogger on Tumblr – and specifically her interactions with the blog *Historical Slut* – has changed her mind,
and she now sees the wave metaphor as unnecessarily separating women's
organizing and discrediting the feminist work that continues to happen
between the supposed waves. She says,

> I feel like in school or formal history settings the wave metaphor makes
> it seem like you had all these feminists in the 20s and then they just
> died out until the 1970s! … But when you actually learn the history of
> women's movements, you realize that Alice Paul was working all the
> way into the 30s and 40s, you realize that things were a happening all

the time – it really complicates the wave metaphor – where do things start or end? It's constant.

Madison's point is an important one, because it again highlights how feminist work can become erased through relying on dominant historical narratives. She concludes, "I don't know if we're in the third wave now, or if it ended, or what's going on, but I'd like my feminist work to be valued, just as much as if we're in a wave."

Conclusion: Reinvigorating (Digital) Feminist Histories

This chapter outlined four major ways in which girl bloggers are creatively engaging with history via their blogging practices: (1) by writing about particular historical feminist figures; (2) by connecting present feminist issues with past feminist struggles; (3) by telling history in new ways using the architecture of the web; and (4) by performing as historiographers through rewriting feminist histories. These practices, I maintain, allow the bloggers to complicate the wave metaphor, understand their own feminist identities in more fluid ways, and challenge the "disarticulation" (McRobbie 2009) and generationalization (Scharff 2012) of feminism prevalent within our postfeminist culture. I contend that we must understand girl feminist bloggers as historiographers, conscientiously intervening into hegemonic history by re-writing histories of feminism on their blogs, and in doing so, educating other girls about important aspects of feminist history.

We must understand these practices within a larger cultural framework where feminism and it's histories are often absent from school curricula, and derided with a postfeminist popular culture which suggests that feminism is something of the past. Consequently, girl feminist bloggers' production and circulation of feminist histories – as well as their own contributions to history through sharing their personal stories – is an important part of their activist practice, fulfilling both an educational function as well as generating feelings of belonging that extend into both the past and the future.

Notes

1. Madison positions Kathleen Hanna as a historical figure, despite the fact that she remains active in feminist politics today. This is likely due to the fact that most bloggers know Hanna through her participation in riot grrrl as the singer of Bikini Kill, who broke up in 1996 (a year when most of my participants were toddlers or small children). Consequently, these young bloggers seem to view her as a historical figure, although this characterization is not accurate.

2. Access to contraception was also a national hot button issue during the time of my research, as President Obama's Affordable Care Act (ACA) added contraception to a list of preventative services covered by the ACA without patient co-pays, as of August 1, 2011. It is this legislation that the bloggers discuss as "no cost" birth control.

3. See Lister et al. (2003) for an expanded discussion about interactivity within digital media.

4. This post was written before the latest assaults on women's reproductive rights in the U.S. in 2011 and 2012. Julie includes the following link for more information on the history of birth control in the United States: http://www.plannedparent hood.org/aboutus/who-we-are/history-and-successes.htm.

5. *Our Bodies, Ourselves* began as a stapled newsprint pamphlet in 1970. Twelve women created the booklet during a workshop on "women and their bodies" at a Boston area women's liberation conference in response to the male dominated field of medicine. The DIY booklet was an underground success and was later published as an expanded edition by Simon & Schuster and renamed *Our Bodies, Ourselves*. I highlight this important history here because it demonstrates both the pedagogical function of feminist media, as well as the power of DIY media production to influence social transformation. See http://www.our bodiesourselves.org/about/history.asp for more information about this history.

6. I am not including the URL to Amandine's posting in order to protect her privacy. However, the video was created by Soomo Publishing and can be viewed on their website at http://soomopublishing.com/suffrage/. Other information about the making of the video can also be found here.

7. The "Planned Parenthood Saved Me" campaign was launched by Deanna Zandt in early February 2012 after the Susan G. Komen Foundation announced they would be ceasing to fund Planned Parenthood in late January 2012. In order to publicize how important Planned Parenthood is to the lives of American women, Zandt asked women to send her their stories about how Planned Parenthood has "saved" them and published them on her Tumblr blog. She received many touching stories about Planned Parenthood helping women through the aftermath of sexual assault, providing life-saving medical screenings that found early stage cancer, and making available contraceptive and family planning information that prevented unwanted pregnancies. Zandt received the 2012 Maggie Award from Planned Parenthood for her efforts. See http://plannedparenthoodsavedme.tumblr.com/.

   The #YesAllWomen Twitter hashtag was popularized after Elliot Rodger cited his hatred of women and sexual rejection as the reason for murdering six people in California in May 2014. Employing the hashtag, thousands of women around the world shared their experiences of gender-based violence and experiences with misogyny. The campaign was extensively covered in the mainstream press and arguably brought significant attention to the problem of misogyny, harassment, and gender-based violence.

8. A similar article titled "How to Make a Zine" appeared in *Rookie* magazine in May 2012, suggesting the popularity of zines among young feminist bloggers.

9. Based upon my own theoretical orientation, I have drawn more heavily on Stanford Friedman's discussion of a poststructuralist approach to feminist historiography; however, it is important to recognize that there are multiple ways that one may approach feminist historiography.

10. I am suggesting that this is a topic in need of further research. How might we as feminist scholars produce girls' history as public knowledge? How might we better educate girls on their contributions to the movement? These are crucial questions for feminist scholars interested in the future of feminist activism.

11. See Hewitt 2010; Dicker 2008; and Piepmeier 2009 for comprehensive discussions about the usefulness of the wave metaphor in feminist scholarship.

12. Julie's comments are interesting considering the label of "fourth wave feminism" that appeared on her website at the time of this writing. I suspect that this discrepancy may suggest the marketing appeal of the wave metaphor, rather than any interest among young feminists themselves in the label.

13. Of course, not all third wave feminists emphasized the distinction between themselves and the women liberationists. For example, I previously discussed how Kearney (2006) described the connections that many riot grrrls forged with older feminists through their zinemaking. Some of the perceived divides between the feminists of the women's liberation movement and the third wavers may be manufactured by writers such as Katie Rophie, whose feminist credentials are questionable, despite her own identification with the label (see Henry 2004). Nonetheless, the shift from girls and women using the third wave label in feminist publications to the lack of wave identification as evidenced by many feminist blogs point to an interesting shift worthy of further study. See Piepmeier (2009) for a discussion of this debate.

References

Baumgardner, Jennifer, and Amy Richards. 2000. *Manifesta: Young Women, Feminism, and the Future.* New York: Farrar, Straus and Giroux.

Bly, Lyz. 2012. "Introduction: Scholars, Archivists and Invisible Alliances." In *Make Your Own History: Documenting Feminist and Queer Activism in the 21st Century*, edited by Liz Bly and Kelly Wooten, 1–2. Los Angeles: Litwine Books.

Burgess, Jean, and Joshua Green. 2009. *YouTube: Online Video and Participatory Culture.* Malden: Polity.

Chidgey, Red. 2012. "Hand-Made Memories: Remediating Cultural Memory in DIY Feminist Networks." In *Feminist Media: Participatory Spaces, Networks and Cultural Citizenship*, edited by Elke Zobl and Ricarda Drueke, 87–97. Germany: Transcript.

Cowman, Krista. 2009. " 'There Is So Much, and It Will All Be History:' Feminist Activists as Historians, the Case of British Suffrage as Historiography, 1908–2007." In *Gendering Historiography: Beyond National Canons*, edited by Angelika Epple and Angelika Schaser, 141–162. Frankfurt: Campus Verlag.

Dean, Jodi. 2006. "Blogging Theory." *Bad Subjects*, 75. Accessed March 1, 2013. http://bad.eserver.org/issues/2006/75/dean.htm.

Dean, Jodi. 2010. *Blog Theory: Feedback and Capture in the Circuits of Drive.* Malden: Polity Press.

De Certeau, Michel. 1984. *The Practice of Everyday Life.* Berkeley, CA: University of California Press.

Dicker, Rory. 2008. *A History of U.S. Feminisms.* Berkeley: Seal Press.

Duncombe, Stephen. 1997. *Notes From the Underground.* New York: Verso.

Foucault, Michel. 1980. *Language, Counter-memory, Practice: Selected Essays and Interviews By Michel Foucault.* Edited by Donald Bouchard. Cornell: Cornell University Press.

Henry, Astrid. 2004. *Not My Mother's Sister: Generational Conflict and Third-Wave Feminism.* Bloomington: Indiana University Press.

Hewitt, Nancy. 2010. "Introduction." In *No Permanent Waves: Recasting Histories of U.S. Feminism*, edited by Nancy Hewitt, 1–12. New Brunswick: Rutgers University Press.

Heywood, Leslie, and Drake, Jennifer. 1997. *Third Wave Agenda: Being Feminist, Doing Feminism.* Minneapolis: University of Minnesota Press.

Hunter, Jane. 2002. *How Young Ladies Became Girls: The Victorian Origins of Girlhood.* New Haven: Yale University.

Jenkins, Henry. 2006. *Convergence Culture: Where Old and New Media Collide.* New York: New York University Press.

Jenkins, Henry, Sam Ford, and Joshua Green. 2013. *Spreadable Media: Creating Value and Meaning in a Networked Culture.* New York: New York University Press.

Kearney, Mary Celeste. 2006. *Girls Make Media.* New York: Routledge.

Kearney, Mary Celeste. 2014. "Historicize This! Contextualism in Youth Media Studies." In *Youth Cultures in the Age of Global Media,* edited by David Buckingham, Sara Bragg and Mary Jane Kehily, 53–68. New York: Palgrave Macmillan.

Keller, Jessalynn. 2012. "Virtual Feminisms: Girls' Blogging Communities, Feminist Activism and Participatory Politics." *Information, Communication & Society* 15(3): 429–447.

Lesko, Nancy. 2001. *Act Your Age! A Cultural Construction of Adolescence.* New York: Routledge.

Lister, Martin, Jon Dovey, Seth Giddens, Iain Grant, and Kieran Kelly. 2003. *New Media: A Critical Introduction.* New York: Routledge.

McRobbie, Angela. 2009. *The Aftermath of Feminism: Gender, Culture and Social Change.* Thousand Oaks: Sage.

Paletschek, Sylvia. 2009. "Opening Up Narrow Boundaries: Memory Culture, Historiography and Excluded Histories from a Gendered Perspective." In *Gendering Historiography: Beyond National Canons*, edited by Angelika Epple and Angelika Schaser, 163–177. Frankfurt: Campus Verlag.

Paradez, Deborah. 2009. *Selenidad: Selena, Latinos, and the Performance of Memory.* Durham: Duke University Press.

Piepmeier, Alison. 2009. *Girl Zines: Making Media, Doing Feminism.* New York: New York University Press.

Pike, Kirsten. 2011. "'The New Activists:' Girls and Discourses of Citizenship, Liberation, and Femininity in Seventeen, 1968–1977." In *Mediated Girlhoods: New Explorations of Girls' Media Culture,* edited by Mary Celeste Kearney, 55–73. New York: Peter Lang.

Q. 2012. "Riot Grrrl Pioneer Kathleen Hanna," December 12. http://www.cbc.ca/q/blog/2012/12/12/riot-grrrl-pioneer-kathleenhanna/.

Sandoval, Chela. 2000. *Methodology of the Oppressed.* Minneapolis: University of Minnesota Press.

Sangster, Joan. 1994. "Telling Our Stories: Feminist Debates and the Use of Oral History." *Women's History Review* 3(1): 5–28.

Scharff, Christina. 2012. *Repudiating Feminism: Young Women in a Neoliberal World.* Surry: Ashgate Publications.

Schilt, Kristen. 2003. "'I'll Resist with Every Inch and Every Breath:' Girls and Zine Making as a Form of Resistance." *Youth & Society* 35(1): 71–97.

Siegel, Deborah. 1997. "Reading Between the Waves: Feminist Historiography in a 'Postfeminist' Moment." In *Third Wave Agenda: Being Feminist, Doing Feminism*, edited by Leslie Heywood and Jennifer Drake, 55–82. Minneapolis: University of Minnesota Press.

Stanford Friedman, Susan. 1995. "Making History: Reflections on Feminism, Narrative, and Desire." In *Feminism Beside Itself,* edited by Diane Elam and Robyn Wiegman, 11–53. New York: Routledge.

Steiner, Linda. 1992. "The History and Structure of Women's Alternative Media." In *Women Making Meaning: New Feminist Directions in Communication*, edited by Lana Rakow, 121–143. New York: Routledge.

Terranova, Tiziana. 2005. *Network Culture: Politics for the Information Age.* London: Pluto Press.

Valenti, Jessica. 2009. "The Fourth Wave(s) of Feminism," personal blog, November 14. http://jessicavalenti.com/2009/11/14/the-fourth-waves-of-feminism/.

Zeilinger, Julie. 2012a. *A Little F' d Up: Why Feminism Is Not a Dirty Word.* Berkeley: Seal Press.

Zeilinger, Julie. 2012b. Author website. Accessed February 23, 2013. http://www.juliezeilinger.com.

5 Performing a Public Politics
Feminist Girl Bloggers and New Citizenship Practices

"Feminist communities like the FBomb, as well as individually curated blogs, allow young women to become comfortable with not only developing our opinions and ideas, but to publicly publish them – to refuse to buy into a culture that encourages our silence and subservience."
—Julie Zeilinger, March 15, 2013, FBomb

"Revenge of the Teenage Girl" was the cover story headline on the September 27, 2014 issue of the Canadian newsmagazine *Macleans*, printed in bold beside an image of a defiant teenage girl clad in jeans and a plaid shirt. The accompanying story by Anne Kingston describes how "the voices of teenage girls have taken on cultural currency," and details how girls, many of them bloggers and avid users of social media, are increasingly involved in feminist activism online and in their schools and communities. Girls are portrayed as agents of social change, a refreshing departure from the dominant mediated representations of teenage girls.

I introduce this chapter with the *Macleans* article because it aptly illustrates the increasing presence of adolescent girls as public, political figures – one of the arguments I will make throughout this chapter. Yet, I also extend this argument, suggesting that the vocal politics practiced by many teenage girls, including the feminist girl bloggers I discuss throughout this book, must be regarded as a practice of citizenship – a way for girls to participate in the public sphere as political agents. I develop this argument by exploring how feminist girl bloggers produce discursive space within mainstream commercial popular culture to perform feminism publically, a strategy that represents a shift away from the traditional notion of girls' more passive, private, and apolitical "bedroom culture" (McRobbie and Garber 1991) and raises significant questions about what it means for girls to *be public* and create *public culture* within our contemporary neo-liberal and postfeminist context. Several questions then guide this inquiry: In what ways are girl feminist bloggers fashioning a new type of girlhood activism through their public engagement with mainstream media? How are hegemonic discourses of girlhood being challenged by such practices? And finally, how might girl feminist bloggers' public subjectivities demonstrate a practice of citizenship?

I begin this chapter by outlining feminist scholarship on citizenship, highlighting the need to develop a conception of citizenship that grants agency to teenage girls. I then discuss two hegemonic contemporary discourses that shape the ways in which girls' public engagements are often framed, focusing particularly on how digital media technologies intersect with both of these discourses: (1) A postfeminist "girl power" discourse prominent since the late 1990s that encourages girls to "live large" through public visibility and display (Hopkins 2002; Harris 2004); and (2) A protectionist discourse that warns girls of making their bodies *too public*. I will discuss this specifically in relation to warnings about the threats related to new media technologies, such as sexting, cyberstalking, and other breaches of privacy. These contradictory discourses suggest a precarious public positioning of girls within a contemporary new media culture, one in which girls are rewarded for being seen as active, yet not heard as political or activist voices.

I then turn to discuss three girl feminist bloggers – Julie Zeilinger, Jamie Keiles, and Tavi Gevinson – as indicative of girl feminist bloggers' ability to perform a public feminist girlhood. Drawing on a discursive and ideological textual analysis of these girls' blog posts, media coverage, and business practices, I outline how these bloggers have utilized entrepreneurial strategies to publicize their media production and to vocalize their feminist politics, complicating neoliberal discourses of girlhood. I argue that Julie, Jamie, and Tavi have successfully created political spaces within public media culture, challenging "can-do" girlhood (Harris 2004) through a specifically activist agenda. This distinguishes these bloggers from many girls visible in popular media culture, often in roles within the entertainment industry, who do not perform as political activists publicly. Nonetheless, I call attention to the cultural and social capital needed to partake in such public activism, contending that many girls are excluded from this type of activism due to a marginalized position with regards to classed, raced, sexual, religious, ethnic, and/or other identities.

Next, I turn to my case study of Tavi Gevinson in order to explore these issues in more depth, analyzing relevant media coverage since her emergence as a fashion blogger five years ago at the age of twelve until the launch of *Rookie Yearbook One* in September 2012. I locate and examine three dominant discourses that were used by adult journalists, bloggers, and fashion insiders in an attempt to contain Tavi's[1] threat to patriarchal and adult-controlled popular culture. I argue that unlike many publicly visible girl celebrities, Tavi was deemed threatening because of her disruption of both postfeminist can-do and protectionist discourses related to public girlhood via the agency she has exercised over her media production and career, and later, her feminist politics. I contend that her adoption and performance of a feminist subjectivity became significant for Tavi's negotiation of public space and represents a significant intervention in popular culture. Consequently, this case study makes visible the ways in which feminist media production practices, such as blogging, provides both the discursive and technical skills for girls to challenge hegemonic discourses of girlhood and circulate alter-ative discourses about who a girl is and what a girl can be.

I conclude this chapter by arguing that Julie, Jamie, and Tavi have fash-ioned a new type of girlhood feminist activism that disrupts both can-do and protectionist discourses of public girlhood via their blogging prac-tices, thereby challenging public/private, visible/invisible, vocal/silent, and commercial/alternative cultural binaries. In doing so, girl feminist bloggers open up a public space for girls to not only access feminism, but practice citizenship as feminist, political, and activist actors in their own right.

Reframing the Girl Citizen

In her seminal book *Citizenship: Feminist Perspectives* Ruth Lister (1997, 3) argues that "behind the cloak of gender-neutrality that embraces the idea [of citizenship] there lurks in much of the literature a definitely male citi-zen and it is his interests and concerns that have traditionally dictated the agenda." Lister contends that citizenship is a gendered concept that operates simultaneously as a mechanism of both inclusion and exclusion relating to gender, as well as class, race, ability, and sexuality. However, both Lister and Rian Voet (1998) argue that the concept remains a fruitful one for femi-nist engagement, offering, "an invaluable strategic theoretical concept for the analysis of women's subordination and a potentially powerful political weapon in the struggle against it" through a focus on (women's) agency (Lister 1997, 195).

It is Lister's focus on agency that I'm interested in, and which she argues connects definitions of citizenship as a status and as a practice. Understanding citizenship as a status recognizes the set of rights, including social and reproductive rights, that one carries. Citizenship as a practice, however, refers to one's political participation, including what Lister calls the "informal politics" in which women are more likely to engage. These informal politics include a range of activities, such as local community organizing around health and education of children, and other actions outside of the formal political sphere of government. One of Lister's key contributions is to acknowledge the dialectical relationship between these two traditions of citizenship by arguing that "citizenship as the expression of agency contributes to the recasting of women as actors on the political stage" (199). This argument suggests that valuing the multiple ways that women act in and between private and public spheres is essential to a femi-nist model of citizenship.

While this scholarship highlights how citizenship has been gendered and recognizes the multiple practices of citizenship, it does not thoroughly address girls. In other words, while including gender (as well as race, class, nationality, and sexuality to a certain extent) as a category of analysis, Lister and Voet retain an adult-centric approach to citizenship. However, citizen-ship has recently become an increasingly important – and contentious – issue for youth studies scholars (Aapola, Gonick, and Harris 2005; Harris 2012b). Indeed, citizenship in its most basic and long-standing sense, referring to participation in formal political institutions centered around rights and responsibilities, has always excluded children and youth, understanding them as minor, and thus, future citizens or citizens in training (Banet-Weiser 2007; Harris 2012b). Yet, increasingly young people are expected to be working toward economic self-sufficiency in preparation to become productive, independent citizens as national governments reduce their responsibilities to their constituents – a cultural context that calls into question traditional notions about what it means to be a citizen (Aapola, Gonick, and Harris 2005).

Cultural studies scholars have also argued for the need to "decenter notions of citizenship" by conceptualizing multiple sites and modes of discourse as representing valid citizenship practices (Dimitriadis 2008, x). This intervention has resulted in a more expansive conceptualization of citizenship that now often encompasses consumer and cultural dimensions (Miller 2007; Burgess, Foth, and Klaebe 2006). Consequently, "cultural citizenship" has gained prominence in much of this literature, yet remains vague in its application to particular practices. For example, Elisabeth Klaus and Margreth Lunenborg (2012, 204) define cultural citizenship as encompassing:

> all those cultural practices that allow competent participation in society and includes the rights to be represented and to speak actively. Media as a particular form of cultural production is both an engine and an actor in the processes of self-making and being-made, in which people acquire their individual, group-specific and social identities.

This definition highlights how producing media both fosters cultural citizenship and can be a practice of citizenship itself. This has significant implications as digital technologies have expanded the opportunity for people to produce their own media, a practice that has been taken up in particular by youth and young adults. Jean Burgess, Marcus Foth, and Helen Klaebe (2006, 1) argue that new media provide fresh spaces for "the greater visibility and community-building potential of cultural citizenship's previously 'ephemeral' practices." Thus, the significance of new media lies in its ability to facilitate everyday active participation in a networked, open, and flexible cultural public sphere that encompasses entertainment, leisure, consumption, and political activities. In this sense, cultural citizenship practices in a new media age mean community-building through social networking platforms, sharing content through web 2.0 technologies, and conversing about a television program via a popular blog, rather than voting, attending a rally, or even talking about political candidates online.

Young people's participation in these alternative modes of citizenship is complicated by an increasingly pervasive neoliberal cultural climate over the past fifteen years. Harris (2004, 71) argues that this is especially true for girls, who are depicted as "leading the way for youth citizenship … forging their nations, becoming responsible self-made citizens, and are expected to either lead a revival in youth participation in the polity or make successes of themselves without state intervention." This conception of citizenship is informed by neoliberal policies that promote citizenship as marked by individual responsibility, active participation in the market economy, proper consumption practices, and the ability to engage in flexible self-reinvention as dictated by a rapidly changing economy (Harris 2004; McRobbie 2009). This model of citizenship is highly regulative, promoting managed forms of participation and consumption and limiting girls' engagement to adult-approved initiatives and civic engagement programs (Harris 2004). Although girls may be highly visible as neoliberal consumer citizens, they have little agency in terms of defining their own politics and enacting their own strategies for change. Instead, postfeminist discourses privilege consumer citizenship for girls via their emphasis on the body and the makeover paradigm, encouraging girls to purchase fashion, beauty, and other lifestyle products as an exercise of 'empowered' postfeminist consumer citizenship (Harris 2004; McRobbie 2009).

Thus, scholarship that addresses citizenship often leaves girls in a precarious position, excluded from traditional definitions of citizenship, yet hailed as consumer citizens by commercial media informed by neoliberal and postfeminist discourses. In this chapter I seek to advance an alternative conception of citizenship for girls that addresses their particular social and cultural positioning and recognizes the various modes of agency accessible to them. Drawing on the scholarship I've outlined in this section, I understand citizenship as a practice in which girls agentially "speak up in the public sphere" (Klaus and Lunenborg 2012, 204) in order to articulate their own ideas, desires, and criticisms. This definition will inform my understanding of citizenship as I map how girls' feminist blogging functions as a practice of citizenship for girls. In this sense, I take up Caroline Caron's (2011) call for feminist scholars to develop a politicized vocabulary to account for a variety of girls' cultural practices as generating political identities and political participation. In doing so, I hope to highlight how both a gender-and-age conscious analysis is significant when developing theories of contemporary citizenship.

Between Postfeminist and Protectionist: Contemporary Discourses of Public Girlhoods

Girls' citizenship practices are situated amidst cultural discourses that shape public understanding of girlhood; the postfeminist can-do girl is one such discourse. Anita Harris (2004, 16) argues that neoliberalism has produced a new idealized subject position for young women: the can-do girl. According to Harris, the can-do girl is "self-inventing, ambitious, and confident," successful at school (and later in the workplace), and consumes the right products, including beauty, fashion, and lifestyle goods that allow her to maintain a highly disciplined body that conforms to hegemonic femininity. While Harris does not use the word 'postfeminist' in her discussion, the can-do girl is unequivocally postfeminist through her mobilization of individualism, choice, and empowerment; self-surveillance and discipline; and femininity as bodily property (Gill 2007).

While the can-do girl is empowered by feminist gains and is expected to take advantage of them (e.g. have a successful career), she is not encouraged to be a political activist or to engage in collective movements for social change. Instead, the can-do girl exercises citizenship through individual responsibility, consumption, adult-managed leadership programs, and the apolitical entrepreneurial activities, such as launching her own fashion line. Jessica Taft (2011, 23–24) explains that the 'empowerment' encouraged of the can-do girl is "focused on incorporating girls into the social order as it stands, rather than empowering them to make any meaningful changes to it." Unlike traditional discourses of girlhood that emphasized passivity, empowered girls are active, yet their activity is informed by an individualized worldview and a focus on personal, rather than collective, change. The can-do girl's politics are thus privatized, an issue that Harris recognizes as part of the reshaping of public space associated with neoliberalism.

The can-do girl discourse is prescriptive in how girls should occupy public space, encouraging girls to be "highly visible in public" via not only the display and positioning of their bodies within the public sphere, but also through the constant display of an 'authentic' inner self, such as through public declarations of responsibility, personal transformation, and self-scrutiny (Harris 2004). Whereas opportunities for girls' political engagements become privatized, Harris (2004) maintains that girls are conversely encouraged to perform their intimate lives publicly. Girls who "live large" in public dominate contemporary celebrity culture, a phenomenon that Sarah Projansky (2014, 6) articulates as the "spectacularization of girlhood," whereby girls are discursively produced and socially regulated as fabulous and/or scandalous objects on display for public consumption. The can-do girl is then situated within this broader cultural context where public girlhood is articulated through celebrity culture, a phenomenon that I'll return to later in the chapter.[2]

Web 2.0 platforms have been significant in opening up new spaces for girls to engage with the public sphere. To Harris (2004, 162), "The Internet allows young women to actively manipulate the borders between public and private, inside and outside, to attempt to manage expression without exploitation, and resistance without appropriation." Banet-Weiser (2011, 2012b), however, connects girls' digital visibility with many of the postfeminist ideals I described earlier in relation to the can-do girl, arguing that today's digital citizen realizes self-empowerment through her capacity and productivity in similar ways to the postfeminist subject. She maintains that girls' visibility within the public sphere via digital media production is often determined by their ability to "self-brand," producing oneself as a product that can be circulated and commodified (also see Keller 2015). Consequently, Banet-Weiser (2012b) contends that rather than fostering more opportunities for girls to perform a diversity of identities publicly, new media spaces have become branded sites that often restrict girls' expression of identity to narrow performances of can-do girlhood (and other postfeminist hegemonic femininities) via disciplinary practices such as "feedback."[3]

Alongside the proliferation of the can-do girl discourse we see the mobilization of another discourse related to girls' positioning in public space. I am referring to this as a protectionist discourse that suggests girls are now *too public*, vulnerable to multiple risks assumed to be primarily the result of girls' increased use of new media technologies and desire to be visible. While "cyberbullying" has gained media attention recently, the dangers surrounding girls' public presence online and via their mobile phones is most often framed as a problem related to girls' sexuality and potential sexualization by adult men (Shade 2007, 2011). Educational experts, policymakers and journalists have portrayed girls as sexually disinhibited by new media technologies, resulting in girls supposedly engaging in risky and non-normative sexual behavior (Hasinoff 2013). These discourses suggest that girls should not be expressing their desires online, and also that girls are too public in their self expression and must be reined in by concerned adults.

As Leslie Regan Shade (2011) argues, these characterizations of girls' use of new media technologies as out of control and potentially dangerous have resulted in a protectionist discourse that prescribes adult intervention in the form of monitoring, tracking, and controlling girls' use of the Internet and mobile phones. Shade describes several examples of spy software, GPS technology, and smartphone apps designed to monitor and contain girls' new media use, which she argues deny girls' agency and technological-savvy.[4] Perhaps ironically, this protectionist discourse suggests that whereas girls must be taught to diligently guard their privacy when using new media technologies, these same girls have few privacy rights in relation to their parents' surveillance of their online lives.

Feminist scholars (Marvin 1990; Kearney 2005; Cassell and Cramer 2008; Shade 2011; Hasinoff 2013) have analyzed the lengthy history of moral panics surrounding girls' uses of new technologies over the past century, understanding them as connected to the politics of space and often proliferating during times of girls' and women's increased public presence and access to the public sphere. Yet, I want to consider this most recent protectionist discourse as related to the girls' "loss of voice" rhetoric that gained widespread attention in the mid-1990s, which I describe in chapter one. Also employing a protectionist framework, the loss of voice discourse perceives adolescent girls as suffering from low self-esteem, an inability to voice their opinions and vulnerable to social and cultural pressures to conform to traditional femininity. Accordingly, teenage girls need adult intervention to 'empower' girls in order to 'save' them from their seemingly dire situation. The contradiction between these two discourses is interesting; as one warns against girls' highly visible and overly-confident public displays of sexuality, the other portrays girls as insecure, voiceless, and absent from public life. I am arguing that despite their seemingly contradictory messages, both discourses reveal a similar anxiety about girls' positioning in public life; namely, that girls should be guided toward "managed participation" (Harris 2004) by adults in order to ensure a public presence that avoids being too public or inappropriately public by upsetting normative performances of female adolescent sexuality and comportment.

Earlier in this chapter I outlined what I see as two primary discourses that relate to the performance of public girlhood. Although postfeminist discourses promote a model of can-do girlhood that celebrates visibility, independence, and one's ability to "live large" through digital media, we simultaneously hear that girls have gone too far, are now too public via their uses of new media technologies and must be monitored and protected by parents and other adults. Consequently, girls are situated in a precarious position where they are encouraged to publicly perform a visible can-do girlhood, yet avoid becoming too public through inappropriate displays or participating in the wrong public spaces, something that I'll explore further when I discuss Tavi. The tension between these postfeminist and protectionist discourses will be illustrated throughout this chapter, as I argue that girl feminist bloggers are able to navigate these tensions through their mobilization of feminist politics through blogging and that this process functions as a practice of citizenship.

Creating Political Spaces Via a "Vocal Politics"

In chapter two I argued that making feminism visible is understood by many girl feminist bloggers as an important activist strategy. I build upon this discussion here by demonstrating how girl feminist bloggers utilize both self-produced and commercial media to negotiate hegemonic discourses of girlhood and establish themselves as vocal, productive citizens. Whereas girl feminist bloggers have been able to successfully create spaces for girls to publicly perform feminism, we must consider their strategies in relation to the privileging of visibility, display, and individual entrepreneurship promoted by postfeminist and neoliberal discourses.

During the years of my research, several feminist girl bloggers, including Julie Zeilinger, Jamie Keiles, and Tavi Gevinson, have made concerted efforts to insert their voices into public conversations, often serving as young feminist commentators and experts in mainstream adult-dominated media, such as radio shows, television segments, newspaper articles, and magazine features. Their engagement with the mainstream media, while often incorporating a critique of such media, is a significant part of their activist strategy that positions them as very active public figures and, as I'll argue, demonstrates a citizenship practice that defines girl feminist bloggers. I will first discuss Julie and Jamie's practices here, before moving on to explore Tavi's public feminist politics through an in-depth case study.

Julie Zeilinger has an impressive list of media credentials. In the six years since launching the *FBomb*, Julie has been featured in such media outlets as *The Daily Beast*, *Salon*, and *More Magazine*, where she was listed as one of the "New Feminists You Need To Know." In 2010, she was named one of the *Times of London*'s "40 Bloggers Who Really Count" and has participated in numerous panels, including the "Women in the World" summit in New York City in March 2012. Julie released her first book, *A Little F'd Up: Why Feminism Is Not a Dirty Word* with Seal Press in 2012, which received significant coverage in the *Huffington Post*, *Forbes Magazine*, the *Melissa Harris-Perry Show* (MSNBC), and *Glamour Magazine*. She continues to edit the *FBomb*, despite starting her undergraduate degree at Barnard College in fall 2011, and also maintains her own promotional website, where, at the time of this writing, she was described as "one of the leaders of the fourth wave feminist movement" (Zeilinger 2012b). In 2014, Julie released a second book, *College 101: A Girls' Guide to Freshman Year* and embarked on a national speaking tour in 2015.

Jamie Keiles gained significant mainstream media attention after her blogging project, *The Seventeen Magazine Project*, became a viral success online in June 2010.[5] Jamie used *Seventeen* magazine as a guide for daily living for the month before her high school graduation, blogging daily about her experience. National Public Radio's "All Things Considered," Canadian Broadcasting Corporation's *Q*, *Bust Magazine*, and her local Fox News affiliate, among other media outlets, covered Jamie's "experiment," and her blog quickly garnered hundreds of comments based on the publicity. As a result of this overwhelming public interest in the *Seventeen Magazine Project*, she then launched an initiative called "Hey Mainstream Media," a photo submission project encouraging people to use handmade signs to critique narrow media representations of femininity and masculinity. In September 2010, *Woman's Day* magazine named Jamie as one of the eight most influential bloggers under age 21. Jamie has written for Tavi's *Rookie* magazine, *Chicago Weekly*, and pop culture blog *The Hairpin* and has recently graduated from the University of Chicago.

Throughout this book I have demonstrated how girl feminist bloggers have used blogging to create their own spaces to perform feminist identities and activism. As we can discern from the examples of Julie and Jamie, a significant part of this practice involves what I'm calling the performance of 'vocal politics' within public space. I employ this concept to refer to the way in which girl feminist bloggers speak publicly about being a feminist and the need to take action to make gender equality a reality. These bloggers often perform their vocal politics publicly by using mainstream commercial, and often traditional, media to publicize their own blogs and feminist politics.

In 2009 Julie actively courted media attention for the newly launched *FBomb* by sending out a press release to both traditional media outlets, as well as other blogs. She tells me,

> I think often times when bloggers start out they either underestimate the power of the already established blogosphere or feel that the only way to establish themselves is to do so independently – that they can only be successful if they make it on their own. I think both are pretty limited ways of thinking. When I started the *FBomb*, I sent out a press release to let other people know – in the blogosphere and in terms of other media – about what I was doing, I figured that some people might be interested and write about the *FBomb*, thus generating interest and audience, which is exactly what ended up happening.

Julie's comments and actions are fascinating to consider in that they demonstrate her conscious attempt to produce an audience for the *FBomb*. The strategy of using a press release to generate publicity for one's feminist blog no doubt assumes the logic of neoliberal entrepreneurship, whereby individuals are expected to brand themselves through visibility and media circulation (Banet-Weiser 2012b). Releasing a press release is also a classed practice, requiring the resources of both time and money, as well as the cultural and social capital needed to understand the workings of the media industry. Consequently, while this tactic worked for Julie, many other girls would not be able to employ such a strategy to publicize their own blogs.

For example, whereas Amandine performs a vocal politics through her blog and actively participates in events such as the NOW Conference in summer 2012, due to her religious identity and attendance at a conservative religious school she is unable to cultivate the same public visibility as Julie. Consequently, Amandine never posts pictures of herself online and does not use her last name in correspondences related to her blog, making the celebrity achieved by Julie impossible for Amandine at this point in her life. Julie also likely attains easier access to mainstream media than some girls, due not only to her class position, but her race and normative body type correspond to the hegemonic ideals privileged in popular culture. Consequently, we must keep these limitations in mind, as they no doubt shape *which* girl feminist bloggers attain mainstream visibility.

While distributing a press release to generate an audience for one's blog seems indicative of a performance of can-do girlhood, I argue that bloggers like Julie complicate this assumption by utilizing their public personas as a platform to perform a vocal feminist politics to a wide audience. In doing so, girl feminist bloggers make feminism an accessible discourse to girls (as well as boys, men, and women) who may not encounter feminism in their daily lives. To wit: Julie's decision to write and publish a book is another example of her desire to engage with a larger audience through traditional commercial media; a decision that also sees Julie participate in the publishing industry more broadly by hiring a publicist, generating 'buzz' through the *FBomb* (which contained a link to the book's Amazon.com page), and engaging in promotional labor such as interviews with major commercial media outlets (Figure 5.1).

Figure 5.1 Julie promoting her book on television, author screen shot. Used with permission from Julie Zeilinger.

Julie's book publicity facilitated her coverage in many publications including *Teen Vogue*, the popular teenage counterpart to *Vogue Magazine*, and a magazine that rarely addresses feminist politics. The May 2012 article, appearing on the magazine's website, was titled, "Teen Author Julie Zeilinger on Her Feminist Blog and New Book," and was formatted as a question and answer with Julie, who responded to questions about topics such as her own interest in and definition of feminism; girls' supposed fear of the term; specific feminist issues in Julie's book; the relationship between fashion and feminism; and the women's health care debate (Tishgart 2012). Unlike most other teen magazines that utilize a postfeminist discourse of 'empowerment' rather than 'feminism' (Keller 2011), the *Teen Vogue* article directly engages with feminism and links to the *FBomb* website, providing readers the opportunity to explore feminism beyond the scope of the article. Julie's ability to produce political space within the pages of a fashion magazine that reaches thousands of teenage girls is significant, as she is making feminism an accessible discourse to many *Teen Vogue* readers who may not otherwise encounter feminist politics in their daily lives.

Although Jamie did not initially court media attention for her blog in the same way that Julie did, she later used her public profile and the connections that she made as a feminist blogger as a platform for her feminist politics. For example, after the media attention she received from the *Seventeen Magazine Project* in June 2010, Jamie continued being active in the feminist blogosphere both through her Tumblr site and her blog *Teenagerie*, where she maintained a significant following. She used her experience with producing media and speaking to mainstream media, as well as her name recognition, to organize and publicize the June 2011 Chicago SlutWalk, where she was able to create more public space for her vocal feminist politics. While Jamie's use of her public persona differs from Julie's, both bloggers demonstrate an interest in maintaining a public visibility from which to speak as political citizens.

It is this interest in cultivating a public *political* identity that departs from postfeminist girlhood subjectivities, which Harris (2004) describes as not only being apolitical, but specifically disconnected from feminist politics. Both Julie and Jamie publicly perform a feminist identity and advocate for other girls to do the same. Furthermore, both bloggers demonstrate girls' right to be present in online public space, maintaining their blogs independent of their parents or other adults. This differs from other feminist websites such as SPARK (www.sparksummit.com), which includes blog posts by feminist girls, yet is organized and managed by adult women. Both Julie and Jamie's success then also reveals the fallacy of protectionist discourses that suggest adult supervision and management is necessary to prevent girls from harming themselves through their online public presence.

Julie and Jamie's strategies also complicate the notion of girls' "bedroom culture," a concept coined by Angela McRobbie and Jenny Garber (1991) to highlight the ways in which girls participate in cultural practices within the private spaces of their bedrooms. While many of the bloggers I interviewed do blog in their bedrooms, their practices challenge early articulations of bedroom culture as primarily consumptive, and reveal how "bedroom culture" is also productive (Kearney 2007a; Baker 2011). Girls are reconfiguring the private space of the bedroom to create "new publics that can better serve their needs, interests, and goals" (Kearney 2007a, 138). Moreover, they also suggest a necessary rethinking of conceptualizing girls' online practices as "virtual bedroom culture," as suggested by Jacqueline Reid-Walsh and Claudia Mitchell (2004). Although Reid-Walsh and Mitchell do acknowledge both the public and private dimensions of girls' self-created websites, they disregard how girls' websites function as spaces for girls such as Julie and Jamie to perform a vocal politics in the public sphere.

Julie's comments that I quote earlier in this chapter suggest that girls such as herself are involved in practices of cultural production that they do not want to remain private; indeed, they hope their voices can be heard among a larger public sphere in order to produce social change. Jamie feels the same. In a December 2011 interview with *The Harvard Independent* she says, "I am pretty confident that the future of social justice will come when there is a shift in who is producing media" (Hou 2011). In this sense, girl feminist bloggers create blogs as a strategy to "broadcast" themselves beyond the confines of their bedroom and immediate peer groups with the hopes of making feminism accessible to more girls and enacting social change, a strategy that Kearney (2006) also links to riot grrrl practices like producing zines and music.

Girl feminist bloggers are not the first or only girl activists historically who have been invested in cultivating a public visibility through combining an engagement with commercial media with their own media production. Instead, girl feminist bloggers can be understood as part of a continuum of girlhood feminist activism. Kirsten Pike (2011) examined how teenage girls regularly wrote columns in *Seventeen* magazine during the women's liberation movement, using the popular commercial magazine for girls as a space to advocate for gender equality and feminist politics. Pike recognizes the girl writers as performing their own form of "do-it-yourself citizenship," where girls engage in "civic action and dialogue by circulating their own ideas, stories, and opinions [about feminism and gender equality] to a broader network of readers" (68). More recently, riot grrrls have cultivated a public visibility for their feminist politics, most notably through their music, with several bands gaining mainstream popularity and commercial success. As rock bands, these groups were sonically loud, producing political spaces in whatever public spaces they played, as well as within the music industry. Riot grrrl coverage in the early 1990s glossy magazine *Sassy* was also crucial for popularizing the movement. While plenty of girls across the country were introduced to feminist politics via the magazine, *Sassy*'s coverage of riot grrrl was not uncontroversial, as the underground nature of riot grrrl and its connections to anti-establishment youth culture like punk meant that some riot grrrls viewed the *Sassy* coverage as co-opting and commercializing the movement (Jesella and Meltzer 2007).

This controversy points to an assumed divide between mainstream commercial popular culture and "subcultural" or alternative culture. Catherine Driscoll (2002, 280) argues that this binary fails to account for the ways in which girls' culture exists between these tensions. She argues, "Feminism itself belongs to the popular culture field, a point feminist discussion of popular culture often seems to ignore even in fields where the influence of feminism is most palpable." This has been especially true for third wave feminism, which emphasizes the importance of popular culture as a site for feminist politics (Heywood and Drake 1997). Thus, rather than view Julie, Jamie, and Tavi's cultivation of celebrity within the realm of popular commercial culture solely as a postfeminist strategy informed by the mantra of "living large," I would argue that their actions are indicative of both a longstanding girls' culture and the influence of third wave feminism, which has always emphasized the integration of feminism within popular culture (Keller 2011).

By cultivating celebrity and producing political spaces outside of their blogs, the girl bloggers I discuss in this chapter perform a public feminist girlhood that differs from many of the highly visible girls we usually see in public culture. We frequently see girls within mainstream media, but they are often only granted access to public space based upon their perceived commercial value to companies such as the Walt Disney Company – a corporation that has been highly invested in the production of girl celebrities (Blue 2013; Sweeney 2008). For example, Kathleen Sweeney (2008, 69) describes former Disney girl celebrities such as Christina Aguilera, Britney Spears, and later, Raven Symone and Hilary Duff, as an "unexpected cash cow" for Disney. As Morgan Blue (2013) documents, Disney's success with girl celebrities has encouraged the corporation to continue producing highly visible girl celebrities, such as Miley Cyrus, Selena Gomez, and Demi Lovato via multiple media and merchandising platforms, including television shows, music, movies, fashion lines, and other branded products ranging from paint colors to prepackaged salads.[6]

The commercial value of girlhood is often contingent on a performance of a can-do girlhood that is apolitical and informed by hegemonic femininity, yet active and entrepreneurial (Harris 2004). Indeed, girls' performances as active "public citizens" constitute a significant aspect of Disney's mobilization of girlhood fame, including for celebrities such as Symone, Cyrus, and Gomez (Blue 2013). For example, Blue describes how Symone has participated in girl-focused civic engagement with a "feminist bent," yet nonetheless presents herself as uncontroversial, safely securing her position as publicly *active*, yet not *activist*. Blue (2013, 45) contends that while Symone has worked on commercially sponsored body acceptance campaigns, "she may also be encouraging girls to connect body acceptance with consumerism while perpetuating neoliberal discourses that individualize the systemic and institutional inequalities that organize U.S. society." Thus, Symone performs a can-do girlhood that is publicly visible and active, but not invested in politics or advocating for progressive structural social change.

Why has the celebration of girls' visibility not resulted in more instances of girls that are politically vocal within public space, like Julie, Jamie, or as I'll soon describe, Tavi? This inquiry illuminates the difference between girls' visibility as a defining feature of postfeminist can-do girlhood and girls' agency – what I argue is central to the model of girls' citizenship advocated in this chapter. Whereas a sense of agency grants girls the ability to be vocal as political citizens, Harris (2004) argues that visibility does not guarantee one's access to voice. She points to the connection between can-do visibility and a protectionist discourse that prescribes management of girls' public selves, a relationship where visibility can function as a "trap" of surveillance rather than as liberation (Foucault 1977). With this in mind, I turn to my case study of Tavi Gevinson, whose extensive media coverage and productive career as a fashion and feminist blogger, as well as the editor in chief of *Rookie* magazine, demonstrates how girls' use of public space remains contentious, yet potentially valuable for the advancement of feminist politics.

Tavi Gevinson and the Politics of Public Girlhood

Since launching her fashion blog *Style Rookie* in 2008 at the age of eleven, Tavi Gevinson has become a "media mogul" (Bazillian 2013), cultivating a devoted following of fans through her witty fashion reviews that paved the way to front row seats at international Fashion Week catwalks and an array of other writing and speaking opportunities. In September 2011, she launched *Rookie* (http://rookiemag.com), an online feminist-oriented pop culture magazine for teenage girls that indicated a shift in Tavi's focus from fashion to cultural critique more broadly. Although Tavi always identified as feminist, the development and launch of *Rookie* saw her frequently engaging in public feminist critiques of media and promoting feminism as necessary for girls through both her *Rookie* posts and public talks. Since *Rookie*'s launch Tavi has released three printed *Rookie Yearbooks,* embarked on a cross-country "*Rookie* Roadtrip" to meet her readers, and has widened her cultural production to include singing, modeling, and acting in both film and theatre.

Tavi Gevinson is not representative of most of the girl feminist bloggers that I've described in this book, in that few have received the kind of celebrity and name recognition as Tavi. Her exceptional situation nonetheless serves as a useful case study that accomplishes three things: (1) It makes legible the contradictory discourses that shape the ways in which teenage girls are both celebrated and restricted within public space; (2) it demonstrates how girls utilize media production as bloggers to cultivate a "vocal politics" and critique hegemonic discourses of girlhood; and (3) it maps how this 'vocal politics' functions as a practice of citizenship through the creation of public space where girls can be not only *seen* but *heard* as political subjects, feminists, and activists. Thus, I employ this case study to parse out the larger thematic issues that are relevant to the feminist girl bloggers I discuss throughout this book, despite the fact that they have not achieved Tavi's level of public attention or celebrity.

The following discussion is based upon my discursive and ideological textual analysis of approximately sixty purposefully chosen media stories about Tavi, spanning from her debut as a fashion blogger in the spring of 2008 until September 2012, when she released *Rookie Yearbook One.* I discuss my findings in this section using the following thematic discourses: (1) Tavi as an extraordinary girl; (2) Tavi as minimized, small, and ultimately insignificant; and (3) Tavi as a fangirl. I suggest that together these discourses function to position Tavi as what I'm calling 'a girl out of place,' occupying public space in a way that challenges postfeminist norms of girlhood through her role as a media and cultural producer and her refusal to perform an apolitical "girl power" subjectivity. Tavi's performance of a public feminist identity has allowed her to challenge hegemonic discourses of girlhood and create her own public space where she invites other girls to be political, activists, feminists, and ultimately, citizens in their society.

One of the prominent discourses used to discuss Tavi within commercial media is one in which the teenage blogger is framed as an extraordinary girl, a discourse that Jessica Taft (2011) also identifies as frequently used by adults to describe girl anti-globalization activists. Indeed, words such as "wunderkind" are consistently used by journalists to position Tavi as a prodigy who has demonstrated talent beyond her role as fashion critic; showcasing a keen understanding of online media at a young age, using it to expand her brand into numerous media projects, and gaining mainstream visibility that many adults never achieve. Central to this discourse is the idea that Tavi represents a deviation from 'normal' or 'average' girlhood. Tavi, accordingly, is presented as special and more creative, smarter, dedicated, and harder working *than other girls her age*. This idea that Tavi is inherently different from most girls is emphasized continually throughout her media coverage and reproduces the invisibility of the many other girls who are engaged in productive, creative, and political projects.

For example, in a July 8, 2010 *Blackbook* blog post, an anonymous staff blogger details Tavi's visit to the magazine's New York office in order to style a shoot for the publication. The blogger writes, "Her voice belongs, of course, to that of a teenage girl, and she carries herself that way. But hype be damned, she is not like other teenage girls" (Haramis 2010). Thus, while Tavi is celebrated in many of these articles, she is consistently positioned in opposition to her girl peers. While Tavi and her work is praised for being "mature, intuitive, and inspired," the implication is that most teenage girls are immature, conforming, and have little cultural insight (Haramis 2010). Moreover, in doing so journalists reinforce hegemonic and dominant notions of girls as culturally unproductive, emphasizing Tavi as an exceptional case, rather than indicative of the creative skills many girls exercise in their daily lives.

Although often seemingly complimentary, the exceptional girl discourse can transform into mocking and condescending jabs. In a 2008 piece in the *New York Times* Elizabeth Spiridakis (2008) writes, "Meet the next generation of style bloggers. They might not be able to drive yet, but their fashion sense is so incredible it's actually intimidating." But Spiridakis' tone hardens in the next paragraph when she quips, "As an almost-30-year old style blogger myself, I have to ask: Whom will I envy next? Kindergartners?" Spiridakis' snarky shift implies that while regarding the fashion advice of tween bloggers as serious cultural work is currently trendy, it is actually ridiculous, an equivalent to celebrating the style of a young child. Yet Spiridakis confesses that she's intimidated by the young fashion bloggers, hinting that Tavi and her peers are potentially threatening to Spiridakis' own status as an adult style blogger. While Spiridakis celebrates Tavi's "creative, supportive, [and] confident" demeanor, she simultaneously attempts to contain the threat her girlishness presents to the public space of the adult-dominated fashion industry. Thus, Spiridakis simultaneously celebrates and contains Tavi's status as prominent fashion blogger, a complex move that dominates much of Tavi's media coverage.

While Tavi is consistently positioned as an extraordinary girl in media accounts, many of these stories simultaneously attempt to contain Tavi through a minimizing or diminutive discourse. While these discourses seem contradictory, I argue that they complement one another by recognizing

Tavi's accomplishments as indicative of can-do girlhood, yet ultimately attempting to silence her by employing a protectionist discourse that maintains girlhood as located in the private sphere (Harris 2004). Thus, whereas the extraordinary girl discourse paints Tavi as a larger-than-life figure in constant circulation, this minimizing discourse is paired with language that emphasizes Tavi's smallness, such as "petite tastemaker" (Schulman 2012), "pint-sized" (Graham 2012), "pocket-size child" (Spiridakis 2010), and "size of a pixie" (Schaer 2009). This language is supposedly describing Tavi's small stature, but the consistent use of such terms must be understood as a specifically ageist and gendered framing of Tavi, rather than as offering objective descriptors merely relaying an observable fact. The constant framing of Tavi through these terms serves to link Tavi's physicality with a state of disempowerment, a position of dependence, and a lack of agency – qualities that are often problematically associated with children – and specifically girls – in dominant social discourses and media representations (Sanchez-Eppler 2005; Nash 2006).

This discourse is connected to the contemporary protectionist discourse used to frame girls who publicly exert themselves in ways that are too public, which I outlined earlier in this chapter. For example, in an August 2008 *USA Today* article "Young fashion bloggers are worrisome trend to parents," Amanda Kwan employs a protectionist discourse to discuss young fashion bloggers, suggesting that parents must closely monitor their children's online activities and providing a sidebar with tips on "How to Keep a Young Blogger Safe." Kwan describes a then twelve- year-old Tavi posting images of herself to her fashion blog, commenting: "To some wary adults, [Tavi is] in a world where she doesn't belong. Unlike a typical social network page, a blog can be seen by anyone. And at least one young fashion blogger says she's been recognized by strangers on the street – a worrisome turn for adults worried about privacy and predators." By suggesting that Tavi is "in a world where she doesn't belong," Kwan problematically implies that the public space of the Internet, which "can be seen by anyone," is not for girls, reproducing traditional binaries that affirm public space as both masculine and adult.

When Tavi is supposedly upset by negative comments written about her online, Kwan explains her reactions as indicative of her gender and age, despite the fact that many adults would also be distraught upon encountering mean-spirited personal comments on the Internet. Citing Addie Schwarz, the CEO of a "kid-safe" social network, Kwan writes, "Such negative responses [to online comments] are the reason why children shouldn't be blogging, Swartz says. 'Whoever may comment and whatever feedback you may get – girls are very impressionable, especially girls in this age that we're … talking about.'" Although it is not surprising that Swartz has a stake in presenting blogging as dangerous and personally damaging to girls, her economic motive goes unquestioned by Kwan. Instead, Kwan's article minimizes the agency of young bloggers like Tavi, prescribes parental surveillance as necessary to ensure Tavi's safety and even suggests that Tavi has no legitimate right to occupy the public space of the Internet.

Kwan's article is not unique in questioning the legitimacy of Tavi's public presence. Scott Schuman, a prominent fashion photographer and blogger at *The Sartorialist*, has also employed ageist and sexist discourse to minimize Tavi's cultural power. In a September 2011 interview Schuman responds to a question about the influence of young fashion bloggers:

> I don't think her [Tavi's] audience is that big. I think her success is a lit-tle bit of a conspiracy by established print media that wanted to show that this blog thing is not that important, that it's done by a bunch of twelve year olds. But a lot of us are serious grown-ups. I think it's great that Tavi can create a blog and write for other people that are like-minded – probably other kids around her age – but I don't know how that is going to help a 26-year-old, if she has never had a boyfriend or any of that kind of stuff. She's just a kid, so she can talk about art and stuff only in an abstract way (*The Talks* blog 2011).

Schuman later apologized for his offensive remarks, but his original com-ments demonstrate how positioning Tavi as "just a kid" is employed to minimize her accomplishments, and I would argue, the threat she poses to Schuman's own career and masculine, adult cultural authority. By suggest-ing that only people who are Tavi's age read her blog, Schuman attempts to protect the dominant binary that celebrates cultural authorities as male, adult, white, serious, and tasteful, whereas those outside of this identity are viewed as childlike, frivolous, unable to understand art and culture, and often, female.

This binary is also gendered. Indeed, while many of these words used to describe Tavi literally minimize her, they also work concurrently to feminize her. For example, words used to describe Tavi, like "pixie" and "blogette," are distinctively feminine and highlight Tavi's femininity as a defining feature of her public presence, effectively linking femininity to smallness. Similarly, Schuman's dismissal of Tavi's cultural critique because "she has never had a boyfriend" implies it is men and boys that are the influential force in women and girls' cultural production, and without them, females cannot possibly be legitimate cultural actors. Consequently, Schuman's comment also heterosexualizes Tavi, while still entertaining suggestions of lesbianism due to her perceived lack of romantic relationships with men, despite her young age.

The *minimizing Tavi* discourse also relies on gendered tropes to posi-tion Tavi's blogging as private and inconsequential, reifying a normative understanding of girls' cultural practices as located in the private sphere, while the public sphere remains a masculine and adult realm. Spiridakis (2008) describes tweens' fashion blogging as "today's equivalent of doing your hair 20 ways before bedtime. Only you use a digital mirror." This analogy is significant, as Spiridakis mobilizes the trope of the girl's bedroom in an attempt to contain girls' blogging within the privacy of their bedrooms. Although McRobbie and Garber (1991) and later Kearney (2007) have demonstrated that bedroom culture has public and political potential, Spiridakis' prose does not acknowledge this and instead implies that girls' blogging has no real public implications, just as doing one's hair "20 ways before bedtime" is a narcissistic and irrelevant act. This framing of Tavi by a young adult female writer is interesting because it reveals how common it is for girls' cultural practices to be viewed as private, personal, irrelevant, and beauty-oriented rather than public and political, an assumption that I refute in this book.

In addition to physical descriptors that highlight Tavi's small size and feminize her, other words are used to discredit and minimize Tavi by dismissing her celebrity as merely a trend. In a December 2009 article journalist Lesley M.M. Blume called Tavi a "novelty" three times, implying that Tavi is merely attracting fleeting amusement that the fashion world will soon tire of. Blume goes on to publicly doubt Tavi's legitimacy, commenting, "She's either a tween savant or she's got a Tavi team" (as quoted in Odell 2009). Blume's dismissal of Tavi's talent and agency highlights how this discourse attempts to contain her threat to the established fashion hierarchies, suggesting that a girl could not possibly successfully participate in the fashion industry outside the role of consumer. Blume's questioning of Tavi's authorship is not uncommon and is a tactic often used to discredit the cultural contributions of women and members of other marginalized groups (Haddad 2011). It is Tavi's status as girl that becomes the basis for her dismissal by both adult women and men already established in the fashion industry. Thus, instead of using Tavi as an example of the creative and cultural agency that many girls exercise in their everyday lives, adults like Blume frame Tavi as a short-lived fluke, reproducing dominant understanding of girls as passive, flighty, consumers dependent on adults rather than serious agential cultural producers.

Finally, the increasing popularity of blogging as a cultural practice has fostered another dominant discourse used to construct Tavi: that of bloggers as fannish, obsessive, and thus, inauthentic, unreliable, and uncritical cultural commentators. Whereas fashion journalism has a lengthy history in popular culture, fashion blogging is a relatively new phenomenon, becoming popular only within the past decade. Thus, many industry insiders who have worked in fashion since long before the emergence of the fashion blogosphere argue that bloggers lack the rigor, expertise, and established dedication of older fashion journalists and editors. For example, in a story about Tavi at Paris fashion week, *The Independent*'s Susie Mesure (2010) cites magazine editor Robert Johnson as saying, "Bloggers are so attractive to the big design houses because they are so wide-eyed and obsessed, but they don't have the critical faculties to know what's good and what's not. As soon as they've been invited to the shows, they can no longer criticize because then they won't be invited back." Likewise, David Graham writes in a March 2012 *Toronto Star* article, "Bloggers are the new critics. Often dazzled by celebrity culture, at best they offer snappy if uninformed commentary." Graham lists three young women, including Tavi, as leaders of this growing and supposedly uncritical fashion blogosphere.

Johnson's use of the words "wide-eyed" and "obsessed" to describe fashion bloggers and Graham's characterization of bloggers being "dazzled by celebrity culture" negatively position fashion bloggers as fans rather than experts or critics, and draws on longstanding problematic assumptions of fans as shallow, mindless consumers, and celebrity obsessed (Jenson 1992). This characterization has been particularly true of girl fans, whom as Barbara Ehrenreich, Elizabeth Hess, and Gloria Jacobs (1986) note, have been portrayed by (often male) adults as merely conforming to the masses and/or unable to control their own frenzied response to their celebrity crush. Furthermore, Johnson's assertion that fashion bloggers "don't have the critical faculties to know what's good and what's not" is unfounded and incorrectly assumes that print fashion editors and journalists are always impartial, critical, unenthused and have no connections with designers and fashion companies.[7]

Johnson and Graham's critiques are informed by and make visible larger cultural binaries, including those of critic/fan, producer/consumer, high culture/low culture, traditional/new media, and professional/amateur. These binaries maintain cultural hierarchies, which often privilege the voices of adult, wealthy, white males (and sometimes females) as purveyors of desirable cultural tastes, as evident in the comments I've outlined throughout this section. Because many fashion bloggers are girls and young women, the previous comments can be read also as specifically gendered, drawing on longstanding notions of girls and women as fans and consumers of mass/low cultural products, rather than media producers or sophisticated audiences (Kearney 2006). Thus, this discourse positions blogging as a fannish, uncritical, and ultimately a low-culture feminine practice, effectively containing Tavi's cultural authority and maintaining the positioning of adult men like Schuman and adult women like Blume as cultural experts.

The positioning of an expert or professional in relation to an amateur is situated within dominant discourses about class and gender. David Buckingham, Maria Pini, and Rebekah Willett (2009) argue that despite popular rhetoric claiming that the distinction between amateur and professional is being blurred by the proliferation of easy-to-use media technologies, this binary continues to exist, yet is complicated by various "grades" of amateur media-makers. They distinguish an amateur, an every-day user who does not intend to distribute their work, from a "serious amateur," the latter as someone wanting to improve their practice, investing in more expensive equipment, as well as the time needed to do so. Thus, Buckingham, Pini, and Willett note that the serious amateur is a classed category marked by middle and upper-middle class taste sensibilities and often gendered male, yet lacking in the knowledge of an expert. While Tavi may be seen as a serious amateur, and as an upper-middle class white girl who has the cultural and social capital to occupy such a position, her age and gender complicate this positioning often reserved for aspirational middle-class men and boys.[8] Consequently, Tavi is discursively constructed not as a professional or even a serious amateur, but as an amateur, a lucky fan whose media products should be consumed by friends and family – not by the wider public.

"People got really mad about a giant pink bow!" Tavi as a Girl out of Place

I argue that the three discourses I outline above are often employed together by those writing about Tavi to suggest that she is occupying public space in a way that is inappropriate for a girl. I want to emphasize two aspects of this sentiment. First, that Tavi's body is positioned in public; and second, that she is mobilizing her public body in an inappropriate way. Consequently, it is not solely the fact that Tavi is a public figure that makes adults uncomfortable, as the can-do girl is encouraged to occupy certain public spaces. Instead, it is the way in which Tavi chooses to inhabit public space – as a media producer with a vocal politics – that upsets some of the logic of the can-do girl as a consumer and adult-managed phenomenon.

In late January 2010, the fashion blogosphere exploded with news of Tavi's accessory of choice for the exclusive Christian Dior Fall 2010 Paris Fashion Week show: a giant pink bow designed by Stephen Jones and positioned on top of her head (Figure 5.2). Tavi's bow made headlines for allegedly blocking the catwalk views of several prominent fashion editors and writers seated behind the blogger. The angered editors' quick use of social media to broadcast the incident to others in the fashion industry soon resulted in an extensive online debate among fashion editors, bloggers, and fans that went beyond the ethics of a front row guest sporting a large headpiece, and instead focused on the politics of age and the authenticity of bloggers as cultural commentators.

Prominent fashion heavyweights were eager to question the appropriateness of Tavi's coveted seat, and even some fellow fashion bloggers took the opportunity to delegitimize Tavi's front-row celebrity status. In a January 25, 2010 blog post Kristin Knox, fashion blogger at *The Clothes Whisperer* writes,

> Oh the irony of a grown-up correspondent's view of the runway being blocked by someone little older than a child and no taller than Frodo (sorry *Grazia*). Who needs a booster seat when you've got Stephen Jones befitting you bespoke headgear? Couture my ass, Christian [Dior] would be rolling in his grave. I mean, with all this school this girl is missing to become Chicago's best traveled eighth-grader, can she even spell the word?

Figure 5.2 The view behind Tavi's bow, author screen shot. Image reprinted from
@Grazia_Live.

Interestingly, many comments depart from the topic of Tavi's bow and
instead focus on her *legitimacy* as a cultural authority. Indeed, numerous
other writers for publications such as *Toronto Life* magazine and *Blackbook*
magazine, as well as popular blogs, such as *Jezebel*, weighed in on the controversy, revealing the real issue at stake: *What right does a 13-year-old girl
blogger have to be sitting in the front row of the Dior haute couture show?*
While writers often draw on Tavi's physically small stature to describe
the blogger, few mentioned her small size within the context of the Dior controversy. Instead, fashion insiders discussed Tavi in reference to her age, with
several editors describing her as being a "13-year-old." For example, *Flare*
editor Lisa Tant tweeted: "Sobbing to think that a 13-year-old gets a front-
row seat to cover couture. No justice in this world" (Goldenberg-Fife 2010).
While their descriptions hint at Tavi's supposedly extraordinary status, they
also carry a subtle implication that the front row of a prominent fashion
show is no place for a 13-year-old. By highlighting Tavi's age rather than
her creative accomplishments, editors such as Tant appear to be attempting
to use Tavi's age to discredit her. I'm also arguing that these editors may
mention her age as a means of disparaging her decision to wear a large pink
bow as a choice made by an amateur fashion week fan, rather than a serious
cultural commentator.

These comments perpetuate the hegemonic and dominant discourses
of girlhood which I outlined throughout this chapter, positioning girls as
lacking in sophisticated cultural knowledge and thus unable to participate
as culturally productive citizens (Kearney 2006). While editors – and even

fellow bloggers – imply that Tavi, as a blogger, has no right to occupy a position formerly reserved for a professional journalist, I suggest that it is Tavi's
status as *media producer combined with her girlhood* that is problematic to
these adult insiders. Indeed, snagging a seat in the front row of a Dior show
is coveted because of the high culture connotation of couture fashion, which
includes a sophistication beyond the mass commercial appeal associated
with girls, and an expert taste that is cultivated through years of experience
in the industry (McRobbie 1998). Thus, dominant discourses of girlhood
suggest that Tavi has no right to be in the front row of a Dior show, and
it is this logic we see being reproduced by annoyed adult fashion editors.
Despite being a prolific blogger, demonstrating both her cultural knowledge
and writing talent, Tavi is unable to occupy the position of fashion expert
because of her status as a girl blogger.

Rather than portray herself as older in order to 'pass' as an adult, Tavi
embraces her girl subjectivity. Thus, the girlishness of the pink bow is important to consider. By choosing this particular accessory Tavi is explicitly
drawing attention toward her status as girl, distinguishing herself from the
other attendees. I read this move as a strategic choice by Tavi to embrace
and make visible her girlhood, perhaps anticipating the backlash that her
front row status may generate. Instead of trying to minimize her girlhood in
order to appear older and conform to dominant notions about who should
receive runway-side seats, Tavi challenges this logic by overtly claiming a
right to be in the front row as a girl by sporting the ultimate feminine girlhood accessory: a large pink bow.

However, Tavi's claim to girlhood is complicated by her dyed gray-blue
hair during this period, described by the *New York Times* as signature to her
"outré granny" look, complemented by her small size, glasses, and eclectic
fashion choices (Schulman 2012). Like girlhood, old age occupies a marginalized positioning within both the fashion industry as well as the public
sphere more broadly. Tavi's choice to adopt signifiers of old age may then
be read as an attempt to reclaim a space for old age within public space in
much the same way that she does for girlhood. However, her ability to mobilize both simultaneously also suggests a complicating of age that creatively
plays on the hype that Tavi is "wise beyond her years" (Weinger 2013). This
specific trope has been used by journalists and fellow bloggers to describe
Tavi throughout the entirety of her career, and is a part of the extraordinary
girl discourse I outlined earlier that suggests Tavi possesses a wiseness not
common to girls. Thus, by dying her hair gray, yet retaining signifiers of girlhood, Tavi encourages us to consider how girls can perform both a wiseness
associated with old age and youthful girlishness.

We may also read Tavi's gray hair as a conscientious challenge to postfeminist beauty norms that privilege signifiers of hegemonic femininity, such
as long, sleek, and (often) blonde hair. By purposefully choosing to dye her
hair gray (a hair color that many women try to hide due to its association
with old age) Tavi refuses to conform to the idealized feminine body norms

associated with can-do girlhood. Furthermore, the fact that she is presenting a non-normative girlhood within a cultural space known for its promotion of hegemonic feminine bodies, suggests that Tavi's gray hair may be an act of resistance that is both provocative and progressive.

Tavi is astute to the ways in which these discourses have shaped her experiences. In a 2012 video interview Tavi recounts the Dior controversy, claiming,

> Once people got mad because I was physically taking up space because I wore a giant bow on my head and whoever was sitting behind me said something about it, even though I was really short at the time. And so that became a whole, "she has no right to be there" thing because I'm not a fashion expert or whatever. People got really mad about a giant pink bow! (PBS 2012)

Here, Tavi acknowledges the politics of space that saturates this story, implying that her status as a girl did not allow her to be "expert," no matter how well she wrote or how creatively she was styled. My discussion throughout this section can then be viewed within the larger debate about the gendered politics of space, which is also framed by race, class, age, and other identity inequalities, and raises questions that include: Who is entitled to occupy public space, and in what contexts? Whose bodies are allowed to be seen in public? Feminist scholars have long been concerned with the politics of space, arguing that women have historically been encouraged to take up less public space, whereas men are taught to actively embrace it (Bordo 1993; Young 1990). This ideal has influenced the ways that women and girls' bodies are understood within the public sphere and shapes the discourse that suggests Tavi is taking up public space to which she has no right.

Fashion is a feminized industry and girls and young women play a key role in sustaining the industry through the consumption of fashion products. However, girls also participate in the industry in non-consumer roles, most notably as models. The different meanings implied by Tavi's body occupying a seat in the front row of a couture show and the body of a girl similar in age strutting down the catwalk is made clear in an exchange between Tavi and the editor-in-chief of *Vogue* magazine, Anna Wintour. In an August 2012 interview Tavi recounts how Wintour once asked her when she goes to school, implying that the appropriate public space for Tavi to be occupying is the high school – not the front row at Fashion Week. Tavi explains, "I just felt like, 'When do your models go to school?' I'm the same age as the models and I'm missing school to travel and write and voice an opinion" (quoted in Alani 2012).

This exchange makes visible how it is not only Tavi's presence in the fashion industry that's offensive to Wintour and the other editors I've cited throughout this chapter, but her role as a writer with a public voice. In contrast to the teenage models who passively display clothes on the catwalk and are paid to be *visible but not vocal*, Tavi is an active cultural producer whose agency is not mobilized through her feminine body, a quality of postfeminist empowerment (Gill 2007). Instead, Tavi's agency is enacted through "voic[ing] an opinion" via her writing skills, creativity, and cultural knowledge. Thus, while Tavi's body occupies a public space where other young female bodies are present and often celebrated, her positioning as a cultural producer that employs a vocal politics complicates her positioning as a girl within the public space of fashion. It is this agency and use of media production to voice one's opinion that is central to my conception of citizenship.

Tavi's Feminist Politics

Thus far I have discussed how others have discursively constructed Tavi through commercial media and have identified several dominant discourses that have consistently framed her public image. However, Tavi is a productive case study because she has creatively challenged and resisted many of the discourses used to frame her, demonstrating an agency that is informed by her feminist politics and is illustrative of the citizenship I'm articulating in this chapter. In this section I focus on Tavi's feminism, analyzing the ways in which she has mobilized her politics as a blogger to challenge the critiques levied against her and exercise her right to public space. In doing so, I argue that she's modeling a practice of citizenship for girls that privileges their right to voice in the public sphere.

In a July 2010 talk at the ideaCity10 conference in Toronto, Tavi surprised her adult audience by discussing girls, media representations, and feminism rather than her anticipated topic, fashion. She told the audience that, "The most subversive thing a magazine could do today … would be to be honest and encourage teen girls to be vocal" (Gevinson 2010a). Tavi's discussion of feminism is passionate, and she advocates for girls to adopt the feminist label: "The fact of the matter is that teen girls have always been told to keep quiet, and it would be such a different world if half of the population hadn't always been told to not be vocal. But it's not the 'Age of Women' unless it can be the age of girls too, so teen girls need to be a part of [feminism] as well" (Gevinson 2010a).

At the time, the audience was unaware that they were witnessing the presentation of the blueprints for what would in just over a year become *Rookie* magazine, Tavi's popular culture-focused website for teenage girls. After her presentation, the male MC asked her "if she could talk about fashion a bit" because the audience wanted to hear about who her favorite designers are. Tavi conceded, yet refused to name-drop which designers she's met, making the MC visibly uncomfortable. This somewhat awkward ending to Tavi's presentation suggests that Tavi's decision to step outside of her publicly constructed persona into a more political and perhaps controversial position made some in her adult audience uncomfortable. After all, she was supposed to talk about *fashion, not feminism!*

Later in summer 2010, Tavi posted what she called "An open letter to *Seventeen* magazine, also, WHY ARE YOU UGLY WHAT IS WRONG

WITH YOU [caps in original]" on her blog *StyleRookie*. In it she criticizes the popular teen magazine for implying that becoming "fat and ugly" is the worst thing that can happen to a teenage girl, writing, "Teenage girls are worth more than looks, and we don't need another media outlet telling us otherwise. ... PS. I'm just taking a guess here, but could it be at all possible that your valuing looks over intelligence or happiness is somehow related to your advertising content?" (Gevinson 2010b). She also began posting about feminism and feminist issues like girls' media representation, rape culture, and female role models on her blog. For example, she writes about media for teen girls:

> We need a voice that can shift through the bullshit and weed it out. There needs to be more feminism. There needs to be less emphasis on boys. *Seventeen* doesn't emphasize companionship, it emphasizes boys, and that is exclusive to straight people. I think it is important to encourage girls to be loud. There can't be all these negative messages. A big thing [to be addressed] is the beauty standard and slut shaming. There are so many double standards here (as quoted in Cadenas 2010).

Tavi has also spoken out in support of restricting runway work to models over sixteen-years-old and marched in Chicago's SlutWalk to raise awareness about rape culture and victim blaming. Her March 2012 TedxTeen talk focused on the importance of strong female characters in media, and she enthusiastically advocated for her audience to understand feminism as a "process" and a "conversation" rather than an intimidating "rulebook." Her presentation revealed the continual role that feminism plays in her work, as well as her ongoing commitment to promoting feminism as a viable and positive politics for teenage girls.

Central to Tavi's positioning of herself as a feminist is her consistent adoption of a girlhood subjectivity, often making reference to herself as a girl and advocating for not just feminist media, but a *feminist girls' media culture*. This is significant because it is this subjectivity that distinguishes her from the adult feminist voices that are usually dominant when feminism is talked or written about publicly. In interviews, for example, Tavi often makes clear that she's speaking from the position of a girl, and in doing so, is able to explore and critique ideas about girls based on her own subject position. In a 2012 interview Tavi is explicit about calling out the ageist and sexist assumptions that understand girls as ignorant of political and social issues. "I think it's alarming or surprising for people to realize that teenage girls are much more aware of certain things than they thought," she says.

Her own sense of gendered power relations is revealed throughout the interview, as Tavi considers the limited subjectivities available to girls based upon sexist ideas about girlhood. She argues, "If you're a girl you have to show some kind of insecurity, to like, show that you're an okay person and that you're not too sure of yourself or whatever. Because that would make you threatening to other people and people don't want to be threatened by a girl, because that would be insulting." Although she doesn't specifically mention her own experience in the fashion industry, her comments can easily be read as reflecting the ways in which adult fashion insiders were threatened by her confident performance of girlhood, and by extension, their often insulting, sexist, and ageist comments made about her. Tavi's ability to vocally embrace girlhood and feminism simultaneously challenges her adult critics who attempted to silence her through hurtful remarks and unfair critiques. In doing so, Tavi is reframing girlhood as a positive, powerful, and feminist subjectivity and challenging the dominant discourses that suggest girlhood is a time of silence and powerlessness. She is practicing a feminist girl citizenship through both her vocal politics and embracing of girlhood, asserting her right to public space and voice.

Tavi's discussion of girlhood is refreshing because, unlike many adult feminists who can't understand why girls have not adopted a feminist position, Tavi avoids criticizing her girl peers, instead understanding their behavior as indicative of larger patterns of gendered socialization and societal power imbalances. When asked about feminism and girls in 2012, Tavi responds,

> I do think there's a stigma attached to the word feminism, if you say I'm a feminist, because most people do probably think that women should be paid equally and people would probably not call themselves a sexist, but it's just that word that they can't get behind because ... if you're a feminist you're angry for no reason or man-hating or whatever, and taking up space. And no one wants to be that person. Especially if you're a girl – you're taught not to feel like an inconvenience to anyone else. When you speak out against something, even just a guy friend making some sexist joke, they will probably feel defensive and threatened. And girls aren't taught that it's okay to speak out. You're not supposed to be that person, you're not supposed to be threatening or whatever to a guy like that (PBS 2012).

Tavi's discussion highlights girls' hesitancy to adopt the feminist label as a somewhat rational and reasonable choice, given their social context. In doing so, she suggests that it is not individual girls' low self-esteem or apolitical nature that prevents them from being vocal citizens, but the patriarchal culture in which they live. Her stance represents a significant departure from the girls' loss of voice discourse that focuses on individualizing girls' perceived problems, as I discussed in chapter one.

Tavi's Feminist Media Production

Tavi has incorporated her feminist girlhood subjectivity into both her blog and more recently, *Rookie*, which she launched in September 2011. Unlike the personal blog format of *StyleRookie*, *Rookie* employs a regular staff, has new content three times a day every weekday, and even occasionally has celebrities write feature columns. Although closer in structure to the online versions of the mainstream glossies, the feminist nature of *Rookie* distinguishes it from most other publications for girls. For example, whereas it is not uncommon for editors of teenage magazines to embrace words like 'empowerment' in place of feminism (Keller 2011), Tavi breaks from this tradition by admitting that "On *Rookie*, everything is through a feminist lens, we're a feminist site" (PBS 2012). Tavi tells PBS that the decision to start *Rookie* was because she felt like "there just wasn't anything today that was honest to an audience of teenage girls or respected their intelligence." And apparently, others agree. *Rookie* became a quick success, registering over one million page views in the first five days after its launch and making headlines in both the blogosphere and in mainstream media, including positive reviews in *The New York Times*, *Ms. Magazine*, and the BBC, among others (Amed 2012).

Although it is not my intention to provide a comprehensive analysis of *Rookie* here, I want to emphasize the way that *Rookie* functions as a public space that Tavi has created for girls to talk about feminist issues, including, sexual harassment ("First Encounters with the Male Gaze"), rape culture ("How We Dress Does Not Mean Yes"), eating disorders ("The Year of My Eating Disorder"), sexuality and queer culture ("Choose Your Own Adventure"), female friendships ("Getting Over Girl Hate"), and activism ("Why Can't I Be You: Shelby Knox, feminist activist"). *Rookie* also consistently celebrates women and girl musicians, comedians, actors, and writers and often provides how-to lessons for readers on succeeding in these often-sexist industries ("last Night (Being) a DJ Saved My Life"), promoting readers to be active producers of culture rather than just consumers.

Rookie is built around the celebration and cultivation of a feminist *girlhood* subjectivity specifically. While girlhood is celebrated in obvious ways (such as featuring "Girl Gangs" as the monthly theme for November 2011), it is also visible in the way *Rookie* pays tribute to longstanding girl culture traditions (the "dear diary" section), girl style ("How to Bejewel Your Tights"), and girl icons ("In Defense of the Spice Girls"). Most importantly, though, *Rookie* celebrates girls' same-sex friendships through a regular column called "Girl Crush," where girls send in a tribute to their best friend, which is featured on the site along with photos of the friends and an interview. The column appropriates the idea of the heterosexual 'crush' and instead mobilizes it as a way for girls to celebrate their friendships and privilege girls, rather than boys. This practice can be understood as continuing important traditions of cultural and third wave feminisms, while suggesting the importance of online spaces for girls to maintain and develop friendships, as I discussed in chapter three.

Unlike mainstream teen magazines, *Rookie* does not promote a singular model of girlhood as the 'correct' way to be a girl. Whereas magazines like *Seventeen* promote normative feminine beauty standards and the seemingly perfect celebrities that embody them, *Rookie* writers often subvert these standards, celebrating the tomboy style of *To Kill a Mockingbird's* Scout Finch ("Secret Style Icon: Scout Finch"), the awkwardness of becoming a teenager ("The Importance of Being Awkward"), and respect for the inner geek ("Literally the Best Thing Ever: Star Trek: The Next Generation"). *Rookie's* presentation of girlhood as diverse, fun, and active, its valuing of (commonly degraded) girl culture, and its celebration of girl friendships and camaraderie can be viewed as significant in creating a discursive space for a public feminist girlhood subjectivity.

Tavi is not the first person to utilize the position of girlhood to adopt a feminist subjectivity. The riot grrrl movement also relied on a girl subjectivity as a dominant position with which to critique issues such as violence, beauty and body image, media representations, sexual double standards, and the right to cultural space and means of production (Kearney 2006). Commercial "girl power" rhetoric, whereas problematic in many respects, could also be understood as privileging girl subjectivities, although significantly more limited ones than riot grrrl (Currie, Kelly, and Pomerantz 2009; Zaslow 2009; Hains 2012). As Harris (2004) notes, girl power informs the can-do girl subjectivity, which offers girls a distinct mode of performing a girled citizenship that relies on a body consistent with hegemonic femininity, the consumption of mainstream girl products, and a public presence that upholds neoliberal values such as entrepreneurship, self-invention, and personal responsibility. However, it is Tavi's emphasis on girlhood as a *political* subjectivity, her public embracing of activism (she claims that "activism, activism, activism!" must be part of media for girls)[9], and her rejection of hegemonic femininity that distinguishes her performance of girlhood from the commercial girl power subjectivity that informs can-do girlhood.

While actively embracing a girl feminist subjectivity has certainly distinguished Tavi from other girl and young women celebrities, it is perhaps her role as cultural producer, rather than just a consumer, that makes adults like Scott Schuman so uncomfortable and hostile toward her. In a 2009 blog post, *Jezebel* writer Jenna Sauers raises this possibility when she smartly observes that prominent fashion writer Lesley M.M. Blume's negative comments about Tavi reveal that Blume "would no doubt prefer that Tavi were reading her young adult novels, rather than competing with her for free-lance gigs" (Sauers 2009). Thus, while adults like Blume have characterized her as a short-lived trend, Tavi has continued to make engaging media, most recently in her role as editor-in-chief and founder of *Rookie*, becoming competition for many adults attempting to sell their own ideas to the desirable teenage girl market.

While Tavi is a fascinating media figure in her own right, this case study makes apparent the high stakes for girls who wish to be vocal media producers within a media culture that often values girls' visibility over their voices – especially when those voices are explicitly political, feminist, and not afraid to call out the patriarchal practices of corporate media, such as

Seventeen magazine. In this sense girls like Tavi and the other bloggers discussed in this book must be seen as citizens who are not only speaking up in the public sphere, but are actively attempting to change that public sphere in order to create a space where more girls' voices can be heard.

Conclusions: Feminist Blogging as a Practice of Citizenship for Girls

Elisabeth Klaus and Margreth Lunenborg (2012) define cultural citizenship as "a set of strategies and practices to invoke processes of empowerment in order to subversively listen and speak up in the public sphere" (204). I have drawn on their definition in my own conception of citizenship, as their emphasis on the ability to speak up in the public sphere is particularly significant for girls, who continue to occupy a precarious position in public space.

This idea has guided my inquiry into how girl feminist bloggers have used public space to advocate for feminist politics. In this chapter I demonstrated how girl feminist bloggers such as Julie Zeilinger, Jamie Keiles, and Tavi Gevinson have utilized entrepreneurial strategies to vocalize their feminist politics and promote their feminist blogs. In doing so, they challenge both postfeminist can-do and protectionist discourses of girlhood – a prospect that can be threatening to adults, as demonstrated in my case study of Tavi. Furthermore, by publicizing their blogs through mainstream commercial media, Julie, Jamie, and Tavi have made feminism accessible to a wide range of girls who may not have encountered feminist politics within their daily lives. It is this performance of a vocal politics as part of a public girlhood that characterizes the citizenship I define here.

Although I do acknowledge the convergence of some of the bloggers' strategies with postfeminist ideals, I am uncomfortable with framing girls' online practices as primarily about self-branding, attaining celebrity visibility, and performances of postfeminist hegemonic femininity. Indeed, this framework ignores the politics that girls such as Julie, Jamie, and Tavi advocate through the public space they generate via new media. This does not mean that we should ignore the structural inequalities that shape *which* girl feminist bloggers have access to mainstream visibility; indeed, Julie, Jamie, and Tavi all are white, middle-class, and possess normative body types privileged within popular culture. This issue suggests a significant limitation of a feminist activist strategy that relies solely on attaining mainstream visibility and celebrity status, a point worthy of further research by feminist media scholars (see Keller 2015). Nonetheless, the public visibility of alternative girlhoods generated through participatory culture, such as the feminist girlhood subjectivities performed by the bloggers I've discussed in this chapter, remind us of the necessary inclusion of girls' public voices and vocal politics for challenging postfeminist popular culture.

Notes

1. Because I refer to all the bloggers by their first names, I will continue this practice with Tavi.
2. See Hopkins 2002; Harris 2004; Banet-Weiser 2011, 2012b; Blue 2012, 2013 and Projansky 2014 for comprehensive discussion of the relationship between girls and celebrity culture.
3. Feedback is a fundamental part of social media, whereby visitors (both anonymous and known) to a site or profile leave a comment. However, Banet-Weiser (2011, 288) notes that often times feedback functions as a "neoliberal disciplinary strategy" that can operate as a strategy of "surveillance, judgment and evaluation," such as rating girls looks on their YouTube videos. She argues that girls often gain "value" (positive comments, compliments, praise) for performing normative standards of femininity. See Banet-Weiser (2011, 2012b) for discussion.
4. Many of these technologies have gendered names, such as "Girl Ambition," a parent-monitored social networking environment, and "Anne's Diary," a subscription only website for girls 6–12 years old. Consequently, there is little confusion that these programs are meant for parents with daughters, not sons.
5. See Keller 2012 for a discussion of the *Seventeen Magazine Project*.
6. Whereas it is beyond the scope of this chapter to comprehensively discuss the history of girl celebrities, it is important to note that the entertainment industry has been one public space where girls have been visible figures. Girl stars such as Shirley Temple (1930s), Patty Duke (1950s and 1960s), and Mary Kate and Ashley Olsen (1990s) are all prominent examples of girls who have occupied public space as entertainers. See Blue (2013) for a comprehensive discussion.
7. This implication that 'real' fashion editors and journalists working for print magazines do not receive gifts and incentives is problematic, as they often receive gifts, complimentary samples, and event invitations from designers and fashion companies. It is common practice at most magazines to keep these gifts and accept event invitations. For example, when I was an intern at a New York-based fashion magazine, I received a free pair of Seven jeans (retail value of about $250) for attending a free breakfast from a beauty company releasing a new teeth-whitening product.
8. Although I describe Tavi as 'white,' I want to clarify that she is of Jewish ethnicity. However, because she doesn't often discuss her Jewish identity, nor is it mentioned in press reports, Tavi is often 'read' as white.
9. Tavi said this as part of her ideaCity10 talk, where one of her PowerPoint slides outlines how her ideal magazine for teen girls would approach politics, listing "Activism activism activism" as one of the bullet points.

References

Ahmed, Imran. 2012. "The Business of Blogging: Tavi Gevinson." *The Business of Fashion*, April 24. Accessed March 3, 2013. http://www.businessoffashion.com/2012/04/the-business-of-blogging-tavi-gevinson.html.

Aapola, Sinikka, Marnina Gonick, and Anita Harris. 2005. *Young Femininity: Girlhood, Power and Social Change*. New York: Palgrave.

Alani, Anaheed. 2012. "Smells Like Teen Spirit." *Bust Magazine*, August/September. 76: 39–45.

Baker, Sarah. 2011. "Playing Online: Pre-Teen Girls' Negotiations of Pop and Porn in Cyberspace." In *Mediated Girlhoods: New Explorations of Girls' Media Culture,*171–187. New York: Peter Lang.

Banet-Weiser, Sarah. 2007. *Kids Rule!: Nickelodeon and Consumer Citizenship.* Durham: Duke University Press.

Banet-Weiser, Sarah. (2011). Branding the Post-Feminist Self: Girls' Video Production and YouTube. In *Mediated Girlhoods: New Explorations of Girls' Media Culture,* edited by Mary Celeste Kearney, 277–294. New York: Peter Lang.

Banet-Weiser, Sarah. 2012b. *Authentic TM: The Politics of Ambivalence in a Brand Culture.* New York: New York University Press.

Bazillian, Emma. 2013. "16-Year Old Media Mogul is Expanding Her Empire, Including Online Mag *Rookie.*" *Adweek*, April 14. Accessed September 27, 2014. http://www.adweek.com/news/advertising-branding/16-year-old-mediamogul-tavi-gevinson-expanding-her-empire-148565.

Blue, Morgan Genevieve. 2012. "The Best of Both Worlds? Youth, gender and a post-feminist sensibility in Disney's *Hannah Montana.*" *Feminist Media Studies* 13(4): 660–675.

Blue, Morgan Genevieve. 2013. "Performing 21$_{st}$-century girlhood: Girls, postfeminist discourse and the Disney star machine." PhD diss., University of Texas at Austin.

Bordo, Susan. 1993. *Unbearable Weight: Feminism, Western Culture, and the Body.* Berkeley: University of California Press.

Buckingham, David, Maria Pini, and Rebekah Willett. 2009. "'Take Back the Tube!:' The Discursive Construction of Amateur Film-and Video-Making." In *Video Cultures: Media Technology and Everyday Creativity*, edited by David Buckingham and Rebekah Willett, 51–70. New York: Palgrave MacMillan.

Burgess, Jean, Marcus Foth, and Helen Klaebe. 2006. "Everyday Creativity as Civic Engagement: A Cultural Citizenship View of New Media." Paper presented at the *Communications Policy and Research Forum,* Sydney, Australia, November 25–26.

Cadenas, Kerensa. 2010. "Tavi Gevinson is Fashionable, Feminist and Just 14." *Ms.* Blog, October 8. Accessed March 17, 2012. http://msmagazine.com/blog/2010/10/08/tavigevinson-is-fashionable-feminist-and-just-14/.

Caron, Caroline. 2011. "Getting Girls and Teens in the Vocabularies of Citizenship." *Girlhood Studies* 4(2): 70–91.

Cassell, Justine, and Meg Cramer. 2008. "High Tech or High Risk: Moral Panics About Girls Online." In *Digital Youth, Innovation, and the Unexpected,* edited by Tara McPherson, 53–75. Cambridge: MIT Press.

Currie, Dawn, Deirdre Kelly, and Shauna Pomerantz. 2009. *'Girl Power:' Girls Reinventing Girlhood.* New York: Peter Lang.

Dimitriadis, Greg. 2008. "Series Editor Introduction." In *Next Wave Cultures: Feminism, Subcultures, Activism,* edited by Anita Harris, ix-x. New York: Routeldge.

Driscoll, Catherine. 2002. *Girls: Feminine Adolescence in Popular Culture and Cultural History.* New York: Columbia University Press.

Ehrenreich, Barbara, Elizabeth Hess, and Gloria Jacobs. 1986. *Re-making Love: The Feminization of Sex.* Garden City, NJ: Anchor Press.

Foucault, Michel. 1977. *Discipline & Punish.* Translated by Alan Sheridan. New York: Vintage Books.

Gevinson, Tavi. 2010a. "How We Can Apply What We Learned from the Teen Girls of the 90s to Create a Good Magazine for Teen Girls Today." Talk at *IdeaCity10,*

Toronto, Canada, July. Accessed April 1, 2012. http://www.ideacityonline.com/talks/tavi-gevinson-on-feministfashion-magazine/.

Gevinson, Tavi. 2010b. "An Open Letter to Seventeen Magazine, also, WHY ARE YOU UGLY WHAT IS WRONG WITH YOU." *StyleRookie,* July. Accessed April 2, 2012. http://www.thestylerookie.com/2010/07/open-letter-to-seventeen-magazine-also.html.

Gill, Rosalind. 2007. "Postfeminist Media Culture: Elements of a Sensibility." *European Journal of Cultural Studies* 10 (2): 147–166.

Goldenberg-Fife, Natalie. 2010. "Thirteen-year-old Makes *Flare* Editor Cry." *Toronto Life,* January 28. Accessed March 9, 2012. http://www.torontolife.com/daily/style/random-stuffgoods/2010/01/28/thirteen-year-old-makes-flare-editor-cry-hm-organic-line-isnot-organic-jimmy-choo-emulates-tommy-ton/.

Graham, David. 2012. "Fashion Week: The Beleaguered Art of Fashion Criticism." *Toronto Star*, March 7. Accessed March 23, 2012. http://www.thestar.com/life/fash ion_style/2012/03/07/fashion_week_the_beleaguered_art_of_fashion_criticism.html.

Haddad, Candice. 2011. "Immigration, Authorship, Censorship, and Terrorism: The Politics of M.I.A.'s US Crossover." In *In the Limelight and Under the Microscope: Forms and Functions of Female Celebrity,* edited by Su Holmes and Diane Negra, 280–302. New York: Continuum.

Hains, Rebecca. 2012. *Growing Up With Girl Power: Girlhood on Screen and In Everyday Life.* New York: Peter Lang.

Haramis, Nick. 2010. "Tavi Gevinson Styles Her First-Ever Fashion Editorial for *Blackbook*." *Blackbook* blog, July 8. Accessed March 12, 2012. http://www.blackbookmag.com/fashion/tavi-gevinson-styles-her-first-everfashion-editorial-for-blackbook-1.33742.

Harris, Anita. 2004. *Future Girl: Young Women in the Twenty-first Century.* New York: Routledge.

Harris, Anita. 2012b. "Citizenship Stories." In *Keywords in Youth Studies: Tracing Affects, Movements, Knowledges*, edited by Nancy Lesko and Susan Talburt, pp. 143–153. New York: Routledge.

Hasinoff, Amy. 2013. "Sexting as Media Production: Rethinking Social Media and Sexuality." *New Media & Society* 15: 449–465.

Heywood, Leslie, and Jennifer Drake. 1997. *Third Wave Agenda: Being Feminist, Doing Feminism.* Minneapolis: University of Minnesota Press.

Hopkins, Susan. 2002. *Girl Heroes: The New Force in Popular Culture.* London: Pluto Press.

Hou, Yuqi. 2011. "This is What a Feminist Looks Like." *The Harvard Independent*, December 1. Accessed January 15, 2013. http://www.harvardindependent.com/2011/12/thisis-what-a-feminist-looks-like-the-indy-interviews-jamie-keiles-co-organizer-ofslutwalk-chicago-1201/.

Jenson, Joli. 1992. "Fandom as Pathology: The Consequences of Characterization." In *The Adoring Audience: Fan Culture and Popular Media*, edited by Lisa Lewis, 9–29. New York: Routledge.

Jesella, Kara, and Marisa Meltzer. 2007. *How Sassy Changed My Life: A Love Letter to the Greatest Teen Magazine of All Time.* New York: Farrar, Straus and Giroux.

Kearney, Mary Celeste. 2005. "Birds on the Wire." *Cultural Studies* 19(5): 568–601.

Kearney, Mary Celeste. 2006. *Girls Make Media.* New York: Routledge.

Kearney, Mary Celeste. 2007. "Productive Spaces." *Journal of Children and Media* 1(2): 26–1 141.

Keller, Jessalynn. 2011. "Feminist Editors and the New Girl Glossies: Fashionable Feminisms of Just Another Sexist Rag?" *Women's Studies International Forum* 34(1): 1–12.

Keller, Jessalynn. 2012. "Virtual Feminisms." *Information, Communication and Society* 15 (3): 429–447.

Keller, Jessalynn. 2015. "Girl Power's Last Chance? Tavi Gevinson, Feminism, and Popular Media Culture." *Continuum: Journal of Media and Cultural Studies.* DOI: 10.1080/10304312.2015.1022947.

Kingston, Anne. 2014. "New Girl, Go Girl." *Macleans*, September 27. Accessed January 10, 2015. http://www.macleans.ca/society/new-girl-go-girl.

Klaus, Elisabeth, and Margreth Lunenborg. 2012. "Cultural Citizenship: Participation Through Media." In *Feminist Media: Participatory Spaces, Networks and Cultural Citizenship*, edited by Elke Zobl and Ricarda Drueke, 197–212. Germany: Transcript.

Knox, Kristin. 2010. "'New Girl in Town' No More: Tavi @ Couture." *The Clothes Whisperer,* February 1. Accessed March 9, 2012. http://www.theclotheswhisperer.co.uk/2010/01/newgirl-in-town-no-more-tavi-couture.html.

Kwan, Amanda. 2008. "Young Fashion Bloggers Are Worrisome Trend to Parents." *USA Today*, August 12. Accessed March 8, 2012. http://usatoday30.usatoday.com/tech/ webguide/internetlife/2008-08-12-girl-fashion-blogs_N.htm.

Lister, Ruth. 1997. *Citizenship: Feminist Perspectives.* New York: New York University Press.

Marvin, Carolyn. 1990. *When Old Technologies Were New: Thinking About Electric Communication in the Late Nineteenth Century.* Oxford: Oxford University Press.

McRobbie, Angela, and Jenny Garber. 1991. Girls and Subcultures. In *Feminism and Youth Culture*, by Angela McRobbie, 12–25. New York: Routledge.

McRobbie, Angela. 1998. *British Fashion Design: Rag Trade or Image Industry?* New York: Routledge.

McRobbie, Angela. 2009. *The Aftermath of Feminism: Gender, Culture and Social Change.* Thousand Oaks, CA: Sage.

Mesure, Susie. 2010. "Fluff Flies as Fashion Writers Pick a Cat Fight with Bloggers." *The Independent,* January 31. Accessed March 12, 2012. http://www.independent.co.uk/ lifestyle/ fashion/news/fluff-flies-as-fashion-writers-pick-a-cat-fight-with-bloggers-1884539.html.

Miller, Toby. 2007. *Cultural Citizenship: Cosmopolitanism, Consumerism, and Television in a Neoliberal Age.* Philadelphia: Temple University Press.

Nash, Illana. 2006. *American Sweethearts: Teenage Girls in Twentieth-Century Popular Culture.* Indianapolis: Indiana University Press.

Odell, Amy. 2009. "Editors Like Tavi But Don't Take Her Fashion Advice Seriously." *New York Magazine*, December 9. Accessed March 1, 2012. http://nymag.com/thecut/2009/12/tavi_the_13-year-old_fashion_b.html.

PBS. 2012. "*Makers* Profile: Tavi Gevinson." Accessed January 23, 2013. http://www.makers.com/tavi-gevinson.

Pike, Kirsten. 2011. "'The New Activists:' Girls and Discourses of Citizenship, Liberation, and Femininity in Seventeen, 1968–1977." In *Mediated Girlhoods: New Explorations of Girls' Media Culture*, edited by Mary Celeste Kearney, 55–73. New York: Peter Lang.

Projansky, Sarah. 2014. *Spectacular Girls: Media Fascination & Celebrity Culture.* New York: New York University Press.

Reid-Walsh, Jacqueline, and Claudia Mitchell. 2004. "Girls' Web Sites: A Virtual 'Room of One's Own?'" In *All About the Girl: Culture, Power, and Identity*, edited by Anita Harris, 173–182. New York: Routledge.

Sanchez-Eppler, Karen. 2005. *Dependent States: The Child's Part in Nineteenth - Century American Culture*. Chicago: University of Chicago Press.

Sauers, Jenna. 2009. "*Elle* Editor Leads Backlash Against 13-Year-Old Blogger." *Jezebel*, December 10. Accessed April 4, 2012. http://jezebel.com/5423555/elle-editor-leads-backlash-against-13+year+old-fashion-blogger.

Schaer, Cathrin. 2009. "The New Frontline of Fashion: Teenage Bloggers." *New Zealand Herald*, January 22. Accessed February 25, 2012. http://www.nzherald.co.nz/lifestyle/news/article.cfm?c_id=6&objectid=10552921.

Schulman, Michael. 2012. "The Oracle of Girl World." *The New York Times*, July 27. Accessed September 14, 2012. http://www.nytimes.com/2012/07/29/fashion/tavi-gevinson-theoracle-of-girl-world.html.

Shade, Leslie. 2007. "Contested Spaces: Protecting of Inhibiting Girls Online?" In *Growing Up Online: Young People and Digital Technologies*, edited by Sandra Weber and Shanly Dixon, 227- 244. New York: Palgrave MacMillan.

Shade, Leslie. 2011. "Surveilling the Girl via the Third and Networked Screen." In *Mediated Girlhoods: New Explorations of Girls' Media Culture*, edited by Mary Celeste Kearney, 261–275. New York: Peter Lang.

Spiridakis, Elizabeth. 2008. "Post Adolescents." *New York Times*, August 17. Accessed March 7, 2012. http://www.nytimes.com/2008/08/17/style/tmagazine/17tween.html?_r=0.

Sweeney, Kathleen. 2008. *Maiden USA: Girl Icons Come of Age*. New York: Peter Lang.

Taft, Jessica. 2011. *Rebel Girls: Youth Activism & Social Change Across the Americas*. New York: New York University Press.

The Talks blog. 2011. "Scott Shuman: 'Magazines Are Driven By Fear.'" *The Talks*, September 28. Accessed February 15, 2012. http://the-talks.com/interviews/scott-schuman-the-sartorialist/.

Tishgart, Sierra. 2012. "Teen Author Julie Zeilinger on Her Feminist Blog and New Book. *Teen Vogue*." Teen Vogue, May. Accessed September 14, 2013. http://www.teenvogue.com/mylife/profiles/2012-05/julie-zeilinger-feminism.

Voet, Rian. 1998. *Feminism and Citizenship*. Thousand Oaks: Sage.

Weinger, Erin. 2013. "The Girl Who's Wise Beyond Her Years." *Foam Magazine*, January 11. Accessed February 12, 2013. http://foammagazine.com/articles/2774-the-girl-who-s-wisebeyond-her-years.

Young, Iris. 1990. *Throwing Like a Girl and Other Essays in Feminist Philosophy and Social Theory*. Bloomington: Indiana University Press.

Zaslow, Emilie. 2009. *Feminism INC: Coming of Age in a Girl Power Media Culture*. New York: Palgrave MacMillan.

Zeilinger, Julie. 2012b. Author website. Accessed March 1, 2013. http://www.juliezeilinger.com.

Conclusion
Toward a Girl-Friendly Feminist Future

"Feminists still have a lot of work to do in terms of countering the negative stereotype of feminism in the media and the overarching idea that feminism is dead, but I think that teen girls today are completely ready and willing to take on that fight."

—Julie Zeilinger, email interview

As 2014 commenced, the wish of many feminist girl bloggers was seemingly becoming reality: feminist activism was thriving on many college campuses in the United States (Grigoriadis 2014), celebrities were eagerly embracing the once-shunned "f-word" (Valenti 2014), and feminism was increasingly visible within media cultures as hashtags like #YesAllWomen and #BeenRapedNeverReported circulated throughout digital media platforms, their impact extensively covered by traditional media (Cresci 2014; Gallant 2014). But what does this increased visibility of feminism within commercial media cultures mean to the young feminist activists I documented in this book? How do they position themselves within these popular feminist discourses? Is there a relationship between their use of digital technologies and the increasing mainstream visibility of feminist politics? And what might it mean for those of us who study feminism, digital media, and girls? In this conclusion I consider these questions, drawing on two-year follow-up interviews with my study participants, before reflecting on what this moment of "feminist zeitgeist" (Valenti 2014) might suggest for feminist digital media studies as a growing scholarly field.

Contemplating Feminist Futures

Colleagues, friends and family often ask me about the *long-term* impact of girls' feminist blogging. People want to know how this practice improves the material conditions of girls and women or how it betters governmental policies in relation to such issues as pay equity or the feminization of poverty. These questions are important yet impossible to answer, as a research project such as this cannot and is not meant to determine a simple causal relationship between blogging and social change; as media scholars we know that linear media effects models rarely uncover the complexity of people's engagement with media cultures. As a small study that is focused on a non-representative sample of girls, it is not ideal to make generalizations or definitive conclusions. Yet, as I reconnect with several of the participants close to two years after our final interviews their reflections point to the ways in which the practice of feminist blogging may contribute to an ongoing participation in feminist politics and the visibility of feminism we're now seeing within popular media cultures.

Upon contacting the bloggers, I was excited to find all of them still engaged in a wide range of feminist activism, both on and offline. To wit: Amandine continues to be an active blogger, and having graduated from high school, now also participates in several college feminist groups, including one whose aim is to end sexual assault and rape culture on campus. Renee is also now a college student studying ethnic, gender, and labor studies, which according to her, has continued to expand her awareness of feminist and social justice issues. Although she's put her blogging on pause while she's studying, she continues to follow the feminist blogosphere as a reader and is considering writing a column on feminist and social justice issues for her college newspaper. As the oldest blogger in the study, Courtney has graduated from college and is enrolled in a master's degree program in counseling where she is specializing in issues of domestic violence and intimate partner violence. She doesn't currently have time to blog, but she still is active in curating feminist content on her Facebook page and Tumblr blog and keeps abreast of feminist issues via her social media networks.

These examples show that feminist politics remain a significant part of the bloggers' lives, even if they are no longer actively maintaining their own blog. In the follow-up interviews several girls spoke of the ways in which their feminist blogging and emergent feminist identities have shaped their future aspirations. Amandine reports, "Feminism has informed my aspiration to go to law school and use my JD to work for a national feminist activist organization and help women advance their status in the world." Likewise, Madison claims that although she's always wanted to be a lawyer, she now sees herself specifically working on feminist legal issues, such as cases involving sexual assault and domestic violence. Julie also credits feminism and her experience as a feminist blogger for continually motivating her to work toward her goal of being a writer. She reflects, "Since I started feminist blogging, I've definitely transitioned from being very shy and self-deprecating to outgoing and unafraid to advocate for myself. I think in the long run that will undoubtedly help me achieve my aspirations." Based on these conversations it is not a stretch to suggest that the bloggers' feminist identities, intricately connected to their blogging as I discuss in chapter one, are shaping their aspirations in ways that will likely be reflected in the legal, educational, non-profit, and cultural sectors in the coming years.

Whereas feminism continues to positively shape the bloggers' lives, several emphasized that their feminism has changed throughout their blogging and the life transitions that they've experienced over the past two years. Madison discusses her feminism as becoming increasingly more "radical," whereas Amandine admits that she's become more open in her new college environment to what she describes as "third wave" politics. Most significant are the ways in which several bloggers spoke of their feminism becoming more far reaching than gender equality. For example, Renee says,

> My feminism has evolved drastically from my high school days and I'm glad for it. Let's just say intersectionality wasn't the focus of my politics as a feminist in high school. It's true that as a white, straight, middle-class woman feminism was my gateway to other crucial movements that I didn't initially connect with as poignantly as the fight to end sexist oppression. I knew, of course, that fighting racial oppression, allying with LGBTQ folks and others were important. But the mainstay of my feminism was 'equal rights for women!' without asking myself 'which women?'

Renee discusses how several college classes encouraged her to understand feminism as being about challenging intersecting structural inequalities rather than being simply about "equal rights" and "choice." In this sense, she acknowledges that her feminism has "changed for the better" and that she feels much more confident in her feminist views.

Julie also considers her college experience as transformational for her feminist politics. She reflects, "Especially after taking women's studies classes in college, my feminism has become increasingly intersectional. I feel that I've definitely come to understand feminism as the intersection of race, gender, class, [and other identities] in a way that I had previously paid lip service to but hadn't really understood on a deeper theoretical level." Considering my discussion of the lack of diversity in the young feminist blogosphere in chapter three, these comments from Renee and Julie are encouraging and remind us that young people's feminisms evolve as they gain more life experiences and move outside of their childhood environments. Thus, the articulations of feminism I documented throughout this book must not be understood as absolute and unchanging, but as fluid, experimental, and shaped by one's social and cultural context, likely to change as young people encounter new experiences, places, and people.

More Than "Leaning In": Reflections on the Feminist Zeitgeist

At the beginning of this book I analyzed how young feminists negotiated the marginalization they often felt as teenage feminists, using digital media production as a way to experiment with feminist identities that may not be accepted in their high school environments. Yet today, the increased visibility of feminism within popular media cultures means that more teens are likely hearing about feminism and high school girls may even be able to confidently perform a once scorned feminist identity in the company of influential celebrities such as Beyoncé, Lorde, and Emma Watson.[1]

The bloggers were unanimously supportive of this cultural shift, recognizing the need for feminism to be demystified and more accessible to young people – something that many of my study participants attempted to do with their blogging, as I discuss in chapter two. For example, Amandine says, "I think it is great that there is more attention being given to feminism … I mean, the fact that there are mainstream articles being written about rape culture and stuff like that. Words like patriarchy are no longer just within the [vocabulary] of feminist activists and theorists." Other bloggers, such as Courtney and Julie, also recognize the importance of feminist topics such as unattainable beauty standards, reproductive rights, and work-life balance getting coverage within mainstream media.

However, the bloggers are also critical of this mainstreaming of feminism, particularly in relation to the kinds of feminism most prevalent within popular culture. Abby reflects, "I've noticed much more attention to feminism in mainstream media, but it's often a very surface-level feminism. Much ink has been spilled about issues like 'leaning in,' but deep discourse about systemic inequality still has not penetrated the mainstream media. I do think that more discussion of feminism is good though, in most forms it takes." Similarly, Julie feels as though the complexities of feminism are often absent within popular media discussions: "We are not defining it [feminism] and we are not taking the time to explain what it really is … We don't take the time to explain that feminism is actually the intersectional approach to equality and oppression, it is more than just women being like, yeah there should be more women in the music industry or whatever." Abby and Julie's comments point to the bloggers' increased attention to intersectional power relations, as I discussed in the previous section, and suggest that the simplistic version of feminism most visible within popular media cultures is a consequence of a widespread lack of education about feminism.

Julie continues: "So I think it is great that there is more exposure to [feminism] and we are talking about it at all, but … we are still not doing a good job of educating women about feminism." Renee echoes this point as we discuss the recent increase of young celebrities publicly identifying as feminist (see Keller and Ringrose 2015). While Renee claims that these performances of "celebrity feminism" (Hamad and Taylor 2015) ultimately shouldn't matter, she contends,

> You kind of hold your breath because if they [celebrities] are positive on feminism it is kind of like a good feeling … Phew, we have one more high profile person on our side! And when you find out that they are against feminism, your heart kind of sinks because inevitably they will say things like 'Oh I'm not a feminist, I love men, I think men and women should be equal and women shouldn't try to take over.' It's like, what?! It is so frustrating because they obviously have no idea about the subject. So I don't understand why they have never – no actually I understand why they have never learned about feminism.

Renee's comments highlight the problem with relying on celebrities to promote feminism – most of the celebrity girls and women, like their non-celebrity counterparts, have never actually been educated about it. As I've documented throughout this book, this absence of feminism from many elementary and high school curricula is a significant barrier to more girls (and boys) identifying as feminist and must constitute an issue of concern and activism for feminist scholars.[2]

It is not possible to determine exactly *why* feminism is part of the public conversation today in ways that it wasn't when I began this research. There is a temptation to suggest that the Internet is responsible, having provided a platform for the feminist activism I have been analyzing in this book. I do not want to promote this technological deterministic perspective because as I've shown in the previous chapters, technology is always situated within larger social and cultural contexts and debates. Yet, the relationship between feminist blogs and feminist discourses in the mainstream media is worth considering, and the bloggers I spoke to make some convincing arguments about this complex relationship. For example, Julie tells me how she not only sees an increase in the attention to feminism since she began blogging in 2008, but she understands feminist blogs as being crucial to this shift. She contends,

> I think blogs like *Jezebel* have played a huge part in this [the mainstream visibility of feminism]. *Jezebel*, at least when it was founded, was unabashedly feminist and still produces a lot of feminist content, and yet is decidedly mainstream, at this point. I also think that certain conversations – like the underrepresentation of women in the media, unattainable beauty standards, [and] work/life balance – have transcended the feminist sphere and are conversations had across the country and the world. It seems that mainstream media have observed the considerable traffic many feminist blogs get and correctly deduced that if they covered the same issues they can get similarly impressive views on their sites.

Julie's comments are interesting because they hint at feminism being profitable, alluding to girls and women as valuable and influential media consumers. They also point to the changing nature of converged media industries. As more blogs and web-based publications become popular sources for news and cultural commentary, we may see more feminist views being articulated within highly read publications (see Harp, Loke, and Bachmann 2014), a potentially exciting development within digital media cultures that is worthy of future research.

But whereas feminism is increasingly visible within popular media cultures, we're also simultaneously witnessing what Sarah Banet-Weiser (2015) has recently termed "popular misogyny," an overt style of misogynistic discourses and practices increasingly permeating media cultures in the form of men's rights groups, the harassment of feminist bloggers, and hacked photos of nude female celebrities. While Banet-Weiser characterizes popular misogyny as a backlash to the feminist zeitgeist, and even in part due to the pervasiveness of digital media technologies, Amandine instead suggests that digital media has merely made misogyny more visible, which in turn has revived mainstream feminist debate. She discusses the website Reddit as an example of the ways in which misogynistic comments are documented online, which can then serve as 'hard evidence' of the need for feminism. Both Amandine and Banet-Weiser's comments are thought-provoking in that they encourage us to think about the recent visibility of feminism as part of a complex media culture shaped by digital technologies where misogynistic content is increasingly prominent and even accepted as normative "lad culture" (see Renold, Ringrose, Jackson, and Phipps forthcoming 2016).

The Future of Feminist Digital Media Studies

As I've documented throughout this book, feminist media studies scholars have done an excellent job demonstrating how postfeminism as a cultural sensibility (Gill 2007), permeates contemporary media culture and how the resulting media representations and cultural discourses are extremely limiting for girls and young women (Budgeon 2001; Zaslow 2009; Currie, Kelly, and Pomerantz 2009; McRobbie 2009; Hains 2012; Banet-Weiser 2011, 2012; Scharff 2012; Ringrose 2013). But while feminism certainly haunts these discussions, it remains somewhat periphery to inquiries about postfeminism. As scholars such as Rosalind Gill (2007) and Angela McRobbie (2009) have reminded us, we know that feminism must be culturally present in order for postfeminist logic to function, yet there has been little research to date locating girls' feminist politics within such a cultural environment.

This book aims to address this oversight. In addition to making feminist girls visible within scholarly literature on postfeminism, I demonstrate the significance of their feminist and activist identities within a culture where these subjectivities are often disparaged – especially for girls. I have argued that the practice of feminist blogging has been a crucial way for girls to explore feminism, engage in activism, connect with likeminded girls, speak agentially in public, and understand themselves as part of a lengthy historical movement. Blogging can be understood as facilitating resistance and a political subjectivity among girl feminist bloggers in ways similar to the media production practices used by riot grrrls in the 1990s. Consequently, this project builds upon the feminist scholarship on riot grrrl's cultural production (Kearney 2006; Schilt 2003; Piepmeier 2009), in order to contextualize and historicize girl bloggers' feminist activism. In doing so, I intervene in the scholarly work on postfeminism referenced earlier by suggesting that girls' feminist blogging continues a lengthy history of girls' media production that is often marginalized within feminist scholarship in favor of examining girls as cultural consumers, rather than producers.

Yet, the research for this book commenced at a moment when popular discourse about feminism is changing (Valenti 2014; Traister and Shulevitz 2014). As various feminisms continue to be visible within popular media culture, it is necessary to ask how feminist media studies scholars can make sense of Beyoncé dancing in front of the illuminated word "FEMINIST" or the mainstream popularity of Tavi Gevinson's feminist-inspired *Rookie* magazine, as I discuss in chapter five.[3] Do these new articulations of popular feminism present a challenge to our theorizing of postfeminist media culture? Who are these representations of feminism appealing to and which feminisms remain unrepresented in commercial media? What new gendered subjectivities are on offer to girls and women within this cultural moment? And how do they differ and converge with the postfeminist subjectivities we have been analyzing over the past decade?

These questions are of particular urgency for feminist digital media scholars, because feminist politics are increasingly being performed and circulated on digital platforms, as I've discussed throughout this book. Several feminist initiatives, such as the Twitter campaign #YesAllWomen, have been crucial in not only making issues such as violence against women visible, but also eventful – as worthy of documentation and political discussion (Thrift 2014).[4] How these types of feminist digital initiatives complicate our understandings of postfeminist media culture needs to be considered in a sustained and systematic way. Here, I argue for the recognition of girl feminist bloggers as challenging postfeminist discourses of girlhood through their performance of feminist identities and resistance of can-do girlhood via the adoption of political subjectivities. Yet there remains much more to consider in relation to the ways in which feminists are using digital media to subvert normative femininities and perhaps even postfeminist media culture.

The future of feminist digital media studies also calls on us to be particularly attentive to issues of difference, diversity, and intersectionality. As I discussed in chapter three, the young feminist blogosphere is not as diverse as it should be and we can understand this problematic homogeneity (particularly in terms of race) as indicative of structural power inequalities that continue to shape not only who has access to digital technologies, but who has the cultural knowledge, leisure time, and social connections to be made visible within the often complex dynamics of the feminist blogosphere. However, recent feminist initiatives by women of color indicate that this may be changing. As trending hashtags like #SolidarityIsForWhiteWomen and #NotYourAsianSidekick demonstrate, women of color are active contributors to digital feminisms and often use social media to speak to each other across borders and boundaries (Loza 2014).[5] These campaigns are calling into question the way in which mainstream feminism has been equated to white feminism and as Fredrika Thelandersson (2014) argues, point to the potential for productive dialogue between feminists online with the goal of creating a more diverse and intersectional feminist blogosphere. It is these conversations that will be crucial to understanding the future of the feminist blogosphere.

In its focus on American bloggers and their participation in feminist activism within those national borders, this book does not represent the transnational nature of today's media culture, which must also be carefully considered by feminist digital media scholars. Rosalind Gill and Christina Scharff (2011, 9–10) advocate the need to "think transnationally" in order to map how postfeminist and neoliberal discourses operate via transnational power relations. Digital campaigns with seemingly feminist messages such as #BringBackOurGirls must be critically analyzed through the intersections of race, class, and age, but also colonialism (see Loken 2014).[6] Consequently, it is imperative for girls' studies scholars to interrogate the ways in which global power is reinforced, negotiated, challenged, and circulated through online media (see Keller 2012). We may ask: How might feminist girls from non-Western countries engage with feminist blogging as an activist strategy? Is it possible to forge a transnational feminism through the young feminist blogosphere? And, which girls' stories do we hear and which remain excluded from international attention?

Throughout this book I have historicized girls' feminist blogging as continuing longstanding practices of feminist activism, including media production, education, and consciousness-raising. Thus, it is worthwhile to consider how contemporary girls' feminist blogs may function as an archive of girls' feminism in the early twenty-first century for future feminist scholars. How might girl feminist bloggers be functioning as archivists in addition to historiographers, as I discuss in chapter four? What might be the implications of this "living, public archive" (Burgess and Green 2009) of feminism in the Information Age for future feminist girls? In addition to exploring the theoretical questions related to the archival quality of girls' feminist blogs, feminist scholars must also consider the practical questions this idea raises. For example, how can we ensure the survival of girls' feminist blogs for future research by both scholars and girls themselves? Feminists have long recognized the importance of having a record of feminist activism, as evidenced by the numerous archival collections of women's and feminist history throughout the United States, including several collections dedicated to feminist zines. However, as Amy Benson and Kathryn Allamong Jacob (2012) note, we have yet to fully understand how the many feminist electronic documents, such as blogs, will be stored, catalogued, and made accessible to future readers. This is an area of exciting potential, yet requires attention from feminist scholars to ensure that valuable stories do not get lost amidst rapid technological change.

Looking forward into the future seems a suitable place to conclude this book. Indeed, speaking to and reading the work of so many passionate young feminists over the past five years has been inspiring and humbling. I have no doubts that they will carry their politics with them into a feminist future, reminding us that as young feminists they are already here, "still alive and kicking."

Notes

1. Pop singers Beyoncé and Lorde and actress Emma Watson have all received significant media attention for publicly identifying as feminist. See Hamad and Taylor (2015) for discussion of the rise of "celebrity feminism."
2. I want to acknowledge that there are indeed some high school teachers actively trying to incorporate feminism into their curriculum, such as New York City-based "Feminist Teacher" Ileana Jimenez, who blogs about her practices at www.feministteacher.com. However, my point is that this feminist pedagogy is not the norm across the United States and most often occurs at private schools in large cities.
3. Beyoncé performed in front of a glowing backdrop of the word "FEMINIST" at the MTV Video Music Awards on August 24, 2014. The performance generated public debate about not only Beyoncé's feminist politics, but about the increasing visibility of feminist politics within popular culture. See Valenti 2014.
4. As noted in a previous endnote, the #YesAllWomen hashtag began in the wake of a mass shooting in California in May 2014 in which the gunman aimed to target women, whom he blamed for sexual rejection. Girls and women across the world used the hashtag to share their own stories of harassment and misogyny and to frame the incident as indicative of a wider culture of violence against women.
5. In August 2013, Mikki Kendall created the #SolidarityIsForWhiteWomen hashtag in order to start a conversation about the ways in which women of color are often marginalized and excluded from mainstream white feminism, including online feminism. Suey Park launched the hashtag #NotYourAsianSidekick in December 2013 as a way to discuss the experiences of Asian American women within contemporary feminism. See Loza (2014) for analysis of both hashtags.
6. The #BringBackOurGirls hashtag gained prominence in May 2014 after 200 Nigerian schoolgirls were abducted by the militant Islamist group Boko Haram. Started by a group of Nigerian campaigners who wanted to exert pressure on the government to find the girls and bring them to safety, the hashtag quickly trended globally with high-profile Western politicians, activists and celebrities participating in the campaign.

References

Banet-Weiser, Sarah. 2011. "Branding the Post-Feminist Self: Girls' Video Production and YouTube." In *Mediated Girlhoods: New Explorations of Girls' Media Culture*, edited by Mary Celeste Kearney, 277–294. New York: Peter Lang.

Banet-Weiser, Sarah. 2012. *Authentic TM: The Politics of Ambivalence in a Brand Culture*. New York: New York University Press.

Banet-Weiser, Sarah. 2015. "Popular Misogyny: A Zeitgeist." *Culture Digitally*, January 21. Accessed February 28. http://culturedigitally.org/2015/01/popular-misogyny-a-zeitgeist/.

Benson, Amy, and Kathryn Allamong Jacob. 2012. "No Documents, No History: Traditional Genres, New Formats." In *Make Your Own History: Documenting Feminist and Queer Activism in the 21st Century*, edited by Kelly Wooten and Lyz Bly, 123–140. Los Angeles: Litwine Books.

Budgeon, Shelley. 2001. "Emergent Feminist(?) Identities: Young Women and the Practice of Micropolitics." *European Journal of Women's Studies* 8 (7): 7–28.

Burgess, Jean, and Joshua Green. 2009. *YouTube: Online Video and Participatory Culture*. Malden: Polity.

Cresci, Elena. 2014. "#YesAllWomen: How Twitter reacted to the shootings in California." *The Guardian*, May 26. Accessed February 28, 2015. http://www. theguardian.com/technology/2014/may/26/yesallwomen-how-twitter-reacted-to-the-shootings-in-california.

Currie, Dawn, Deirdre Kelly, and Shauna Pomerantz. 2009. *'Girl Power:' Girls Reinventing Girlhood*. New York: Peter Lang.

Gallant, Jacques. 2014. "Twitter conversation about unreported rape goes global." *The Toronto Star*, October 31. Accessed February 28, 2015. http://www.thestar. com/news/crime/2014/10/31/twitter_conversation_about_unreported_rape_ goes_global.html.

Gill, Rosalind. 2007. "Postfeminist Media Culture: Elements of a Sensibility." *European Journal of Cultural Studies* 10 (2): 147–166.

Gill, Rosalind, and Christina Scharff. 2011. "Introduction." In *New Femininities: Postfeminism, Neoliberalism and Subjectivity*, edited by Rosalind Gill and Christina Scharff, 1–17. New York: Palgrave MacMillan.

Grigoriadis, Vanessa. 2014. "How to Start a Revolution." *New York Magazine*, September 22.

Hains, Rebecca. 2012. *Growing Up With Girl Power: Girlhood on Screen and In Everyday Life*. New York: Peter Lang.

Hamad, Hannah, and Anthea Taylor. 2015. "Introduction: Feminism and contemporary celebrity culture." *Celebrity Studies* 6 (1): 124–127.

Harp, Dustin, Jaime Loke, and Ingrid Bachmann. 2014. "Spaces For Feminist (Re) Articulations: The blogosphere and the sexual attack on journalist Lara Logan." *Feminist Media Studies* 14 (1): 5–21.

Kearney, Mary Celeste. 2006. *Girls Make Media*. New York: Routledge.

Keller, Jessalynn. 2012. "'It's a Hard Job Being an Indian Feminist:' Mapping Girls' Feminist Identities and 'Close Encounters' on the Feminist Blogosphere." In *Feminist Media: Participatory Spaces, Networks and Cultural Citizenship*, edited by Elke Zobl and Ricarda Drueke, 136–145. Germany: Transcript.

Keller, Jessalynn, and Jessica Ringrose. 2015. "'But then feminism goes out the window!': Exploring teenage girls' critical response to celebrity feminism." *Celebrity Studies* 6 (1): 132–135.

Loken, Meredith. 2014. "#BringBackOurGirls and the Invisibility of Imperialism." *Feminist Media Studies* 14 (6): 1100–1101.

Loza, Susana. 2014. "Hashtag Feminism, #SolidarityIsForWhiteWomen, and the Other #FemFuture." *Ada: A Journal of Gender, New Media and Technology* 5. Accessed March 1, 2015. http://adanewmedia.org/2014/07/issue5-loza/.

McRobbie, Angela. 2009. *The Aftermath of Feminism: Gender, Culture and Social Change*. Thousand Oaks: Sage.

Piepmeier, Alison. 2009. *Girl Zines: Making Media, Doing Feminism*. New York: New York University Press.

Renold, Emma, Jessica Ringrose, Carolyn Jackson, and Alison Phipps. Forthcoming 2016. "Laddism, Rape Culture and Everyday Sexism: Researching New Mediations and Contexts of Gender and Sexual Violence." Special issue of *Journal of Gender Studies*.

Ringrose, Jessica. 2013. *Postfeminist Education? Girls and the Sexual Politics of Schooling*. London: Routledge.

Scharff, Christina. 2012. *Repudiating Feminism: Young Women in a Neoliberal World*. Surry: Ashgate.

Schilt, Kristen. 2003. "'I'll Resist with Every Inch and Every Breath:' Girls and Zine Making as a Form of Resistance." *Youth & Society* 35(1): 71–97.

Thelandersson, Fredrika. 2014. "A Less Toxic Feminism: Can the Internet Solve the Age Old Question of How to Put Intersectional Theory into Practice?" *Feminist Media Studies* 14 (3): 527–530.

Thrift, Samantha. 2014. "#YessAllWomen as Feminist Meme Event." *Feminist Media Studies* 14 (6): 1090–1092.

Traister, Rebecca, and Judith Schulevitz. 2014. "Feminism Has Conquered the Culture. Now Comes the Hard Part." *New Republic*, September 29.

Valenti, Jessica. 2014. "Beyoncé's 'Flawless' feminist act at the VMAs leads the way for other women." *The Guardian*, August 25. Accessed February 28, 2015. http://www.theguardian.com/commentisfree/2014/aug/25/beyonce-flawless-feminist-vmas.

Zaslow, Emilie. 2009. *Feminism INC: Coming of Age in a Girl Power Media Culture*. New York: Palgrave MacMillan.

Index

Printed and bound by CPI Group (UK) Ltd, Croydon, CR0 4YY

17/10/2024

01775683-0003